T0332121

AI–Driven Intelligent Models for Business Excellence

Samala Nagaraj
Woxsen University, India

Korupalli V. Rajesh Kumar
Woxsen University, India

A volume in the Advances in
Business Information Systems and
Analytics (ABISA) Book Series

Published in the United States of America by
    IGI Global
    Business Science Reference (an imprint of IGI Global)
    701 E. Chocolate Avenue
    Hershey PA, USA 17033
    Tel: 717-533-8845
    Fax: 717-533-8661
    E-mail: cust@igi-global.com
    Web site: http://www.igi-global.com

Library of Congress Cataloging-in-Publication Data

Names: Nagaraj, Samala, 1980- editor. | Kumar, Korupalli V. Rajesh, 1989-
    editor.
Title: AI-driven intelligent models for business excellence / Samala
    Nagaraj, and Korupalli V. Rajesh Kumar, editors.
Description: Hershey, PA : Business Science Reference, 2022. | Includes
    bibliographical references and index. | Summary: "As digital technology
    is taking the world in a revolutionary way and business related aspects
    are getting smarter this book is a potential research source on the
    Artificial Intelligence-based Business Applications and Intelligence"--
    Provided by publisher.
Identifiers: LCCN 2022015764 (print) | LCCN 2022015765 (ebook) | ISBN
    9781668442463 (hardcover) | ISBN 9781668442470 (paperback) | ISBN
    9781668442487 (ebook)
Subjects: LCSH: Business intelligence--Data processing. | Management--Data
    processing. | Artificial intelligence--Industrial applications.
Classification: LCC HD38.7 .A3898 2022 (print) | LCC HD38.7 (ebook) | DDC
    658.4/038028553--dc23/eng/20220408
LC record available at https://lccn.loc.gov/2022015764
LC ebook record available at https://lccn.loc.gov/2022015765

This book is published in the IGI Global book series Advances in Business Information Systems
and Analytics (ABISA) (ISSN: 2327-3275; eISSN: 2327-3283)

British Cataloguing in Publication Data
A Cataloguing in Publication record for this book is available from the British Library.

All work contributed to this book is new, previously-unpublished material.
The views expressed in this book are those of the authors, but not necessarily of the publisher.

For electronic access to this publication, please contact: eresources@igi-global.com.

Advances in Business Information Systems and Analytics (ABISA) Book Series

ISSN:2327-3275
EISSN:2327-3283

Editor-in-Chief: Madjid Tavana La Salle University, USA

MISSION

The successful development and management of information systems and business analytics is crucial to the success of an organization. New technological developments and methods for data analysis have allowed organizations to not only improve their processes and allow for greater productivity, but have also provided businesses with a venue through which to cut costs, plan for the future, and maintain competitive advantage in the information age.

The **Advances in Business Information Systems and Analytics (ABISA) Book Series** aims to present diverse and timely research in the development, deployment, and management of business information systems and business analytics for continued organizational development and improved business value.

COVERAGE

- Performance Metrics
- Business Information Security
- Business Models
- Business Decision Making
- Forecasting
- Information Logistics
- Data Management
- Algorithms
- Geo-BIS
- Legal information systems

IGI Global is currently accepting manuscripts for publication within this series. To submit a proposal for a volume in this series, please contact our Acquisition Editors at Acquisitions@igi-global.com or visit: http://www.igi-global.com/publish/.

Titles in this Series

For a list of additional titles in this series, please visit:
www.igi-global.com/book-series/advances-business-information-systems-analytics/3715

Revolutionizing Business Practices Through Artificial Intelligence and Data-Rich Environments
Manisha Gupta (Sharda University, India) Deergha Sharma (The NorthCap University, India) and Himani Gupta (Jagannath International Management School, India)
Business Science Reference • © 2022 • 300pp • H/C (ISBN: 9781668449509) • US $250.00

Handbook of Research on Foundations and Applications of Intelligent Business Analytics
Zhaohao Sun (Papua New Guinea University of Technology, Papua New Guinea) and Zhiyou Wu (Chongqing Normal University, China)
Business Science Reference • © 2022 • 425pp • H/C (ISBN: 9781799890164) • US $325.00

Utilizing Blockchain Technologies in Manufacturing and Logistics Management
S. B. Goyal (City University, Malaysia) Nijalingappa Pradeep (Bapuji Institute of Engineering and Technology, India) Piyush Kumar Shukla (University Institute of Technology RGPV, India) Mangesh M. Ghonge (Sandip Institute of Technology and Research Centre, India) and Renjith V. Ravi (MEA Engineering College, India)
Business Science Reference • © 2022 • 290pp • H/C (ISBN: 9781799886976) • US $250.00

Business Applications in Social Media Analytics
Himani Bansal (Jaypee University, Solan, India) and Gulshan Shrivastava (National Institute of Technology, Patna, India)
Business Science Reference • © 2022 • 330pp • H/C (ISBN: 9781799850465) • US $195.00

Achieving Organizational Agility, Intelligence, and Resilience Through Information Systems
Hakikur Rahman (Ansted University Sustainability Research Institute, Malaysia)
Business Science Reference • © 2022 • 350pp • H/C (ISBN: 9781799847991) • US $215.00

Handbook of Research on Applied Data Science and Artificial Intelligence in Business and Industry
Valentina Chkoniya (University of Aveiro, Portugal)
Engineering Science Reference • © 2021 • 653pp • H/C (ISBN: 9781799869856) • US $470.00

701 East Chocolate Avenue, Hershey, PA 17033, USA
Tel: 717-533-8845 x100 • Fax: 717-533-8661
E-Mail: cust@igi-global.com • www.igi-global.com

Table of Contents

Detailed Table of Contents

Chapter 1

Lavanya K, Vellore Institute of Technology, India
Bharathi K., Vellore Institute of Technology, India
Preethi Christina A., Vellore Institute of Technology, India
Satyam Chaurasia, Vellore Institute of Technology, India

The use daily of vehicles is rising exponentially and as a result there is an increase in crimes associated with it. Many vehicles are violating the rules of traffic and so an abnormal number of accidents occur leading to a rise in the crime rates linearly. In order for any vehicle to be recognized, its license plate number is needed. Therefore, the vehicle license plate detection plays a notable role. The optical character recognition (OCR) is one effective way to scan number plates and recognize the text found in the digital image, containing the license plate number into machine readable text which can then be used to track the vehicles. The image of the number plate is first captured, processed, and every character present in the number plate is read for perfect recognition. The optical character recognition model is trained using TensorFlow. Spark's in-memory data engine can perform tasks rapidly in multi-stage jobs. Therefore, TensorFlow and Spark are used together to train and apply the OCR model to perform the license plate recognition swiftly.

Chapter 2

Murat Pasa Uysal, Baskent University, Turkey

There is an overestimation of the benefits that may be provided by machine learning (ML) applications. Recent studies report the failures of ML projects, inadequate return on investment, or unsatisfactory project outcomes. Software engineering challenges, business and IT alignment, holistic management of business processes, data, applications, and infrastructure may be some causes. However, the author believe that the integration of ML applications with enterprise components is a serious issue that is often neglected. Therefore, the main argument of this study is that the enterprise integration models are critical for the long-term benefits and sustainability of ML-driven systems. In this study, the author developed an enterprise integration method for ML-driven business systems by using enterprise architecture methods and tools. Finally, this method is applied to an online shopping system in a business case study and presented important findings and insights.

Chapter 3

In the current study, the author implemented cohort analysis methodology of machine learning (ML) to assess the rate of consumers' complaint retention behavior toward firms. The author obtained a three-year range of data on customer complaints from the Consumer Financial Protection Bureau's website. After removing the missing data from the customer complaints dataset, the current study also uses the cohort analysis approach of ML to assess the rate of consumer complaints retained by businesses. According to the findings, organizations retain a significant portion of complaints. This study adds to the body of knowledge on consumer complaining behavior (CCB), especially by creating and deploying unsupervised machine learning-based technique to conceptualize consumers' complaint behavior in the financial service providers industry. Moreover, professionals will benefit greatly from this research.

This chapter aims to investigate pandemic crisis in the various business fields like real estate, restaurants, gold, and the stock market. The importance of deep learning models is to analyse the business data for future predictions to overcome the crisis. Most of the recent research articles are published on intelligent business models in sustainable development and predicting the growth rate after the pandemic crisis. This clear study will be presented based on all reputed journal articles and information from business magazines on the various business domains. Comparison of best intelligent models in business data analysis will be done to transform the business operations and the global economy. Different deep learning applications in business data analysis will be addressed. The deep learning models are investigated which are applied on descriptive, predictive, and prescriptive business analytics.

Chapter 5

    Sapna Chopra, Woxsen University, India
    Samala Nagaraj, Woxsen University, India

Businesses are using innovation to communicate their story online so they can reach hundreds of thousands of users at once. The technology trend is probably here to stay. This means that innovation is still in its infancy and that new types of technical advances are appearing every day. Video content is becoming more popular as a result of the use of cutting-edge technologies in the media and entertainment industries. However, the creation of novel technical ideas may result in a wide range of previously unheard-of digitalized tools and functionalities. Films, print, television, and radio were the key components of media and entertainment. The usage of gesture recognition technology, picture analysis in journalism, film screenplay analysis, and music composition and generation are a few of the new components that make up the media and entertainment environment. Due to the incorporation of innovation and technology, the media and entertainment sector has seen dramatic changes in recent years.

Chapter 6

    Malla Sudhakara, Reva University, India
    Bhavya K. R., Reva University, India
    M Rudra Kumar, G. Pullaiah College of Engineering, India
    N. Badrinath, Annamacharya Institute of Technology and Sciences,
        Tirupati, India
    K. Rangaswamy, Sai Rajeswari Institute of Technology, India

In recent years, digital marketing has surpassed traditional marketing as the preferred technique of reaching customers. Researchers and academics may utilize it for social media marketing and for predicting client buy intent, among other applications. It can boost customer happiness and sales by facilitating a more personalized shopping session, resulting in higher conversion rates and a competitive advantage for the retailer. Advanced analytics technologies are utilized in conjunction with a dynamic and data-driven framework to expect whether or not a customer will make a purchase from the organization within a certain time frame. To increase income and stay ahead of the competition, one must understand customer buying habits. Several sectors offered rules to explore a consumer's potential based on statistics results. A machine learning algorithm for detecting potential customers for a retail superstore is proposed using an engineering approach.

Chapter 7

Swarnasree Vutharkar, Woxsen University, India
C. A. Narasimha Swamy, Woxsen University, India
Krishna Hitesh, Woxsen University, India

Initial public offerings (IPOs) have long been a popular term on Wall Street and among investors. By selling shares of the Dutch East India Company to the general public, the Dutch are credited with launching the contemporary IPO. Since then, firms have utilised IPOs as a means of raising funds from the general public by issuing shares of stock to the general public. IPOs have experienced uptrends and downtrends in issuance over the years. Due to innovation and several other economic reasons, individual industries also undergo uptrends and downtrends in issuance. At the height of the dotcom boom, companies scrambled to list themselves on the stock market as technology IPOs surged. There are essentially two steps in the IPO process. The pre-marketing stage of the offering is the first, and the actual initial public offering is the second. A company that wants to go public will either request private bids from underwriters or make a public announcement to pique interest.

Chapter 8

Swarnasree Vutharkar, Woxsen University, India
Rajesh Kumar K. V., Woxsen University, India

The words "financial" and "technology" are combined to form the phrase "fintech." Despite being a wide expression with numerous interpretations, it typically refers to the growth of a sector when new technology use-cases are developed and put into place to expedite more traditional-looking financial activities. When it first arose in the 21st century, the term "fintech" was used to describe the technology employed in the back-end systems of reputable financial organisations. Since then, nevertheless, there has been a shift toward more client-centered services, and thus, a more client-centric definition. Currently, the term "fintech" is used to describe a wide range of professions and businesses, including investment management, retail banking, education, and non-profit fundraising, to name a few. In this chapter you will be reading the relation between python and finance; SQL and finance; Tableau and finance; Power Bi and finance; and Block Chain and finance.

Chapter 9

The research is mainly focused on forecasting office space utilization trends in the organization using information such as office space count, space occupancy count, holidays, leaves. Space occupancy data is collected using PIR sensors. Descriptive analytics is done using creative visualizations, and model building is done using univariate and multivariate time series methods. Descriptive analytics explains that there is a positive autocorrelation in the data with no outliers and randomness. There exists a pattern of space occupancy for different office locations at different times of the day. Univariate time series models are suitable for forecasting space occupancy for single office locations, whereas multivariate time series model VAR is suitable when considering multiple office locations of a client or multiple office locations of different clients at the same time. Empirical research has exhibited that out of tested models, SARIMAX has shown better performance on multiple test datasets.

In this chapter, the foundation of customer relationship management has been explored along with its history and how it has evolved in the past few years. Metrics to measure CRM are important to check its effectiveness. It also determines the impact of CRM on customer satisfaction and loyalty. The way CRM has helped business over the years has also been discussed. In business-to-business and business-to-consumer, CRM has made a large impact. With CRM technology, both business and relationship areas have been improved.

The present empirical study has explained the part of foreign direct investment (FDI) in India's economic growth in the pharmaceutical sector. The study has detailed information about the relationship, impact, and forthcoming action of the FDI on the Indian economy. This study applies the e-views software concerning statistical tools used are VECM, ordinary least squares, and VAR. It has considered the secondary data with the year starting from 2011 to 2021. The study has evaluated the results as a good association between the FDI and the pharmaceutical sector. This study suggests that it affected the positive long-term connection of FDI in the pharmaceutical industry and the short-term affinity between FDI and GDP. The study also concluded that the outcomes of foreign direct investment would have positive future movements in GDP.

Chapter 12

Sai Sreeja Nainala, Woxsen University, India
Snehamayee Gowribidanur Matam, Woxsen University, India

This chapter explores the role of local brands during the COVID-19 pandemic, the expansion of SMEs all throughout the pandemic, and the needs for all start-ups during the pandemic. The authors have also done research and written about how startups and small businesses have adapted to and used digitalization. This chapter will discuss the effects of regional brands during a pandemic.

Chapter 13

Bhavya K. R., Reva University, India
Malla Sudhakara, Reva University, India
G. Ramasubba Reddy, Sai Rajeswari Institute of Technology, India
L. N. C. Prakash K., CVR College of Engineering, India
Rupa Devi B., AITS, India
Sangeetha M., Reva University, India

The act of digital marketing uses a variety of traditional methods such as analyst consensus, earnings per share estimation, or fundamental intrinsic valuation. Also, social media management, automation, content marketing, and community development are some of the most popular uses for digital marketing. Stock price prediction is a challenging task since there are so many factors to take into account, such as economic conditions, political events, and other environmental elements that might influence the stock price. Due to these considerations, determining the dependency of a single factor on future pricing and patterns is challenging. The authors examine Apple's stock data from Yahoo API and use sentiment categorization to predict its future stock movement and to find the impact of "public sentiment" on "market trends." The main purpose of this chapter is to predict the rise and fall with high accuracy degrees. The authors use an artificial intelligence-based machine learning model to train, evaluate, and improve the performance of digital marketing strategies.

Chapter 14

   G. S. Siva Kumar, Pragati Engineering College, India
   Suneetha P., Pragati Engineering College, India
   Sailaja V., Pragati Engineering College, India
   Srinivas Akula, Pragati Engineering College, India
   Vasantha Lakshmi B., Pragati Engineering College, India
   Ravi Kumar M., Pragati Engineering College, India

The era of the semi-conductor manufacturing industry is from 1970 to recent times. During these decades, the manufacturing process has achieved its greatest heights. At present, it reached its saturation level in terms of VLSI, ULSI, SOC manufacturing techniques. Recently artificial intelligence models are expanding their domains and applications in all the sectors. In this regard, changes in the hardware modeling also play a crucial role. In this chapter, the authors present artificial intelligence on hardware models, how the IC manufacturing industry is turning its conventional methods to add new features, and future directions at the business level.

Preface

Business models have been evolving over the centuries, starting from the production and marketing era to the relationship and intelligence era. Artificial intelligence has radically altered the nature of ideas, innovation, and inventions over the years. Businesses are evolving in response to this change. As we see across industries businesses struggling with a new balance of intelligence power, we also see AI applications and adoption offering them a multitude of new opportunities.

Businesses are also evolving as digital technology revolutionizes the world by adopting digital technologies such as artificial intelligence, digital marketing, and analytical methods. According to this trend, further research on the solutions modern technology may offer businesses is needed in order to implement it across disciplines.

Across nations, business and commerce are already being transformed by AI. Large or small, rich or poor, developed or developing, AI has created a level playing field for countries and economies. While technology and information are universally accessible, each company employs information in different ways—for various objectives and purposes. While digital data and information help companies across industries access intelligence, they must comprehend the other factors that will determine their success in developing AI capabilities. A new technology has levelled the playing field to an extent, but it doesn't mean that businesses can't access intelligence.

From Silicon Valley to China, everyone is talking about AI. The artificial neuron, the first piece of AI, was invented in 1943 by scientist William McCulloch and logician Walter Pitts. Since then, we have made significant strides in developing and understanding models that can comprehend, predict, and analyse.

Businesses already rely on artificial intelligence for automation, data analytics, and natural language processing, among other things. Across fields, these three areas of AI are reducing operational costs and speeding up results.

Businesses can benefit from data analytics, which gives them information they've never had before. Data analytics alleviates repetitive or even deadly tasks. Intelligent search engines, helpful chatbots, and better accessibility for visually impaired people are all made possible by natural language processing.

Businesses are already utilizing AI the following purposes:

1. Copying and cross-referencing information; updating files.
2. Forecasting and providing products to match consumer behavior is what product innovation is all about.
3. Fraud detection.
4. Targeted advertising and marketing messages.
5. Chatbots or telephone customer service can provide support.

A significant impact on marketing services, supply chain management, and manufacturing can be made using AI.

AI will assist patients in healthcare by helping with early detection and immediate diagnoses, as well as streamlining clinic scheduling and safeguarding patient records. On the physician side, AI will play a more significant role in helping with scheduling and safeguarding patient records.

There is still a lot of room for AI to grow in finance and banking, two data-rich fields with great potential for AI-based innovation that still rely heavily on ancient processes.

Customers will demand more data transparency and security as AI makes a significant impact in these fields in the coming years. As customers become aware of how much data is being collected, they will demand to know what data is collected, what it is used for, and how it is safeguarded.

TRANSFORMATION OF THE BUSINESS MODEL

Everything being connected allows businesses to collect more data and gain critical insights, leading to important market evolution. We may see a much-needed evolution in marketplaces, leaner operations, vibrant firms, increased profits, educated consumers, and innovative companies.

Business models are being disrupted by AI in critical ways, and this is something we want to examine. Businesses across sectors and countries are adopting AI in different stages, but most seem to be focusing on using it to improve customer service, process data, predict performance, automate workloads, trade, and much more. Businesses appear to still be focusing on AI applications and adoption, despite their rapid evolution in intelligence capabilities. Furthermore, businesses may create an environment of mistrust and animosity among competitors within their respective industries and nations.

Many nations are unwilling to take an approach to data collection and information accessibility because of the lack of a digital infrastructure. A lack of data, information, and intelligence—all of which are difficult to obtain—may impede businesses from addressing their data, information, and intelligence needs.

Despite the fact that AI has the potential to revolutionize economies and trade across the world, data and information sharing issues may impede its progression. As a result, the creation and adoption of massive data pools and procedures at local, national, and worldwide levels are still up for debate.

Businesses are not the only ones to experience significant changes due to AI; collaboration, competition, and creativity are all being altered in fundamental ways. With most AI initiatives, competitors gain an advantage by perceiving an entirely new opportunity, enhancing current efforts, supplying a neglected customer segment, or inventing new markets, information from connected devices that continuously feeds data about function, usage, production, needs, and much more will be used to create more competitive situations.

THE VERDICT ON AI-DRIVEN INTELLIGENT MODELS FOR BUSINESS EXCELLENCE

The future is coming to each country in which artificial intelligence is an essential component. AI-driven automation trends reflect significant changes in players and actions in the AI industry that signal a shift in interests, influence, and investments in global business politics. There are significant security concerns associated with rapidly automating businesses. As nations must manage their big data resources across cyberspace, aquaspace, geospace, and space (CAGS) in order to increase the AI business transformation, they should focus on enhancing data initiatives to gather more information in order to develop the AI realm more.

This reference work examines how artificial intelligence can be used to improve business performance across almost any industry. Business analysis, machine learning, deep learning, and analytical methods are just a few of the AI approaches discussed in this book. This book is ideal for managers, business owners, computer scientists, industry professionals, researchers, scholars, practitioners, academicians, instructors, and students.

Chapter 1: A CNN-Based License Plate Recognition Using TensorFlow and PySpark

In the world of commerce, ensuring the security of a payment card plays an important role. To protect the payment card's security, a token is typically inserted into the card's magnetic strip at the time of purchase. However, it is important to note that the protection against fraudulent use of the token is not guaranteed. The token is generated through a secret process in a secure environment and is valid only for a certain amount of time. The time period can vary based on the type of card and transaction. As you shop, the card's token is replaced with a new one.

The first two digits of a card's numerical sequence represent the country in which the card was issued, while the last three characters represent the bank that issued the card. The country code is divided into two groups based on the ISO 3166-1 standard: alpha-2 codes and alpha-3 codes. Alpha-3 codes are used by most countries and are very rare.

The future of vision is the automation of vision. With the advent of automatic cars and automated systems we can now do away with the necessity of human vision in many situations. It is this background that led to the development of vision-based number plate recognition systems. While the visibility of number plates varies from country to country, there are some features that are common to most countries.

The aim of this paper is to present a vision-based system for automatic number plate recognition. The proposed system is intelligent enough to recognise and localize the numbers on number plates.

The detection and recognition of number plates with the help of AI Robot has the potential to make driving safer and more efficient. A number of existing approaches exist for the recognition of number plates, including machine learning models. However, there is no single framework that combines all the best features available in the deep learning approach. In this work, we have taken the best features from several existing approaches and developed a vision-based system which exhibits deep learning-based performance.

Chapter 2: An Enterprise Integration Method for Machine Learning-Driven Business Systems

There is an overestimation of the benefits that may be provided by Machine Learning (ML) applications. Recent studies report the failures of ML projects, inadequate return on investment, or unsatisfactory project outcomes. Software engineering challenges, business, IT alignment, holistic management of business processes, data, applications, and infrastructure may be some causes. However, it is thought that the integration of ML applications with enterprise systems is a serious issue that is often neglected. Therefore, the main argument of this study is that the enterprise integration models are critical for the long-term benefits and sustainability of ML-driven systems. In this study, we propose an enterprise integration method for ML-driven business systems by using enterprise architecture methods and tools. Finally, we apply it to an online shopping system in a business case study, and present important insights.

One of the most significant challenges facing organizations is the lack of agility to respond to existing and emerging business opportunities. In order to exploit available opportunities and optimize business performance, it is important to establish a high-performance business system that is adaptable and agile. The rise of Machine Learning and Artificial Intelligence (AI) are expected to revolutionize many businesses in the coming years. These technologies can be applied to increase the efficiency and revenue of businesses by automating routine processes. The success of ML-driven online shopping systems will depend on the integration of AI and ML with business, application, and infrastructure domains. This paper presents an approach that addresses this challenge. It combines multi-dimensional integration with service-oriented architecture to critique and build the business system. Integrating AI and ML with other architectures and domains, we hope to make the business system more adaptive and agile. As a result, we hope to create a business system that is able to overcome challenges associated with the management of ML systems.

Chapter 3: Behavioral Analytics of Consumer Complaints

With financial services being a truly global business, there are huge opportunities for growth in cultural markets that are often overlooked by many firms. There is still a great need and plenty of room to improve financial services in many of the world's less developed or emerging economies and countries. Greater customer satisfaction and satisfaction with financial services can be catalysts for the rapid growth and expansion of financial inclusion programs and services in the global south and southeast. Financial inclusion is an important means of building trust between the public and the private sectors and making the financial system more equitable. The financial systems of these regions are not adequately serving their people, and as a result, there is an enormous amount of potential for financial services development. The ability to leverage technology and financial service innovation will be critical in this endeavor.

Consumers are increasingly demanding retailer brands that meet their expectations of customer satisfaction, and they will likely refuse to purchase from companies that fail to meet these expectations. As a result, businesses are increasingly compelled to establish handling systems that facilitate resolving customers' complaints in a timely fashion. In order to do so, businesses typically look for existing customers who have had experiences with the company and obtain their feedback about the handling processes and customer service. Although the positive effect of a complaint management system on customer satisfaction has been well established in the research literature, there are few studies that have explored the potential sources and functions of customer complaints and the relationship between complaints and quality service delivery. This article focuses on the relationship between customer complaints, quality service delivery, and customer satisfaction as these are considered by marketers and managers as key performance indicators.

Chapter 4: Business Analysis During the Pandemic Crisis Using Deep Learning Models

Artificial intelligence (AI) is being used increasingly in business applications to improve decision-making and create intelligent systems. The AI-based techniques used in any business systems include big data and machine learning. The goal is to gather the available data, process the data, and create intelligent solutions and systems that solve problems automatically. The AI-based solutions have a lot of benefits and advantages over conventional solutions in terms of accuracy and efficiency. AI-based systems are more effective in integrating insights from different sources and creating actionable information for decision-making. A great number of researches have been conducted to improve various AI solutions and AI applications. The outcomes of these studies show that AI solutions have a lot of potential and hold the promise to transform and streamline business activities.

Chapter 5: Business Tech in Media and Entertainment

Businesses are using innovation to communicate their story online so they can reach hundreds of thousands of users at once. The technology trend is probably here to stay. This is as a result that innovation is still in its infancy and that new types of technical advances are appearing every day. Video content is becoming more popular as a result of the use of cutting-edge technologies in the media and entertainment industries. However, the creation of novel technical ideas may result in a wide range of previously unheard-of digitalized tools and functionalities. Films, print, television, and radio were the key components of media and entertainment. The usage of gesture recognition technology, picture analysis in journalism, film screenplay analysis, and music composition and generation are a few of the new components that make up the media and entertainment environment. Due to the incorporation of innovation and technology, the media and entertainment sector has seen dramatic changes in recent years.

Chapter 6: Customer Purchase Prediction and Potential Customer Identification for Digital Marketing Using Machine Learning

In recent years, digital marketing has surpassed traditional marketing as the preferred technique of reaching customers. Researchers and academics may utilize it for social media marketing and for predicting client buy intent, among other applications. It can boost customer happiness and sales by facilitating a more personalized shopping session, resulting in higher conversion rates and a competitive advantage for the retailer. Digital marketing tactics most commonly used to enhance sales include Customer Purchase Prediction (CPP). The goal of CPP is to predict future client purchases, and the results are critical for future commercial activity. Advanced analytics technologies are utilized in conjunction with a dynamic and data-driven framework to expect whether or not a customer will make a purchase from the organization within a certain time frame. To increase income and stay ahead of the competition, one must understand customer buying habits. Several sectors offered rules to explore a consumer's potential based on statistics results. A machine learning algorithm for detecting potential customers for a retail superstore is proposed using an engineering approach. The content of a website is unstructured. Web scraping collects and organizes unstructured content for later analysis. Customer product price and rating prediction is currently a hot research topic. SVM-Linear is a tool for data collection and analysis. Using machine learning methods, investigate and analyze the extracted dataset. The study employs dynamic product ratings and price analysis to produce accurate forecasts.

Chapter 7: Failed IPO Stories – Stories of Initial Public Offering

Initial public offerings (IPOs) have long been a popular term on Wall Street and among investors. By selling shares of the Dutch East India Company to the general public, the Dutch are credited with launching the contemporary IPO. Since then, firms have utilised IPOs as a means of raising funds from the general public by issuing shares of stock to the general public. IPOs have experienced uptrends and downtrends in issuance over the years. Due to innovation and several other economic reasons, individual industries also undergo uptrends and downtrends in issuance. At the height of the dotcom boom, companies scrambled to list themselves on the stock market as technology IPOs surged. There are essentially two steps in the IPO process. The pre-marketing stage of the offering is the first, and the actual initial public offering is the second. A company that wants to go public will either request private bids from underwriters or make a public announcement to pique interest.

Chapter 8: Fin-Cology or Tech-Nance? Emergence of FinTech

The words "financial" and "technology" are combined to form the phrase "fintech." Despite being a wide expression with numerous interpretations, it typically refers to the growth of a sector when new technology use-cases are developed and put into place to expedite more traditional-looking financial activities. When it first arose in the 21st century, the term "fintech" was used to describe the technology employed in the back-end systems of reputable financial organisations. Since then, nevertheless, there has been a shift toward more client-centered services, and thus, a more client-centric definition. Currently, the term "fintech" is used to describe a wide range of professions and businesses, including investment management, retail banking, education, and non-profit fundraising, to name a few. In this chapter you will be reading the relation between python and finance; SQL and finance; Tableau and finance; Power Bi and finance; and Block Chain and finance.

Chapter 9: Forecasting the Space Utilization Trend in Corporate Offices

This chapter describes that how this research paper is focused on developing the forecasting model of office space utilization, using both univariate and multivariate time series approaches. The univariate time series forecasting models ARMA and SARIMAX are best fit to forecast space occupancy for single office location and multivariate time series forecasting model VAR is best fit to forecast space occupancy for multiple clients and their multiple office locations or single client and its multiple office locations.

However, as the test dataset varied the model performance has varied. Hence, more the models are trained, more of office space's demand and supply equation is getting smoother. Based on the other research works the parameters that they have suggested for office space utilization can be taken into consideration in the future, depending upon the social and professional situations then.

The development of a forecasting model help organizations in planning space allocation for the employees who are willing to work from the office every day and those who want to work from office for a few days in a month. As the employee count increases accordingly desk spaces can be managed and becomes easier to maintain safe distance between each desk. As per the methods proposed in this research paper, the focus was more on developing a robust, analytical forecasting model that provides decision support for important, real-time, and critical forecasting and monitoring.

Chapter 11: Indian Economic Growth Concerning the Impact on FDI (Foreign Direct Investment) – Impact of FDI on Indian Economic Growth in the Pharmaceutical Sector

The present empirical study has explained the part of foreign direct investment (FDI) in India's economic growth in the pharmaceutical sector. The study has detailed information about the relationship, impact, and forthcoming action of the FDI on the Indian Economizing. This study applies the E-views software concerning statistical tools used are VECM, Ordinary Least squares, and VAR. It has considered the secondary data with the year starting from 2011 to 2021. The study has evaluated the results as a good association between the FDI and the Pharmaceutical sector.

The positive association between FDI and GDP. This study suggests that it affected the positive long-term connection of FDI in the pharmaceutical industry and the short-term affinity between FDI and GDP. The study also concluded. The outcomes of foreign direct investment would have positive future movements in GDP.

Chapter 12: Local Brand Impact During COVID-19

In the current scenario the role of local brands during the COVID-19 epidemic, the expansion of SME's all throughout pandemic, and the need for all start-ups during the pandemic. We have also done research and written about how startups and small businesses have adapted to and used digitalization. How few firms encountered problems during the epidemic and which others have a chance to succeed in the market and earn money. We also included a few regional advertisements that took place globally. This section will discuss the effects of regional brands during an epidemic.

Chapter 13: Machine Learning-Based Stock Price Prediction for Business Intelligence

Nowadays, the act of Digital Marketing using a variety of traditional methods such as analyst consensus, Earnings per share estimation, or fundamental intrinsic valuation plays a major role. And also, social media management, automation, content marketing, and community development are some of the most popular uses for digital marketing. Stock price prediction is the one and a challenging task since there are so many factors to take into account, such as economic conditions, political events, and other environmental elements that might influence the stock price. Due to these considerations, determining the dependency of a single factor on future pricing and patterns is challenging. We examine Apple's stock data from yahoo API and uses sentiment categorization to predict its future stock movement and to find the impact of "public sentiment" on "market trends". The main purpose of this article is to predict the rise and fall with high accuracy degrees. we use Artificial Intelligence based machine learning model to train, to evaluate and to improve the performance of digital marketing strategies.

Chapter 14: Transformation and Future Directions of the Integrated Chip (IC) Manufacturing Industry Using Artificial Intelligence Models

Critic high tech minerals (CHTMs) are unrefined substances that are fundamental for a future clean-energy change and the assembling of very good quality items.

Electronic devices, one of the quickest developing electronic items, contain different CHTMs. Starting around 2019, India has outperformed the United States to turn into the second biggest electronic gadget market on the planet. An expanding and disturbing number of unreasonable waste electronic contraptions will be created in India soon. In this review, the powerful material stream investigation approach and the Weibull dissemination are taken on to examine the volumes of collected squander electronic devices and the contained CHTMs in light of the separation among electronic gadgets and component telephones in India. Also, a market supply model is embraced to anticipate the future patterns of CHTMs in squander electronic devices. The outcomes show an overall vertical propensity of waste electronic devices volume in India, which demonstrates that different CHTMs contained in electronic devices waste can be appropriately reused or reused. Future ramifications in light of the investigation results are accommodated proficient electronic devices the executives in India.

THE VERDICT ON AI-DRIVEN INTELLIGENT MODELS FOR BUSINESS EXCELLENCE

The future is coming to each country in which artificial intelligence is an essential component. AI-driven automation trends reflect significant changes in players and actions in the AI industry that signal a shift in interests, influence, and investments in global business politics. There are significant security concerns associated with rapidly automating businesses. As nations must manage their big data resources across cyberspace, aquascape, geospacers, and space (CAGS) in order to increase the AI business transformation, they should focus on enhancing data initiatives to gather more information in order to develop the AI realm more.

Samala Nagaraj
Woxsen University, India

Korupalli V. Rajesh Kumar
Woxsen University, India

Acknowledgment

I would like to extend my gratitude to my collaborators Sai Lakshmi Chandra Mounika K., Sai Deepthi Bhogaraju, and Vani Ganapati Hedge for all their hard work in managing the chapters of this book. They made this book available to the public. We are proud to publish *AI-Driven Intelligent Models for Business Excellence*.

Every book and publisher have different chapter acceptance, peer review, and publication procedures. Authors may submit their chapters to IGI Global through the e-Editorial Discovery system. An online editorial system is used to review and publish chapters. After the Editor-in-Chief has reviewed the chapter, he selects reviewers based on their subject expertise and research topic. After one round of peer review by more than three reviewers, a chapter is typeset and published. It then goes through several rounds of revision and review.

I'd like to express my gratitude to books and texts for providing me with dedicated reviewers. Your generosity and expertise have been invaluable in improving this study, and I have saved myself from a multitude of errors; any remaining ones are entirely my own fault.

We would also like to thank the editors and support staff of IGI Global publishers for their assistance in bringing this book to press and publication. Finally, we would like to thank all of the authors for their contribution to this publication. Without your contribution, your hard work, and your submission, this book would not exist.

Creating the editorial team for every new book is a time-consuming process. The editor-in-chief and all other members of the editorial team are volunteers and hold honorary positions. No one is paid. It's tough to get people with specific knowledge and expertise to volunteer when they have full-time jobs. The next step was choosing the correct individuals with the correct expertise and architecture in fog computing applications, architecture, and security for the review team.

I hope that readers will find this book enjoyable and inspiring to start their own fog computing research. I would like to congratulate everyone involved in the writing, review, editorial, and publication of this book once again.

Korupalli V. Rajesh Kumar
Woxsen University, India

Chapter 1
A CNN–Based License Plate Recognition Using TensorFlow and PySpark

Lavanya K
Vellore Institute of Technology, India

Bharathi K.
Vellore Institute of Technology, India

Preethi Christina A.
Vellore Institute of Technology, India

Satyam Chaurasia
Vellore Institute of Technology, India

ABSTRACT

The use daily of vehicles is rising exponentially and as a result there is an increase in crimes associated with it. Many vehicles are violating the rules of traffic and so an abnormal number of accidents occur leading to a rise in the crime rates linearly. In order for any vehicle to be recognized, its license plate number is needed. Therefore, the vehicle license plate detection plays a notable role. The optical character recognition (OCR) is one effective way to scan number plates and recognize the text found in the digital image, containing the license plate number into machine readable text which can then be used to track the vehicles. The image of the number plate is first captured, processed, and every character present in the number plate is read for perfect recognition. The optical character recognition model is trained using TensorFlow. Spark's in-memory data engine can perform tasks rapidly in multi-stage jobs. Therefore, TensorFlow and Spark are used together to train and apply the OCR model to perform the license plate recognition swiftly.

DOI: 10.4018/978-1-6684-4246-3.ch001

INTRODUCTION

The increase in the number of vehicles on the road these days is serving as a reason for the increase in traffic and various crimes associated with it. Since the vehicles involved could not be recognized accurately, various cases of theft, hit and run, robbery, kidnapping, smuggling, on-road fatalities remain unsolved. Identifying the vehicles has various applications in toll payments, parking management, road-traffic monitoring, security and crime identification. Manual monitoring of vehicles is cumbersome, error prone and a daunting task. Therefore, a robust mechanism such as an automated vehicle recognition system is necessary to handle this task efficiently.

Each vehicle is uniquely identified by the number assigned to it which is displayed on the license plate. A license plate contains a unique combination of digits and alphabets. When a number from the number plate is correctly detected, the complete information about the vehicle and its owner can be retrieved. One of the effective methods to scan the number plates is optical character recognition.

It involves using OpenCV, Keras. OpenCV stands for *Open Source Computer Vision Library*. It is a library of programming functions that helps with real-time computer vision. Keras is a highly powerful and dynamic framework that makes testing easier, simplifies neural network usage and offers support to both convolution and recurrent networks. There are 3 steps associated with this process: Detection of the plate, character segmentation and reading the contents of the plate. The detection of the plate is done using Tensorflow object detection. TensorFlow is an end-to-end open source platform for machine learning that comprises of tools, libraries and resources that can be used to build and train models using high level APIs and perform powerful experimentation using research. TensorFlow object detection is a computer vision technique that helps in detecting, locating and tracing objects from a video or an image. The model is trained with 411 images of the car with annotated plates. LabelImg, an image annotation tool allows us to annotate images in Pascal VOC format. The dataset is composed of car images that are found online. Some of the images are taken on the street and data augmentation (Vertical Flip, Brightness modification) is performed using Keras. In character segmentation, two methods are used for more accuracy: The first one comprises of a trained model that has images of license plates where characters are annotated. Around 1400 characters are present in total. In the second method, OpenCV's functions are used to process the plate.

At last, to recognize a character, Convolutional Neural Network is trained with Tensorflow and Keras libraries. There are 35 classes (10 for numbers and 25 for alphabet without "O"). Approximately 1000 images are used for each class. A sample of characters and images are collected and data augmentation (rotation and brightness) is performed.

Big data framework examines large amounts of data to uncover hidden patterns, correlation and other insights. With big data technology it is possible to analyze the data and get results almost immediately, paving the way for intelligent document processing. This enables data extraction to be performed in an accurate manner. Usage of spark enables fast processing, flexibility and quick access to data which helps to produce instant outcome that plays a vital role in character recognition. Thus the usage of a spark environment along with the features of keras and tensorflow provides a robust system that performs effective character recognition of license plates.

LITERATURE SURVEY

In the pre-processing of images with the OCR software, data sets containing non intersecting images are subjected to a neural network. Images and the data required for training are collected, the attributes are detected, then the accuracy of detection is improved. The OCR is then optimised to find different ways in which optimal results can be obtained with fewer failures. (Madhumitha and Dhivya, 2020)

The improved segmentation method involves selecting the image and removing noise. The interested area of image is detected, then the location of the license plate is obtained using edge detection (Heng Sun et al.,2018). Each character in the image undergoes segmentation individually. The template matching method is then used with the help of correlation for recognition of characters in the number plate. (Balaji and Rajesh, 2017)

This paper deals with the detection and recognition of the license plate in a complex background. YOLO detector is used in license plate detection. YOLOv2 and YOLOv3 are trained for the detection process and compared to assess the detection performance (Cheng et al., 2018). Convolutional Recurrent Neural Network (CRNN) is used for recognition. CRNN-12 contains a DCNN which is used to obtain the features and a 2-layer bidirectional Gated Recurrent Unit (GRU) is used to decode the sequences of the feature. Connectionist Temporal Classification (CTC) loss function is used to train CNN and RNN together. This allows end-to-end recognition to be performed without segmentation. (Karwal and Girdhar, 2015)

The image acquisition is done first by capturing images automatically by a camera using raspberry pi. Then license plate extraction followed by license plate segmentation is performed (Rafique et al., 2009). The last step involves the character recognition process. OpenCV and OCR (optical character recognition) platforms are used for converting images into text. (Kashyap et al., 2018)

In handwritten OCR an algorithm is trained on a known dataset, and it discovers how to accurately classify the alphabets and digits (J. Redmon et al.,2016). Classification involves learning a model on a given input data and mapping it to predefined categories or classes. In the context of optical pattern, text categorization, time-series prediction, kernel based learning models have significant relevance (Palekar et al., 2017)

VNPD System algorithm is presented based on template matching. When the image is pre- processed, the image is loaded and converted to gray or binary (Kulkarni et al., 2018). Later, some denoising techniques are performed after which detection of number plate area and segmentation of characters is carried out during candidate area extraction phase. Following that in character recognition, template matching and retrieval of characters is performed. (Shariff et al., 2021)

The image of the number plate is captured and then processed. Each and every character present in the number plate is read in the recognition phase (Singh and Bhushan, 2019). OCR allows the letterings on the image to be scanned and changes it into texts which can be decoded. This paper uses ANPR and its applications for template matching (Ren et al., 2017)

The image for which the number plate recognition is to be done is loaded in RGB format which is then converted to grayscale image and then converted to binary using adaptive thresholding (Dalal and Triggs, 2005). The edges are obtained by subtracting the dilated image from the original image. The characters are then segmented from the number plate image which is used for template matching. Finally, segmented characters are matched with the templates of each character (Dean et al., 2013).

Image processing steps are employed to increase the accuracy of the results from convolutional neural. The smearing algorithm is applied to binary images for plate detection (Erhan et al., 2014).

TensorFlow framework developed using Keras deep learning library is used in the background. The results show that the system performs well and the trained neural network can accurately recognize the license plates (Felzenszwalb et al., 2010).

The object detection is framed as a regression problem to spatially separated bounding boxes and class probabilities associated with them (Girshick et al., 2014). In one evaluation, bounding boxes and class probabilities are predicted directly from full images by a single neural network (Zhai and Bensaali, 2013). This makes more localization errors but is less likely to predict false positives in the background. YOLO has better performance when compared to other detection methods, including DPM and R- CNN (Puranic et al., 2016).

METHODOLOGY

The proposed system has the capability of detecting and recognizing vehicle number plates. The main objective of this segment is to provide an elaborate explanation about how the license plate image is detected, captured and processed. The most widely used device for capturing the images in real time is the surveillance camera. In this prototype, a web camera is used to capture the basic features involved in image detection and recognition.

To detect each character of a number plate, the system is pre- trained to detect alphanumeric characters using machine learning techniques.

Pre-Trained Model Installation

In order to perform license plate recognition, the following technologies are used: PySpark, Tensorflow, OpenCV and OCR detection.

In the Initial step, PySpark is installed. It can be easily integrated with Apache spark and works well with a vast dataset. It enables the usage of Spark and Python APIs in detection and processing, then Tensorflow Object Detection is implemented using PySpark that provides access to pre- trained models for detection. These models can be downloaded from Tensorflow model zoo.

TensorFlow Object Detection API Installation

The Tensorflow object detection API is used here to create a model that will identify and localize the license plate. This helps in training and deploying several object detection models. It also includes a collection of the pre-trained models that were trained on various datasets such as the Common Object in Context (COCO) dataset, KITTI dataset and the Open Image Dataset.

Label Map Creation for Image Annotation

Label mapping is done to annotate images by applying bounding boxes to the relevant objects. A bounding box indicates the reference point for object detection and creates a collision box for the object that has been detected. Rectangles are drawn over images by data annotators. This outlines the object of interest within each image by defining its X and Y coordinates. This process simplifies finding the necessary objects for machine learning algorithms, determine the collision

Realtime Image Detection Using Open CV

For real-time detection of license plates, Open CV is used. It is a tool for image processing and performing computer vision tasks. It obtains the image from the web camera feed and converts it into Numpy arrays for further processing.

OCR Detection and ROI Filter Application

Once the image has been detected, the region of interest (ROI) filter is applied to the detected image. This allows the region of interest to be represented as a binary mask image where the pixels that belong to the ROI are set to 1 and pixels outside the ROI are set to 0.

The image captured is initially in RGB format; it is further converted into greyscale image which has black, white and multiple shades of grey. This can make character recognition a tedious process. Therefore, the greyscale image is again converted into a binary image which makes the characters in the license plate distinct and easy to detect for template matching.

Character Segmentation

Character segmentation process locates the alpha numeric characters on a number plate. The segmented characters are further translated into an alpha numeric text entry using the optical character recognition (OCR) techniques. Once the image of the license plate is detected, this input image is cropped from the starting to the ending point leaving all the extra wide spaces from top to bottom and from left to right. The characters present in the license plate are equally fit in the plate region and for easy comparison of the input characters with the characters present in the template data, the results are converted into the character set that matches the size of the images in the template data. After this is performed, matching metrics are computed.

This matching process is called template matching. The highest match for the character in the license plate is stored. If proper match is not found, rescaling and template matching process is repeated until the highest and accurate match is found. The index for the best match is stored as the recognized character. Template matching can also affect the accuracy of the number plate recognition.

RESULTS

In order to perform license plate recognition, the following technologies are used: PySpark, Tensorflow, OpenCV and OCR detection. Label mapping is done by applying bounding boxes to the relevant objects. The training process comprises of training the existing object detection model. For real-time detection of license plates, Open CV is used.

After the image is identified, the region of interest filter is applied to it and it is represented as a binary mask image. Then, character segmentation process is carried

Figure 1. License plate recognition system workflow

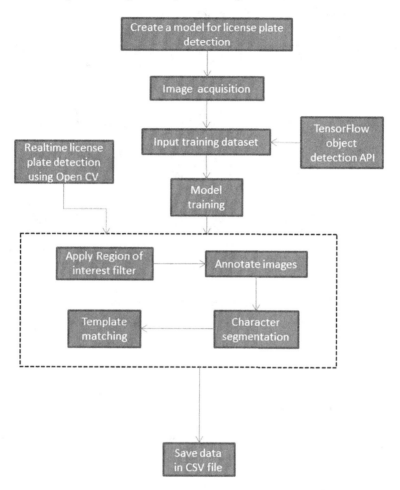

out on the detected image followed by template matching. The index for the best match is stored as the recognized character.

There are a number of additional techniques that could be used for applying OCR techniques with Apache Spark: Utilizing the Tesseract-OCR via PyTesseract is one of the common available techniques. But, there are numerous limitations in PyTesseract. Tesseract is not as precise as OCR using tensor flow. Teserract can sometimes return false positives which is not the case in PySpark. It is not good at analyzing the normal reading order of documents. It might fail to recognize a document that contains two columns and might try to join the text across the two columns. Tesseract does not work really well with images that have undergone some modification (complex or blurred background, lines, partial occlusion, distortion,

Figure 2. Sample of License Plate Dataset

Figure 3. Phases of license plate detection

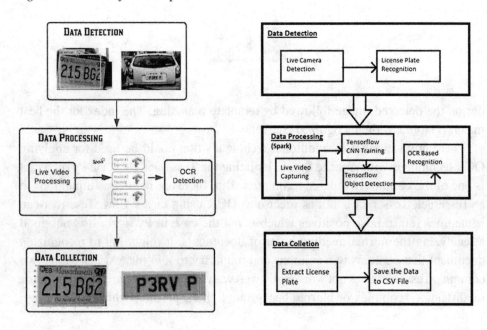

Figure 4. License plate detection to text conversion

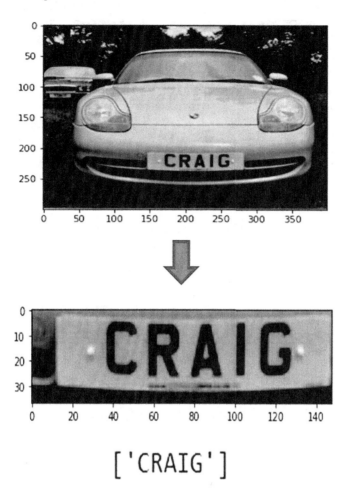

etc.) Tesseract requires a clean image to detect the text, this is where OpenCV plays an important role as it performs the operations on an image like converting a colored image to binary image, adjusting the contrast of an image, edge detection, and many more.

CONCLUSION

In this paper, a system is proposed to detect and recognize the license plates using a web camera. In this system, the license plate images are captured and annotated by applying bounding boxes. Furthermore, the region of interest filter is applied

Figure 5. License plate detection to text conversion

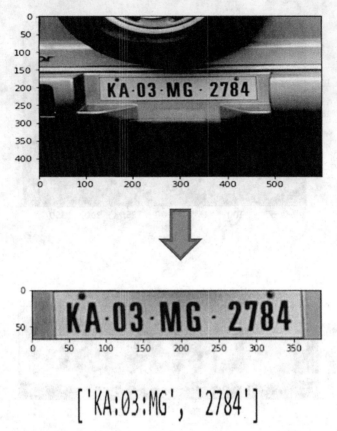

to convert the image into a binary mask image. Following this step, character segmentation process takes place to locate the alphanumeric characters found in the license plate. This is then converted into an alpha numeric text entry by using optical character recognition techniques. The usage of spark in the implementation of license plate detection helps capture and store large amounts of data and process them efficiently. A dataset of 411 license plate images were used to train the model to produce a robust system that performs detection, capturing and processing with utmost accuracy. This proposed license plate detection and recognition method achieves the best results compared to the existing methods in terms of precision and recognition rate.

REFERENCES

Cheng, C., Mei1, L., & Zhang, J. (2018). License Plate Recognition via Deep Convolutional Neural Network. *IOP Conference Series: Earth and Environmental Science, Volume 189, Traffic Engineering and Transportation System.*

Dalal, N., & Triggs, B. (2005). Histograms of oriented gradients for human detection. *IEEE Computer Society Conference on Computer Vision and Pattern Recognition (CVPR'05)*, pp. 886-893 vol. 1, 10.1109/CVPR.2005.177

Dean, T., Ruzon, M., Segal, M., Shlens, J., Vijaya-Narasimhan, S., Yagnik, J. (2013). Fast accurate detection of 100000 object classes on a single machine. *Computer Vision and Pattern Recognition (CVPR)*, pp. 1814-1821, 2013.

Erhan, D., Szegedy, C., Toshev, A., & Anguelov, D. (2014). Scalable object detection using deep neural networks. *Computer Vision and Pattern Recognition,* pp. 2155-2162. 10.1109/CVPR.2014.276

Felzenszwalb, P. F., Girshick, R. B., McAllester, D., & Ramanan, D. (2010, September). Object Detection with Discriminatively Trained Part-Based Models. *IEEE Transactions on Pattern Analysis and Machine Intelligence, 32*(9), 1627–1645. doi:10.1109/TPAMI.2009.167 PMID:20634557

Girshick, R., Donahue, J., Darrell, T., & Malik, J. (2014). Rich Feature Hierarchies for Accurate Object Detection and Semantic Segmentation. *IEEE Conference on Computer Vision and Pattern Recognition*, pp. 580-587, 10.1109/CVPR.2014.81

Karwal, H., & Girdhar, A. (2015). Vehicle Number Plate Detection System for Indian Vehicles. *IEEE International Conference on Computational Intelligence & Communication Technology*, pp. 8-12, 10.1109/CICT.2015.13

Kashyap, A., Suresh, B., Patil, A., Sharma, S., & Jaiswal, A. (2018). Automatic Number Plate Recognition. *International Conference on Advances in Computing, Communication Control and Networking (ICACCCN)*, pp. 838-843, doi:10.1109/ICACCCN.2018.8748287

Kulkarni, Y., Bodkhe, S., Kamthe, A., & Patil, A. (2018). Automatic number plate recognition for motorcyclists riding without helmet. *International Conference on Current Trends towards Converging Technologies (ICCTCT)*, pp. 1-6, 10.1109/ICCTCT.2018.8551001

Madhumitha, M., & Dhivya, P. (2020). Vehicle Recognition and Compilation in Database Software. *International Conference on System, Computation, Automation and Networking (ICSCAN)*, pp. 1-5, 10.1109/ICSCAN49426.2020.9262286

Palekar, R. R., Parab, S. U., Parikh, D. P., & Kamble, V. N. (2017). Real time license plate detection using openCV and tesseract. *International Conference on Communication and Signal Processing (ICCSP)*, pp. 2111-2115. 10.1109/ICCSP.2017.8286778

Puranic, A., K, D., & V, U. (2016). Vehicle Number Plate Recognition System: A Literature Review and Implementation using Template Matching. *International Journal of Computers and Applications, 134*(1), 12–16. doi:10.5120/ijca2016907652

Rafique, M. I. S. & Habib, H. A. (2009). Space Invariant Vehicle Recognition for Toll Plaza Monitoring and Auditing System. *Multitopic Conference INMIC 13th International*, pp. 1-6.

Balaji, G. N., & Rajesh, D. (2017). Smart Vehicle Number Plate Detection System for Different Countries Using an Improved Segmentation Method. *Imperial Journal of Interdisciplinary Research (IJIR)*.

Redmon, J., Divvala, S., Girshick, R., & Farhadi, A. (2016). You Only Look Once: Unified, Real-Time Object Detection. *IEEE Conference on Computer Vision and Pattern Recognition (CVPR)*, pp. 779-788, 10.1109/CVPR.2016.91

Ren, S., He, K., Girshick, R., & Sun, J. (2017, June 1). Faster R-CNN: Towards Real-Time Object Detection with Region Proposal Networks. *IEEE Transactions on Pattern Analysis and Machine Intelligence, 39*(6), 1137–1149. doi:10.1109/TPAMI.2016.2577031 PMID:27295650

Shariff, M. A. S., Bhatia, R., Kuma, R., & Jha, S. (2021). Vehicle Number Plate Detection Using Python and Open CV. *International Conference on Advance Computing and Innovative Technologies in Engineering (ICACITE)*, pp. 525-529, 10.1109/ICACITE51222.2021.9404556

Singh, J., & Bhushan, B. (2019). Real Time Indian License Plate Detection using Deep Neural Networks and Optical Character Recognition using LSTM Tesseract. *International Conference on Computing, Communication, and Intelligent Systems (ICCCIS)*, pp. 347-352, 10.1109/ICCCIS48478.2019.8974469

Sun, H., Fu, M., Abdussalam, A., Huang, Z., Sun, S., & Wang, W. (2018). License Plate Detection and Recognition Based on the YOLO Detector and CRNN-12. *International Conference On Signal And Information Processing, Networking And Computers ICSINC*, pp 66-74

Zhai, X., & Bensaali, F. (2013). Standard Definition ANPR System on FPGA and an Approach to Extend it to HD. *IEEE GCC Conference and exhibition*, pp. 214. 10.1109/IEEEGCC.2013.6705778

Chapter 2
An Enterprise Integration Method for Machine Learning-Driven Business Systems

Murat Pasa Uysal

https://orcid.org/0000-0002-8349-9403

Baskent University, Turkey

ABSTRACT

There is an overestimation of the benefits that may be provided by machine learning (ML) applications. Recent studies report the failures of ML projects, inadequate return on investment, or unsatisfactory project outcomes. Software engineering challenges, business and IT alignment, holistic management of business processes, data, applications, and infrastructure may be some causes. However, the author believe that the integration of ML applications with enterprise components is a serious issue that is often neglected. Therefore, the main argument of this study is that the enterprise integration models are critical for the long-term benefits and sustainability of ML-driven systems. In this study, the author developed an enterprise integration method for ML-driven business systems by using enterprise architecture methods and tools. Finally, this method is applied to an online shopping system in a business case study and presented important findings and insights.

INTRODUCTION

The proliferation of Artificial Intelligence (AI) has enabled new business models and provided innovative solutions for enterprises. As a subfield of AI, Machine Learning (ML) and its successful implementations, may have a great impact on the

DOI: 10.4018/978-1-6684-4246-3.ch002

competitiveness of enterprises. It is possible to see various examples of complex ML-driven business systems in the domains, such as industry, finance, defense, healthcare (Nalchigar et al.,2021). However, recent studies also report the failures of ML projects, their inadequate return on investment, or unsatisfactory project outcomes. There is an overestimation of the solutions and benefits that may be provided by ML applications. Therefore, business systems employing ML solutions can be at a high risk of failure or they can easily fall short of their business objectives (Kelly and Kaskade, 2013).

There may be various causes for the failures of ML applications when they are viewed from the perspectives of different disciplines, such as System Engineering (SyE), Computer Science (CS), Data Science (DS), and Software Engineering (SE) (Ishikawa and Yoshioka, 2019). For example, Ponsard et al. (2017) and Saltz et al. (2017) indicate that the majority of ML studies focus on technical aspects. Bughin et al. (2017) present the factors for transforming an organization towards AI. Ransbotham et al. (2017) report the challenges in the adoption of AI systems as AI-related skills and knowledge, cultural and organizational barriers, limited technological capabilities, lack of management support, and unclear business cases. Some research studies explore ML and DS project management methods from project management perspectives and report their efficiency and implementation challenges (Saltz et al. 2019, Uysal 2021a).

From a historical perspective, ML may be thought of as it is in the early days of SE. Therefore, analyzing and specifying requirements, managing stakeholders' expectations, correct estimations, design of effective test cases, and configuration management can be the major SE challenges when engineering ML-driven business systems (Giray, 2021). Moreover, SE and ML modules can be entangled in various ways, and thus, the development of the ML-integrated modules is usually more difficult than traditional SE modules (Amershi et al., 2019) Therefore, there is a clear need for the integration of ML workflow management into SE practices (Lwakatare et al., 2020). The integration of SE infrastructure with ML processes also speeds up the ML experimentations.

In terms of business and IT alignment, one important challenge is the holistic and integrated management of business processes, data, enterprise applications, and infrastructure. However, regarding the strategies needed for the integration of ML applications with enterprise components is often neglected when developing or maintaining ML-driven business systems (Uysal and Mergen, 2021b). Advances in hardware, software, communication, software applications, and data processing technologies have also paved the way for integrating cutting-edge solutions into business systems, such as Internet of Things (IoT) (Xu, 2011). However, these developments have even worsened the management and integration issues. The majority of the research studies and industrial applications explore ML in specific domains, such as IT, software, finance, industrial production, healthcare, e-commerce, etc. However, they cannot prescribe the seamless integration of ML applications with the rest of the business domain components. Some of the studies propose architectures only for ML-specific data processes, applications, and hardware, however, they fail to address enterprise-wide integration without risking the current structure and business applications.

There are few vendor-specific reference architectures for ML (Google, 2021). However, they are still away from providing holistic and integrative prescriptions for realizing the organizational benefits of ML applications. Consequently, we claim that these integration issues necessitated the support of a relatively new discipline: Industrial Information Integration Engineering (IIIE) (Roode, 2005; Raffai, 2007). Xu (2015) provides the technological and engineering foundations of IIIE along with its interdisciplinary structure. Accordingly, enterprise systems require adopting strategic approaches and integration frameworks, such as enterprise architecture (EA). Thus, EAs can meet the integration requirements of various business stakeholders when designing, implementing, or evaluating information systems (Uysal, 2021c).

Chen (2016) presents the findings of studies from 2006 to 2015. IoT, business systems' interoperability, and various integration technologies are the core research topics. According to this research report, there are two important integration challenges for business systems. The first is taking all of the concerns of stakeholders into account while addressing a wide range of technical and organizational issues. The second is establishing a holistic business and enterprise perspective for ML applications. Therefore, the main argument of this study is that the design and maintenance of enterprise integration models are critical for the long-term organizational benefits, operations, and sustainability of ML-driven business systems. In other words, we need to adopt the principles and use the guidelines of IIIE. Studies on ML refer to various issues, however, there is significantly less research exploring the business systems and ML from an enterprise integration perspective. In this chapter, therefore, an enterprise integration method is proposed for ML-driven business systems. The next parts of this chapter are organized as the background, main focus, solutions and recommendations, future research directions, and conclusions sections respectively.

BACKGROUND

Business Systems and Models

The concept of a system can be defined as a whole that is made up of parts. Although this definition may change from one discipline to another, Systems Science explores those concepts, characteristics, and properties of systems that are not specific to one discipline. For example, one definition of a system adopts a technology-based approach, and it emphasizes a certain functionality that is not shared or possessed by none of the parts. Another approach underlines the combination of system elements along with their mutual interactions and connections. A more comprehensive definition is given by Lin et al. (2012): "a system is an organic whole, which is made up of some elements and their mutual interactions, with certain structure and functionality". Therefore, a system is a collection of components or elements, which are organized for a common purpose. In the same context, a business system may be an organization, company, or an enterprise with a collection of value-added processes, services, technologies, and resources for producing and supplying goods or providing services.

A model is an abstract, physical or conceptual representation of a system, object, or phenomenon. Models help people understand a subject that it represents, and formulate or design a solution to a problem. In the same scope, a business model (BM) may have two essential functions: First, expressing the expectations from people, business processes, and services. Second, helping managers or decision-makers understand and communicate business strategies, implementations, and relevant issues (Nielsen, 2019). The definitions of BM may be grouped into several categories depending on the points of view of a business. For example, they may be regarded as a tool that connects processes, services, resources, and people to assure a company to be profitable in the long term. According to Timmers (1998), and Weill and Vitale (2001), a BM stands for an architecture for a product, services, information flows, and sources of revenues and they focus on business actors, tangible and intangible flows among them. Chesbrough (2007), Skarzynski and Gibson (2008), and Zott and Amit (2008) focus on creating value. Therefore, as a useful tool to link ideas, "a business model is a conceptual framework for identifying how a company creates, delivers, and extracts value. It typically includes a whole set of integrated components, all of which can be looked on as opportunities for innovation and competitive advantage".

The literature reviews on BM provide a variety of findings. Budler et al. (2021) present the results of a bibliometric review. They explore the time-dependent co-evolution of research sub-streams of BMs. They find that the major businesses are strategy, entrepreneurship, and innovation sub-disciplines from which a BM draws. Value networks, Industry 4.0, and sustainability offer various opportunities to increase the inter-connectedness of BM research. From an innovation perspective, business model innovation (BMI) is defined as a radical change in an existing BM for gaining or maintaining competitive advantages. Thus, Zhang et al. (2021) explore the relationships among BMI, its antecedents, and company performance. Accordingly, there is a significant positive association between internal (managerial cognition, internal resources, capabilities, and organization characteristics) and external antecedents (market opportunity, situational factors, value network, and technology innovation) and BM.

In terms of sustainability and circular economy, a great body of knowledge has been started to accumulate. For example, Geissdoerfer et al. (2020) present the history, conceptual foundations, and frameworks of circular business models (CBM) and circular BMI. Cycling, extending, intensifying, dematerializing, and transformation are major circular business model strategies, and the BM concept is mostly based on the value chain concept. Rosa et al. (2019), identify five CBM archetypes and nine classification methods along with five adoption-oriented challenges and four decision-support tools. In the same context, Reis et al. (2021) provide a view of the prevailing and emergent energy community BM archetypes and focus on the main differences between BMs, their strengths, and barriers. Finally, Vaio et al. (2020), explore the role of Artificial Intelligence in the construction of sustainable BMs and development goals. They find that the innovation challenge includes ethical, social, economic, and legal aspects, however, they still suggest the use of AI for the development of SBMs. ML-driven or supported systems, today, have been used for a variety of purposes (classification, regression, and clustering) in sectors such as, finance, e-commerce, production, agriculture, retail, healthcare, etc. Therefore, ML is an important means of creating value as well as achieving or improving competitive advantages (Wodecki. 2019).

Machine Learning

"Big data" means the collection of large and complex data sets. Variety (diversity and types of data), volume (size of data), and velocity (speed of data generation) are regarded as the main characteristic properties. Data science (DS) has evolved from the data management and statistics disciplines (Cielen et al. 2016) since the processing and analysis of big data is difficult by using traditional methods, tools, and techniques. This situation even gets worse and becomes difficult when the amount of data grows, velocity, and variety increase. The data may be structured, unstructured, or machine-generated, and they may also be in the form of video, audio, or image. In this context, Machine learning (ML) is defined as "a field of study that gives computers the ability to learn without being explicitly programmed (Samuel, 1959)" as a subfield of AI. In ML, appropriate data and an algorithm are combined to form a learning model that learns to perform tasks by relying on the patterns in the data. ML is multidisciplinary and borrows some of its techniques from computer science, uses complex algorithms, and includes the processes to build predictive models. Thus, meaningful information can be derived to make better business decisions and valuable insights can be inferred from the knowledge extracted. Since DS and ML are closely related, ML can be linked to the model development phase of a DS project.

In DS, an algorithm is used as a sequence of statistical and mathematical data processing steps to model a solution. In ML, however, this algorithm is first trained to find the right features or patterns in a massive amount of training data. Next, the trained model (data plus algorithm), which also represents a candidate solution to a problem, is used for predictions or making decisions based on testing data. The predictions and decisions become more accurate as the performance of the model becomes better. Therefore, data and a matching algorithm together form a model that has to be fit into a solution space. Learning types in ML are broadly categorized into supervised learning (SL), unsupervised learning (UL), and reinforcement learning (RL). The main stages of an ML project are as follows:

Problem Definition

Initially, a research problem as well as the rationale behind using ML have to be identified. Understanding the context of the business and how ML can contribute is critical for the project's success. Therefore, a project charter frames the goal(s), missions, project scope, timeline, deliverables, success criteria, data sources, and risks.

Data Acquisition

Observation of real-world objects and phenomena related to the research problem is the data to be used during an ML project. The concepts, such as events, facts, measurements, words, numbers, images, and a collection of discrete entities may belong to the data (Zheng and Casari, 2018). Data may be in different forms ranging from text files to databases, which are provided by online or offline data sources. Each part of data presents a limited aspect of reality, and thus the collection of the related data parts enables the big picture of the problem. It is also important to collect and process a large volume of data for model accuracy. Moreover, completeness, accuracy, timeliness, and consistency are the other core criteria for assuring data quality.

Data Processing

This stage includes the data processes, such as data preparation, combining the data retrieved from different sources, cleansing and removing possible errors, labeling, transforming, and integrating. These processes are labor-intensive and can take up much of the project time, which may be up to 80%. Missing values, data entry errors, impossible values, redundant white spaces, and outliers are among the common data errors that have to be eliminated. Missing data can be omitted or imputed from a static or statistical distribution. Transforming data into a suitable form can simplify data modeling. Too many features (variables) can make data processing difficult to manage as they may not add new information or contribute to modeling. In this case, it may be better to reduce the number of features. The main purpose of data processing is to bring the data to a common standard, and thus, the ML models will perform better as the data is better. The success of ML projects is directly dependent on the quality of data.

Feature Engineering

Features (variables) are the representations of raw data and they can be a scalar (numeric value) or an ordered list of scalars. Features play an intermediary role between data and models. ML algorithms (models) are mathematical formulas, which describe the relationships between various aspects of the data and relate the numeric quantities to each other. Therefore, feature engineering (FE) or feature extraction is a process for exploring the most appropriate features from the raw data and also making them available for modeling, training, and testing processes (Zheng and Casari, 2018). Embedding, filtering, and wrapping methods are used for FE. Embedding methods are used during model training processes. Filtering removes the features that are not useful for the models. Wrapper methods allow the use of subsets of features. Combining multiple data inputs may improve the ML models' performances when features are scattered among various data sources. FE can be part of the data acquisition, data processing, or model-building phases of ML. The procedures of FE may be complicated, time and resource-consuming. Therefore, the much of time is usually spent on data processing and FE activities. For this purpose, an ML pipeline can be used as a method of automating ML workflows to develop learning models effectively and efficiently. ML pipelines encapsulate multiple sequential steps and organization-specific ML practices. They can be critical for maintaining multiple learning models and integrating them with software applications. The automated ML pipelines enable automated model development, testing, cooperation, and coordination in ML development teams.

Exploratory Data Analysis

The exploratory Data Analysis (EDA) process is conducted to have a better understanding of the research data. Therefore, statistical analysis and data visualizations are its main methods and techniques (Muller and Massaron, 2015). Data analysts try to describe the data, seek relations between variables, and identify known or unknown patterns. Results are reported by graphs, tables, plots, and various data visualization techniques. EDA is also required for forming research hypotheses, determining, developing, and predictive evaluating models. Thus, EDA gives direction to model development and helps to become more effective in the subsequent modeling and analysis processes (Mukhiya and Ahmed, 2020).

Model Training and Testing

An ML model is the combination of an algorithm and data with appropriate features. ML models are created after training and testing processes. The main purpose of this stage is to use, design, or build models for developing the best solution to the research problem. Therefore, models should be correct, interpretable, and applicable, and represent the problem and solution domain as precisely as possible. Modeling is an iterative process, which includes the selection of a suitable algorithm that maps the input data to the target data, model execution, comparison, and evaluation of the results. A complex research problem may require chaining multiple models. In this case, the output of a model becomes the input for another model, which is defined as ensemble learning.

As aforementioned, SL, UL, and RL are the main types of learning methods in ML (Muller and Guido, 2017). SL occurs when the model learns from labeled training data to make predictions. This is similar to a situation where a student learns with examples of input-output pairs under the supervision of an instructor. k-Nearest Neighbor (k-NN), Regression, Support-Vector Machines, Decision Tree, Random Forest, Naive Bayes, and Neural Networks are the major SL algorithms (Fenner 2020). In UL, ML models learn from the data without reference to labels. The purpose is to identify commonalities in the input data and to determine the patterns, clusters, or distinct groups. UL can also be used in the EDA processes to have a better understanding of the raw data. RL is similar to learning by trial and error. It occurs when the model learns from labeled data through experimentation by giving negative or positive feedback. The idea behind RL is learning by interacting with a dynamic environment (Sutton and Barto, 2015). Programming languages, such as Python, R, Java, and C++ can be used during the training process.

Model Validation and Evaluation

Model validation and evaluation processes are carried out by using quantitative and qualitative methods and techniques. Qualitative methods emphasize the ML process life cycle while quantitative ones focus on the data and learning models (Zheng, 2015). An ML model should have good predictive power and it should generalize well to the unseen data. Overfitting and underfitting are the two common modeling errors in an SL process. Underfitting occurs when the model is too simple and it cannot detect all the aspects of the data. On the other side, overfitting occurs when the model is too complex, and thus the algorithm learns too much by memorizing the training data however, it displays low performance against the testing data. Different ML models for classification, regression, and clustering have also different performance or evaluation metrics. For example, the root-mean-square error is the most commonly used evaluation metric for regression tasks. The accuracy, precision-recall, confusion matrix, area under the curve, and log-loss metrics are used for the classification tasks. Testing is conducted with separate and unused data. The hold-out strategy is based on training the data on the larger part while validation is done by using the smaller and randomly hold-out data set. The cross-validation strategy, on the other hand, divides the data into parts and uses each part one time as test data while the rest is used as training data.

Enterprise Architecture

An "enterprise" is defined as a collection of organizations that have common goals (TOGAF, 2018). It may be a division of a corporation, an entire corporation, a government agency, a department, or organizations connected by common ownership. ISO/IEC/IEEE 42010 defines an "architecture" as "the fundamental concepts or properties of a system in its environment embodied in its elements, relationships, and in the principles of its design and evolution.". An architecture may cross various systems and various functional groups within an enterprise. Depending upon this context, the TOGAF standard defines EA as "the structure of components, their inter-relationships, and the principles and guidelines governing their design and evolution over time." According to Lankhorst (2009), EA is "a coherent whole of principles, methods, and models that are used in the design and realization of an enterprise's organizational structure, business processes, information systems, and infrastructure". Thus, EAs enable organizational alignment through the use of models that are describing various aspects of enterprises and represent the different views of stakeholders.

Today, it is known that exploitation of information technology (IT) and digital transformation are vital means to achieve business success and competitive advantage. EAs can meet these requirements by providing a strategic context for the improvement of digital capability as a response to ever-changing business environments. An EA provides an integrated and holistic view of an enterprise by linking distinct enterprise knowledge domains and bringing information together. Moreover, an effective EA governance enables organizations to establish the balance between business/IT operational efficiency and business/IT transformation. There are different frameworks for EA design and development, such as Zachman (2008), DoDAF (2010), TOGAF (2018), etc. They provide guidelines, methods, and techniques while presenting the concepts, definitions, and a basis for EA design and development. In terms of management discipline, EAs should establish capabilities in the areas, such as IT management, service management, performance management, financial and resource management, risk, and quality management. EAs also include the following benefits:

- Effective data, information, process, and technology integration,
- Proactive control, monitoring, and management,
- Stakeholder management and value creation through monitoring, measuring, evaluation, and responding to change,
- Increased transparency and accountability,
- Controlled risk management,
- Maximum use of existing EA components,
- Improvement of business process performance and operations,
- Improvement of user productivity,
- Improvement of portability and scalability,
- Improvement of interoperability,
- Improvement of security,
- Decrease in the costs.

The Open Group Architecture Framework (TOGAF)

The TOGAF standard is an open and foundational industry framework. It provides guidelines, methods, and tools for the design and development of any kind of EA. Its main document is composed of various parts, such as architecture development method (ADM), ADM guidelines and techniques, architecture content framework, enterprise continuum and tools, and architecture capability framework. TOGAF supports four architecture domains: business architecture, data architecture, application architecture, technology, and infrastructure architecture. ADM is a repeatable, iterative, and cyclic EA development process, which realizes the architecture contents, their transitioning, and governing. Preliminary, architecture vision, business architecture, information systems, technology architecture, opportunities and solutions, migration planning, implementation governance, and architecture change management are the main phases of ADM. Since architecture development is a cyclical and continuous process, these steps are executed repeatedly for the target architecture as shown in the case study below. The steps of ADM adapted to this study are as follows:

- Step-1: Define business strategy, drivers, goals and principles,
- Step-2: Select reference models, viewpoints, and tools,
- Step-3: Develop baseline architecture description,
- Step-4: Develop target architecture description,

- Step-5: Perform gap analysis,
- Step-6: Define candidate roadmap components,
- Step-7: Resolve impacts across the architecture landscape,
- Step-8: Conduct formal stakeholder review,
- Step-9: Finalize and create the architecture definition document.

Requirements analysis and specification of a target EA is usually the initial process. A target EA represents the final state and future descriptions of a baseline EA. Determining the scope and breadth of the EA is an important challenge. Therefore, a complete EA may be expected to address all of the domains (business, data, application, and technology); however, all-inclusive or enterprise-wide architecture may be too complex and resource-consuming. In this situation, focusing on a particular segment or specific enterprise domain(s) may be suggested. Special notice should also be given to the depth and appropriate level of the EA. For the sake of usefulness and simplicity, this level can be relevant to the extent it includes the required details while excluding the unnecessary components. The design of EA as a federation of architectures can be another option, however, this time, it would bring extra challenges for the integration processes, consistency, and maintenance.

A target architecture represents the outcome of an EA project, the main goal, and stakeholders' concerns for functional and non-functional requirements. Foundation architectures consist of guideline principles, patterns, and generic and ready-to-use architectural solutions. Therefore, architects can make use of the foundation and common systems architectures, or organization-specific architectures when developing target architectures. Another choice would be the use of industry-specific architectures; however, they are still incomplete in terms of system functionalities and enterprise architectural requirements. A gap analysis is conducted to identify the differences between the current and target EA. The results of this analysis are important for determining the transition architectures, which describe the increments according to the architectural descriptions of preliminary and vision phases. Transition architectures are evolutionary in nature, and therefore, they converge on the target EA. If the project requires a large-scale transformation, it would be advisable to address the urgent issues that have high priority and that are aligned with the project's scope. For example, an initial focus may be given to the information systems, data, and application architectures.

Data architecture illustrates how data are created, stored, and transported. It mainly consists of data objects used by business functions, processes, and services. The level of data complexity, requirements for data migration and integration as well as the support needed for data exchange are included. Therefore, architecture definition documents comprise all or some of the logical and physical data models along with the conceptual diagrams. The application architecture domain layer supports its above layer, which is the business architecture layer. How the enterprise applications function and how they handle the operational and integration requirements are highly critical. The TOGAF standard recommends the use of diagrams, such as business, data flow, use-case, realization, and migration. Therefore, enterprise architects can also consider the followings: (a) creating a list of applications as a portfolio, (b) decomposing complicated applications into simplified applications when needed, and (c) relating the enterprise application architecture to the enterprise business and data architectures by using tools, such as matrices and maps.

Change and transition management of EAs is another critical success factor for the design, development, and maintenance processes. To consider the gaps between the baseline and target architectures, a migration and implementation plan with an architecture road map are created. The migration plan shows how to move from the baseline and transition EAs to the target EA. The required changes are grouped into logical work packages in transition architectures. The candidate solutions indicate the construction and specification of the new architectures at the corresponding level of the target EA. The assessment of dependencies between EA elements, estimating costs and benefits, and time and resource requirements are important activities when trying to ensure conformance with the target EA. Therefore, the target EA is created, deployed and delivered as a series of EA transitions. This also provides a reflection on the business priorities, an early realization of the expected benefits, and minimizing the possible risks during implementation.

Industrial Information Integration Engineering

Architecture is a formal description of the structure of a system, which is composed of different components, interrelationships, and guidelines for the design and development processes. On the other hand, the concept of enterprise is defined as a collection of organizations with common goals, missions, and objectives to provide products and services. Therefore, an EA describes the organizational structure, business processes, information systems, infrastructure, and the relationships between an organization and its environment (Lankhorst, 2009). The artifacts of an EA define the logical organization of enterprise processes, business functions, information flow, and data architecture. The concept of enterprise integration (EI) has emerged from the methods and frameworks used for EAs. EI ensures that the interactions between enterprise structures and components help to achieve enterprise goals and objectives. However, EI requires the application of engineering knowledge belonging to various engineering disciplines, such as systems engineering, industrial engineering, information systems engineering, management, etc. As a result, a new engineering discipline has been born: Industrial Information Integration Engineering (IIIE). IIIE "is a set of foundational concepts and techniques that facilitate the industrial information integration process", and it "comprises methods for solving complex problems when developing IT infrastructure for industrial sectors, especially with respect to information integration (Xu, 2015)" (Figure 1).

Figure 1. Industrial Information Integration Engineering

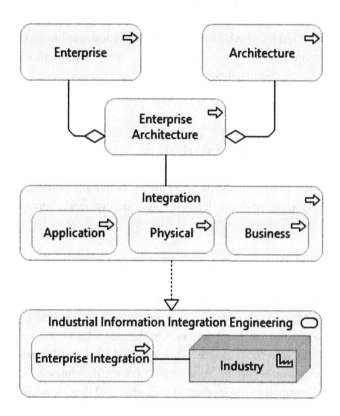

MAIN FOCUS OF THE CHAPTER

The purpose of this study is to propose an approach and an enterprise integration architecture (EIA) for ML-driven online shopping systems. Therefore, this approach will enable us to deal with the complexity of ML systems as well as their integration with business, application, and infrastructure architectural domains. A layered, multi-dimensional, and service-oriented integration method is proposed for ML-driven business systems. The layered integration includes a business process integration layer, a data integration layer, an application integration layer, and an infrastructure integration layer. The multi-dimensional integration view contains horizontal and vertical integration activities and it forms the scope of the EI process. Horizontal integration aims the cross-functional cooperation within an enterprise while vertical integration combines the processes, data, and interactions at different integration layers. Service-Oriented Architecture (SOA) allows the definition and representation of processes and functions at different layers in terms of IT services. This approach can also provide seamless integration and interoperability of an enterprise owning heterogeneous systems. Finally, we develop the EIA based on a generic business scenario. ArchiMate Language Specification (Archimate 3.1, 2019), Archi IDE (Archi, 2021), TOGAF, and ADM are the main methods and tools used during the design and development processes. The ADM is a generic method, therefore, we modified it to suit the specific needs of the business scenario.

Business Scenario

The success of any EA project depends on the extent to which it is linked to the business requirements and the degree how it supports achieving business goals. Therefore, the case study and the design and development of the EIA for the ML-driven business system are dependent on a generic business scenario as presented below:

Business Problem

Company X is an e-tailer and owns an online shopping system for selling different products from various vendors. It adopts a transaction fee revenue model, and thus, it receives a transaction fee from sellers. On the other hand, recent developments in information and web technologies have enabled the establishment of low-cost e-commerce business enterprises. As a consequence, this situation led to an increase in the number of competitors in its market segment, and thus, it would be difficult to become profitable in near future. To achieve a competitive advantage and customer satisfaction, the company intends to offer intelligent services to its customers, such as product recommendation, personalization, customization, and product matching. These services will also enable effective customer segmentation as well as various financial predictions. Therefore, the company decided to gradually transform its e-business system into an ML-driven e-business system. However, it is not sure about "what-to-do" and "how-to-do". Most importantly, how to integrate new ML applications without risking its current business environment, enterprise applications, and technological infrastructure.

Business and Technical Environment

The company's e-commerce model is business to customer (B2C) and it owns IT infrastructure, server nodes, and applications. It also uses an enterprise resource planning (ERP) application along with additional enterprise applications for its business processes.

Business and IT Goals, Objectives and Desired Outcomes

The company's business and IT goals are as follows:

- To achieve a competitive advantage,
- To improve customer satisfaction through personalization, customization, product matching,
- To improve profitability,
- To make effective and more correct financial predictions,
- To improve business process performance and operations,
- To improve business and IT manageability,
- To decrease business and IT risks,
- To maintain the efficiency and operability of its current IT applications and infrastructure,
- To decrease long-term IT costs.

As indicated above, the company also wants to decrease the expenses related to IT ownership, IT operations, and maintenance costs. Therefore, it would be reasonable for adopting cloud computing principles, such as software-as-a-service (SaaS), platform-as-a-service (PaaS), or infrastructure-as-a-service (IaaS).

Human and Computer Actors in the Business Case

The human actors are customers, business managers, business management team, IT managers and staff, and ML application developers. The main computer actors are the desired ML application supporting the online shopping system, the company's ERP, and enterprise applications.

SOLUTIONS AND RECOMMENDATIONS

Target Architecture

The target EIA for Company X includes five logical groups of EA components that are arranged as EA layers (Figure 2):

- Business elements, drivers, goals, principles and stakeholders: This layer includes the company's main business strategy, business drivers, e-business model elements, and stakeholders.
- ML-driven business system drivers, goals, principles and stakeholders: This layer includes ML-related stakeholders, drivers and goals, IT-related drivers and goals, SOA, cloud principles, and information integration principles.
- Business actors, roles, interfaces, services and processes: This layer includes business actors, roles and processes, IT processes and services, online shopping processes and services.
- Enterprise applications, ML experimentation processes and applications: This layer includes enterprise processes and applications, ML experimentation, ML pipeline processes, and applications.
- Technology and infrastructure: This layer includes system servers and nodes, infrastructure services, communication networks, and application programming interfaces (API).

Business Strategy

Business Stakeholders, Drivers, Goals and Principles

The purpose of this layer is to determine the business strategy and related EA elements for the ML-driven online shopping system (Figure 3). Stakeholders, drivers, goals, and principles are the main motivational EA elements. Drivers are the internal or external conditions that would motivate the company to define its goals and apply the required changes to achieve them. Business managers, customers, IT managers and staff, e-business model management team constitute the stakeholders. Choosing Company X's online shopping system is defined as the customers' main motivating driver. Personalization and customization, ease of managing product delivery, and ease of product search may be the goals of customers. Profitability is the business managers' main driver, which is affected by the goals such as increasing sales revenue and charging a transaction fee. In terms of e-business models, the eight key elements are adopted as the business principles and rules that would support the way in which

Figure 2. Target EIA

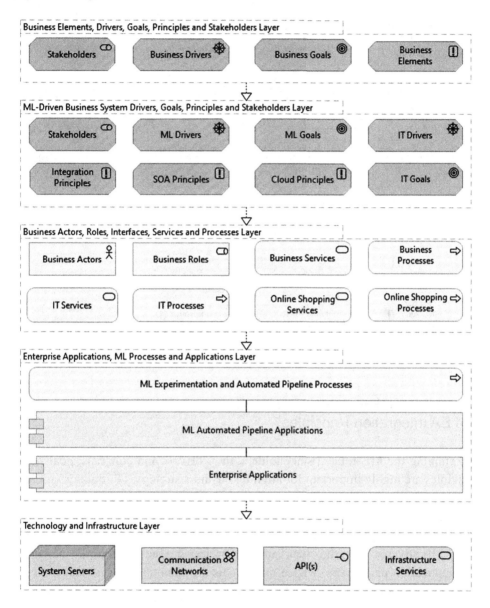

the company fulfills its missions. These principles are value proposition, revenue model, market opportunity, market strategy, competitive environment, competitive advantage, organizational development, and management team (Laudon and Traver, 2020). However, they are usually influenced by organizations' missions and plans, external constraints, current systems and technologies, and industry trends.

Figure 3. Business strategy, stakeholders, drivers, goals and principles

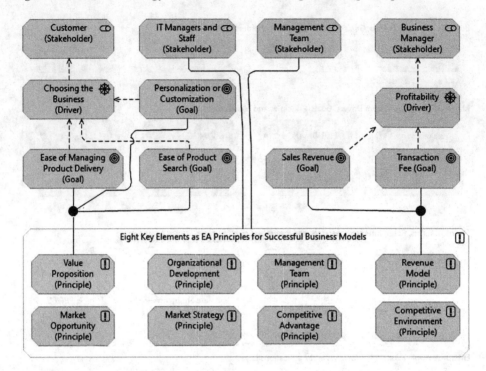

ML-related Stakeholders, Drivers, Goals and EA Integration Principles

Determining the ML-related stakeholders, their drivers and concerns, goals, and principles are highly important for aligning business strategy, IT strategy, and ML strategy (Figure 4). The management team, ML developers, the company's IT managers, and application developers are the technical stakeholders. ML pipeline, easy model development, quality, and availability of data are the goals that affect the driver ML processes. On the other hand, IT services are the driver for IT managers and application developers, whose main goals are maintaining the quality of IT services, and ensuring the availability and sustainability of IT operations. The eight key e-business model elements are the drivers of the management team. The goals for ML application usage are: Customer segmentation, product recommendation, fraud detection, product matching, sell and financial predictions, and personalization.

In terms of EA principles, ML EIA design and development principles should support the business goals for ML. A multi-dimensional, layered, and SOA is adopted for the information integration processes. The layered integration is accomplished by the business process integration layer, data integration layer,

Figure 4. ML-driven business system drivers, goals, principles and stakeholders

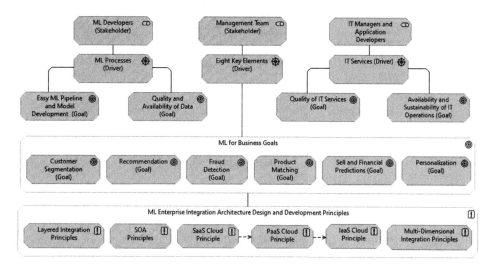

application integration layer, and infrastructure and technology integration layer. The multi-dimensional integration includes vertical and horizontal integration., and it frames the scope of the integration processes. Horizontal integration provides cross-functional cooperation. Vertical integration, on the other hand, enables the integration of processes, data, applications, and infrastructure at different layers. SOA allows functional integration so that heterogeneous business systems and ML application components can invoke each other and use the services provided by its upper or lower layers. Cloud computing principles have also great contributions. In Software-as-a-Service (SaaS), the control over storage, servers, applications, operations, and configuration management is given to a third party, such as Amazon Web Services (Amazon 2021) and Google Cloud Platform (Google, 2021). In the case of Platform-as-a-service (PaaS), the company has control over the management of ML applications and data to some extent. However, the service provider is still responsible for the data storage, infrastructure, and operating systems used for ML applications. Finally, the infrastructure-as-a-service (IaaS) principles allow the control over the data storage, application server management, and access to the ML application infrastructure via interfaces.

Business Process Architecture

This layer includes business and IT processes, user service bus, interfaces, and user roles (Figure 5). In other words, business and IT processes are realized by the business services that serve the users via desktop and mobile interfaces. Business

Figure 5. Actors, roles, interfaces, services and processes

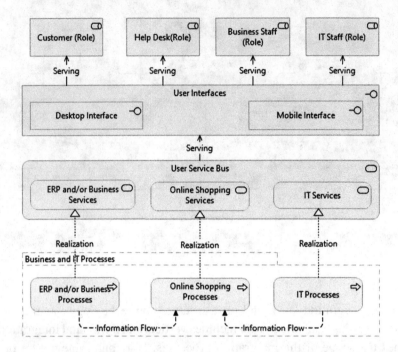

and IT processes are composed of ERP and/or business processes, online shopping processes, and IT processes, which are connected by information flow relationships. User Service Bus includes the services that are realized by their corresponding business and IT processes.

The online shopping process may start with one of the processes, such as viewing items, searching items, browsing items, or recommending items. After deciding on an item and customer authentication, the customer may add the searched item to the shopping cart, and continue her/his shopping or conduct the payment process. The payment can be made via credit card or wire transfer (Figure 6).

ML experimentation includes data analysis, data validation, data preparation, model training, model evaluation, model validation, and ML pipeline deployment processes. Consequently, these processes are realized into a ML service that supports the online shopping processes. There are information flows between business and IT processes (Figure 7).

Aforementioned, data processing and its architecture are highly critical. Therefore, business and online shopping data are prepared and then realized as a data service for both ML applications and their experimentation processes as shown by Figure 8.

Figure 6. Online shopping processes

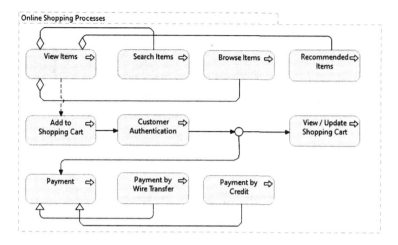

Application Architecture

At this layer, there are two main service realizations, which collaborate to form an enterprise applications service bus as shown in Figure 9. The first one is the service realization of enterprise applications and ERP. The second service realization includes the automated ML pipeline application components that are again realized as ML service(s) through the service collaboration. In a ML pipeline, ML codes are split into more manageable and integrated components and they are used for producing, updating, and deploying ML models. In this way, it is easy to execute, iterate, and monitor ML processes in the context of the pipeline. The ML application components are (a) data analysis, (b) data validation, (c) data preparation, (d) model training,

Figure 7. ML experimentation processes

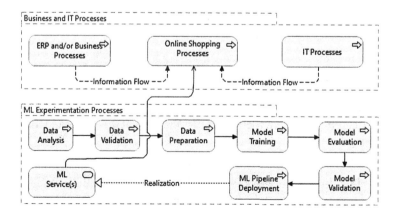

Figure 8. Data architecture and ML experimentation processes

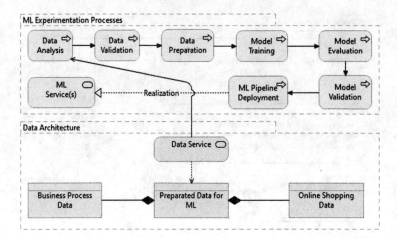

(e) model evaluation, (f) model validation, (g) model serving, and (h) monitoring performance of an ML service. An enterprise may use ERP or distinct enterprise applications depending on its organizational structure, resources, and IT strategy. Thus, enterprise applications would be: human resources IS, finance and accounting IS, customer relationship management IS, supply chain management IS, document management IS, web application(s), mobile application(s), database application(s).

Technology and Infrastructure Architecture

As can be seen from Figure 10, the technology and infrastructure service bus provides the services to its upper layer (enterprise and ML applications layer). This service bus includes database service, web service, network service, and application service. These services are located in the system servers and nodes, which usually communicate by using local area (LAN) or mobile networks. The system servers consist of ML deployment server(s), database server(s), network server(s), web server(s), application server(s), file server(s).

FUTURE RESEARCH DIRECTIONS

Our future research efforts will focus on the limitations of this study and the following research topics:

- Addressing the limitations of this study, i.e. application of the proposed method to a real industrial case study instead of a generic case.

Figure 9. Application architecture

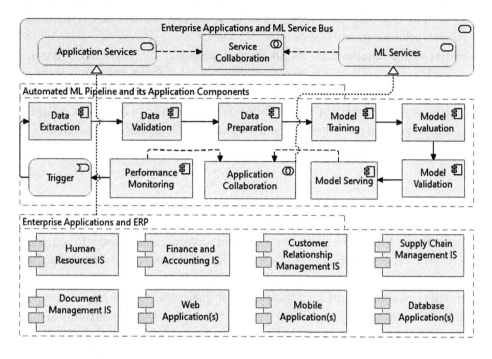

- Transition EAs are not given due to the scope and the limitations of this study. Therefore, future studies will focus on the transition architectures in more detail.

Figure 10. Technology and infrastructure architecture

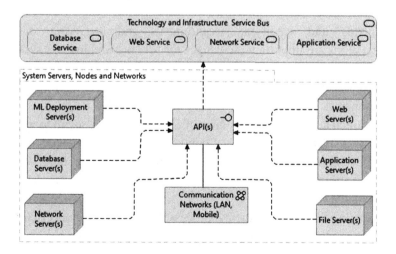

- Application of the proposed method to the systems of different domains, such as industrial production systems, healthcare information systems, and enterprise information systems.
- Exploring requirements engineering approaches for ML-driven systems, such as goal-oriented requirements engineering, value-based requirements engineering, and scenario-based requirements engineering.
- Exploring the applicability, feasibility, and practicality of corrective, adaptive, perfective, and preventive software maintenance methods, and techniques for ML-driven systems.

CONCLUSION

AI, specifically ML, has become very popular in academia and industry. Researchers, practitioners, IT engineers, and business stakeholders have their own understanding, point of view, and different expectations from ML applications. When the characteristic properties, inherent complexity, and technical difficulties of ML applications are added, the situation gets complicated and thus, the success and sustainability of these types of systems become more challenging. In this study, we reviewed the related literature, presented the background of ML and EA, proposed an EI method, and applied it to a generic, online shopping business case. The important insights and main conclusions are as follows:

- There is an overestimation of the benefits that may be provided by ML-driven solutions. Studies report inadequate return on investment or unsatisfactory outcomes of ML projects.
- Business systems with ML solutions may be at a high risk of failure and may fall short of business objectives.
- Analyzing and specifying requirements and satisfying stakeholders' expectations are important challenges for ML-driven business systems.
- Businesses that procure or develop ML-driven systems need to start by defining their AI business strategy and vision, and then specifying the other requirements.
- Holistic and integrated management of enterprise processes, data, applications, and infrastructure is a challenge; however, it is often neglected.
- The developments in technology and advances in the field of ML have increased dimensionality and complexity that also led to additional integration problems.
- Automating SE and ML pipeline processes is a common concern for software and ML application developers.

- Development and deployment processes of ML-driven business systems need to be synchronized with the system development and deployment life cycle processes. Therefore, there is a need for the integration of ML workflow management into SE practices.
- There is not much work that provides guidelines for the seamless integration of ML applications without risking the IT structure of business systems.
- Vendor-specific reference architectures for ML are still away from providing holistic and integrative prescriptions. Therefore, enterprise integration architectures are needed for assuring the long-term benefits and maintenance of ML-driven business systems.
- Various integration issues necessitate the adoption of the IIIE principles. EA knowledge domain can help businesses to understand the big picture of ML-driven systems in view of IIIE.
- IIIE, EA, cloud computing and SOA can contribute to the businesses that want to adopt ML applications. They can provide step-wise transition processes while, at the same time, assuring the return on investment and maintainability of enterprise systems.

REFERENCES

Amazon (2021). *Training ML models*. https://docs.aws.amazon.com

Amershi, S., Begel, A., Bird, C., DeLine, R., Gall, H., Kamar, E., Nagappan, N., Nushi, B., & Zimmermann, T. (2019). Software engineering for machine learning: A case study. *Microsoft Research*. https://www.microsoft.com

Archi 4.9.1 (2021). The Open-Source modelling toolkit for creating ArchiMate models. https://www.archimatetool.com

Archimate 3.1 (2019). Enterprise Architecture Description Language and integrated development environment. https://www.archimatetool.com

Budler, M., Zupi, I., & Trkman, P. (2021). The development of business model research: A bibliometric review. *Journal of Business Research*, *135*, 480–495. doi:10.1016/j.jbusres.2021.06.045

Chen, Y. (2016). Industrial information integration-A literature review 2006–2015. *Journal of Industrial Information Integration*, *2*, 30–64.

Chesbrough, H. (2007). Business model innovation: It's not just about technology anymore. *Strategy and Leadership*, *35*(6), 12–17.

Cielen, D., Meysman, A., & Ali, M. (2016). *Introducing data science: Big data, machine learning, and more, using Python tools.* Manning Publications.

DoDAF. (2010). *The DoDAF Architecture Framework Version 2.02.* U.S. Department of Defense.

Fenner, M. E. (2020). *Machine learning with python for everyone.* Pearson Education.

Geissdoerfer, M., Pieroni, M. P. P., Pigosso, D. C. A., & Soufani, K. (2020). Circular business models: A review. *Journal of Cleaner Production, 277,* 123741.

Giray, G. (2021). A software engineering perspective on engineering machine learning systems: State of the art and challenges. *Journal of Systems and Software, 180,* 1–35. doi:10.1016/j.jss.2021.111031

Google Cloud. (2021). MLOps: Continuous delivery and automation pipelines in machine learning. https://cloud.google.com/architecture/mlops-continuous-delivery-and-automation-pipelines-in-machine-learning

Ishikawa, F., & Yoshioka, N. (2019). How do engineers perceive difficulties in engineering of machine-learning systems? In *Proceedings of IEEE/ACM 6th International Workshop on Software Engineering Research and Industrial Practice.*

ISO/IEC/IEEE 42010 (2011). *Systems and software engineering: Architecture description,* Geneva, Switzerland.

Kelly, J., & Kaskade, J. (2013). Cios & big data what your IT team wants you to know, Infochimps, Inc. http://www.infochimps.com

Lankhorst, M. (2009). *Enterprise architecture at work: Modelling, communication and analysis.* Springer-Verlag Berlin Heidelberg.

Laudon, K. C., & Traver, C. G. (2020). *E-commerce: business. technology society.* Pearson.

Lin, Y., Duan, X., Zhao, C., & Xu, L. D. (2012). *Systems Science: Methodological approaches.* CRC Press.

Lwakatare, L. E., Raj, A., Crnkovic, I., Bosch, J., & Holmströ, H. O. (2020). Large-scale machine learning systems in real-world industrial settings: A review of challenges and solutions. *Information and Software Technology, 127,* 1–17.

Mukhiya, S. K., & Ahmed, U. (2020). *Hands-on exploratory data analysis with Python.* Packt Publishing.

Muller, A. C., & Guido, S. (2017). *Introduction to machine learning with Python.* O'Reilly Media, Inc.

Muller, J. P., & Massaron, L. (2015). *Python for data science for dummies.* John Wiley & Sons, Inc.

Nalchigar, S., Yu, E., & Keshavjee, K. (2021). Modeling machine learning requirements from three perspectives: A case report from the healthcare domain. *Requirements Engineering, 34567*(2), 1–18. doi:10.100700766-020-00343-z

Nielsen, C., Lund, M., Montemari, M., Paolone, F., Massaro, M., & Dumay, J. (2019). *Business Models: Research Overview.* Routledge.

Ponsard, C., Majchrowski, A., Mouton, S., & Touzani, M. (2017). Process guidance for the successful deployment of a big data project: Lessons Learned from Industrial Cases. In *Proceedings of IoTBDS*, 350-355. 10.5220/0006357403500355

Raffai, M. (2007). New working group in IFIP TC8 Information Systems Committee: WG8.9 working group on enterprise information systems. *SEFBIS Journal, 2*, 4–8.

Reis, I. F. G., Gonçalves, I., Lopes, M. A. R., & Antunes, C. H. (2021). Business models for energy communities: A review of key issues and trends. *Renewable & Sustainable Energy Reviews, 144*, 111013.

Roode, D. (2005). *IFIP General Assembly September 2005. Report from Technical Committee 8.* Information Systems.

Rosa, P., & Sassanelli, C. & Terzi Sergio. (2019). Towards circular business models: A systematic literature review on classification frameworks and archetypes. *Journal of Cleaner Production, 236*, 117696.

Saltz, J., Hotz, N., Wild, N., & Stirling, K. (2018). Exploring project management methodologies used within data science teams. In *Proceedings of the Americas Conference on Information Systems (AMCIS).*

Saltz, J., Shamshurin, I., & Crowston, K. (2017). Comparing data science project management methodologies via a controlled experiment. In *Proceedings of the 50th Hawaii International Conference on System Sciences*, 1013-1022.

Samuel, A. (1959). Some studies in machine learning using the game of checkers. *IBM Journal of Research and Development, 3*(3), 210–229.

Skarzynski, P., & Gibson, R. (2008). *Innovation to the core.* Harvard Business School Publishing.

Sutton, R. S., & Barto, A. G. (2015). *Reinforcement learning: An introduction.* MIT Press.

Timmers, P. (1998). Business models for electronic markets. *Electronic Markets, 8*(2), 3–8. doi:10.1080/10196789800000016

TOGAF. (2018). *The Open Group Architecture Framework, version 9.2.* The Open Group.

Uysal, M. P. (2021a). Machine learning and data science project management from an agile perspective: Methods and challenges. In V. Naidoo & R. Verma (Eds.), *Contemporary challenges for agile project management,* (pp. 73–89). IGI Global.

Uysal, M. P. (2021c), Towards an integration architecture for machine learning-enabled health information systems. In *Proceedings of the IFIP International Conference on Industrial Information Integration (ICIIIE 2021),* Norfolk, VA, USA.

Uysal, M. P., & Mergen, A. E. (2021b). Smart manufacturing in intelligent digital mesh: Integration of enterprise architecture and software product line engineering. *Journal of Industrial Information Integration, 23*(1), 1–12. doi:10.1016/j.jii.2021.100202

Vaio, A. D., Palladinoa, R., Hassan, R., & Escobar, O. (2020). Artificial intelligence and business models in the sustainable development goals perspective: A systematic literature review. *Journal of Business Research, 121,* 283–314. doi:10.1016/j.jbusres.2020.08.019

Weill, P., & Vitale, M. R. (2001). *Place to space: Migrating to eBusiness models.* Harvard Business School Press.

Wodecki, A. (2019). *Artificial Intelligence in value creation: Improving competitive advantage.* Springer. doi:10.1007/978-3-319-91596-8

Xu, L. D. (2011). Enterprise systems: State-of-the-art and future trends. *IEEE Transactions on Industrial Informatics, 7*(4), 630–640.

Xu, L. D. (2015). *Enterprise integration and information architecture: A systems perspective on industrial information integration.* CRS Press.

Zachman, J. A. (2008). The concise definition of the Zachman Framework. https://www.zachman.com/about-the-Zachman-framework

Zhang, H., Xiao, H., Wang, Y., Shareef, M. A., Akram, M. S., & Goraya, A. S. (2021). An integration of antecedents and outcomes of business model innovation: A meta-analytic review. *Journal of Business Research, 131,* 803–814. doi:10.1016/j.jbusres.2020.10.045

Zheng, A., & Casari, A. (2018). *Feature engineering for machine learning.* O'Reilly Media.

Zott, C., & Amit, R. (2008). The fit between product market strategy and business model: Implications for firm performance. *Strategic Management Journal, 29*(1), 1–26. doi:10.1002mj.642

KEY TERMS AND DEFINITIONS

Algorithm: A sequence of statistical and mathematical data processing steps.

Model: Data and a matching algorithm that represent a candidate solution to a ML problem.

Training: A ML process whereby a learner algorithm maps a function to the training data.

Machine Learning: A field of study that gives computers the ability to learn without being explicitly programmed.

Enterprise Architecture: The structure of components, their inter-relationships, and the principles and guidelines governing their design and evolution over time.

Industrial Information Integration Engineering: An engineering discipline with a set of foundational concepts and techniques that facilitate the information integration processes.

Chapter 3
Behavioral Analytics of Consumer Complaints

Md Shamim Hossain
(iD) https://orcid.org/0000-0003-1645-7470
Hajee Mohammad Danesh Science and Technology University, Bangladesh

ABSTRACT

In the current study, the author implemented cohort analysis methodology of machine learning (ML) to assess the rate of consumers' complaint retention behavior toward firms. The author obtained a three-year range of data on customer complaints from the Consumer Financial Protection Bureau's website. After removing the missing data from the customer complaints dataset, the current study also uses the cohort analysis approach of ML to assess the rate of consumer complaints retained by businesses. According to the findings, organizations retain a significant portion of complaints. This study adds to the body of knowledge on consumer complaining behavior (CCB), especially by creating and deploying unsupervised machine learning-based technique to conceptualize consumers' complaint behavior in the financial service providers industry. Moreover, professionals will benefit greatly from this research.

INTRODUCTION

Similar to the manufacturing industrial revolution and the rise of the eighteenth century, the service area appears to be at a crossroads in terms of productivity increases and service industrialization. Virtually all service industries will be transformed by promptly developing technology that grows cheaper, faster, smarter, and better (Hossain and Rahman, 2021a; Hossain et al., 2021; Wirtz et al., 2018; Wirtz and

DOI: 10.4018/978-1-6684-4246-3.ch003

Zeithaml, 2018), such as the use of artificial intelligence (AI). Basically, AI is altering digital marketing techniques at a breakneck pace (Mogaji et al., 2020). In the financial services sector, AI is defined as a system aided by technology that evaluates real-time provision circumstances using data collected from physical and/or digital sources to deliver tailored recommendations, solutions, and alternatives to purchasers' problems or inquiries, even intricate ones (Xu et al., 2020). Machine learning (ML) is a subset of AI that involves the automatic recognition of significant patterns in large datasets (Hossain and Rahman, 2022b; Pashchenko et al., 2022). The goal of ML technologies is to make algorithms more efficient by assuring their capacity to learn and adapt based on massive data analytics. Many industries, including financials, will continue to be impacted by machine learning and omnipresent data (Hossain and Rahman, 2022a). When vast amounts of data are entered into the system, machine learning tends to be more accurate in gaining insights and producing predictions (Hossain et al., 2022). The financial services business deals with massive amounts of data from everyday transactions, invoices, payments, vendors, and consumers, all of which are ideal for machine learning. Also, it will be more advantageous for businesses to understand their customers' feelings continuously.

According to marketing philosophy, the growth of consumer pleasure is the lifeblood of marketing practice and theory (Agag and Eid, 2020). Consumers are looking for a positive experience rather than products (Hossain and Rahman, 2022b; Buonincontri et al., 2017). As a result, marketing and sales approaches are focused on increasing customers' satisfaction (Liu and Atuahene-Gima, 2018). Consumer satisfaction has been shown to have a beneficial impact on profitability, competitive advantage, and business performance at the company level (Lee & How, 2019; Agag and Eid, 2020). Consumer feedback indicators (such as customer satisfaction, customer complaints, customer reviews, etc.) are becoming increasingly important in the relationship marketing process since they may forecast customer retention and company performance (e.g., Hossain and Rahman, 2022b; Agag and Eid, 2020; De Haan et al., 2015). Marketing efforts that increase customer feedback metrics are frequently beneficial to businesses (De Haan et al., 2015; Venkatesan et al., 2019). As a result, businesses increasingly conduct frequent customer feedback metrics surveys in order to assess their marketing effectiveness and determine appropriate marketing strategies (De Haan et al., 2015; Agag and Eid, 2020). As a customer feedback tool, complaints should be seen as a positive tool for companies to develop (Istanbulluoglu et al., 2017). Additionally, customer complaint behavior and management are critical for businesses, especially as companies increasingly recognize the significance of establishing long-term customer relationships (Bell and Luddington, 2006). London (1980) mentioned that a customer's complaint is an expression of dissatisfaction on behalf of a customer to a responsible organization. Consumers' reactions to displeasure with any aspect of consumption involvement, which can include both non-behavioral and behavioral complaints (Istanbulluoglu et al., 2017). Retaining existing customers is less expensive in the long run than recruiting new customers, so it's critical to address reasons of dissatisfaction (Rosenberg and Czepiel, 1984). Complaints may help businesses solve problems, enhance the quality of their products and services, and transform unhappy consumers into happy ones (Tax et al., 1998). Consumer satisfaction and customer involvement rise after a purchase when they see justice and effort in the resolution of a complaint (Cambra-Fierro et al., 2016). Furthermore, complaint management methods can be used to protect businesses from negative word-of-mouth (WOM), protect their reputation, and even generate positive WOM and repurchase behavior (Istanbulluoglu et al., 2017). Consumer complaining behavior (CCB) encompasses a wide range of customer responses in the aftermath of dissatisfaction (Arora and Chakraborty, 2020). Moreover, CCB refers to customers' attempts to resolve their unhappiness by informing merchants or service providers of their unpleasant experiences (Popelnukha et al., 2021; Berry et al., 2018). Customer complaints are an important source of information for companies looking to improve their products or services. Customers are prone to feeling unhappy if a company's products or services fail to fulfill their expectations. Complaint handling systems that are well-designed play an important role in allowing vulnerable customers to complain and seek remedy (Brennan et al., 2017). According to customer complaint behavior theory (Crié, 2003), most unhappy consumers remove their patronage and tell others about their poor experiences with products or services (Yang et al., 2018). Thus, customer complaint management is at the core of the customer relationship; it is the most comprehensive tool for altering customer complaints into voices of transformation (Kuster-Boluda et al., 2020).

Ultimately, internet applications frequently amass a large quantity of activity data, which represents information related to user behaviors. To improve sales and guarantee user retention, such activity data is frequently tabulated to give insights into user behavior. In these enormous tables of activity records, data analysts are interested in cohort analysis or discovering anomalous user behavioral tendencies (Jiang et al., 2016). Cohort analysis is a type of behavioral analytics that divides data into similar groups before analyzing it. Within a specific time frame, these groups, known as cohorts, have common qualities or experiences. Data analysts have an additional opportunity to draw important insights into user behavior because of the massive amounts of user behavior information collected across many domains. One of the most often used approaches is cohort analysis, which tries to uncover hidden user behavioral tendencies in time series (Xie et al., 2018). The current study implemented cohort analysis to determine the retention rate of consumers' complaints toward organizations.

Moreover, despite the fact that a few studies have used behavioral analytics to analyze sales data, none of the previous investigations have complemented such investigations for consumer complaints data. The current study used the cohort analysis approach of unsupervised ML to determine the rate of consumer complaints retained by businesses. Customer satisfaction can be improved by promptly and efficiently resolving customer complaints. Furthermore, customer complaints play a significant part in defining their needs, which serves as a beginning point for firms' entire R & D and new product or service development efforts (Singh et al., 2021). Therefore, after downloading consumers' complaints data from the Consumer Financial Protection Bureau (CFPB), the current study implemented unsupervised machine learning techniques to use cohort analysis to measure the complaint retention rate towards organizations.

LITERATURE REVIEW

Customers' Complaint

In the interactive new retail age, service platforms are advancing quickly. Although service platforms make buying easier for customers (Rahman and Hossain, 2022; Hossain et al., 2018), they nevertheless face a number of obstacles due to a lack of laws and generally unstandardized and immature operations when compared to customary commercial marketplaces. Consumer complaints result from the drawbacks of service platform operations (Yan et al., 2021). Consumers do not continually match the things that are being complained about perfectly. They blame merchants' service or product faults on both the platform and the merchants themselves, and consequently complain about both. Customers similarly complain about organizations when the platform's distribution service fails. Investing in consumer assistance will assist businesses in better understanding customer concerns and improving their goods, services, and overall experience. There is always a positive aspect to a customer's complaint. Modern businesses understand the importance of complaints and see them as a great commercial opportunity (Hsiao et al., 2016).

According to Day (1980), CCBs are prompted by perceived dissatisfaction. Consumer judgment is typically defined as an individual's judgment of the gap between expectations and actual outcomes, in which undesirably unmet customer expectations result in dissatisfaction (Kim et al., 2019). Customer complaint management (CCM) is the process of resolving and documenting customer concerns. Consumer relationship management (CRM) is continually improved by businesses in order to handle customer complaints and develop remedies and recommendations (von Janda et al., 2021). Receiving, managing, and encouraging consumer complaints, as well as giving a response to consumers, are critical activities inherent in an organization's CRM system. As a result, businesses may use a variety of platforms to encourage customers to state their opinions strongly (Yang et al., 2018). To enhance an organization's CCM and CRM systems, it's important to understand a few aspects of complaint behavior, such as complaint retention rate and so on. Additionally, according to the majority of recent consumer studies (Morgeson et al., 2020; von Janda et al., 2021; Popelnukha et al., 2021; Jeanpert et al., 2021), just a small percentage of unsatisfied consumers make complaints. Nowadays, where customers may readily submit complaints over the web (Armstrong et al., 2021), it is critical to calculate the consumers' complaint retention rate to better understand the CCB.

The current investigation looked into the CFPB's complaints dataset. Also, Ayres et al. (2013) look at a prior investigation of the CFPB's buyer complaints on a company-by-company basis as well as by zip code demographics. In studying the CFPB data at the government agency level, Littwin (2015) investigates an altered approach to that of Ayres et al. (2013). Notably, the author investigates the reasons why government agencies should practice CFPB complaints and whether these motives validate the resources required for customer complaint handling. She sees three grounds for the CFPB to handle consumer complaints: to build goodwill for the agency, to resolve consumer disputes; and to educate the government agency's regulatory actions. Her regression-based study shows that (1) the CFPB has been successful in providing a venue for customers to resolve disputes; (2) the CFPB is sturdy on regulatory actions and shows a strong obligation to ensure that consumer complaints are addressed by the appropriate firms; and (3) the CFPB's operations are quite well.

Bertsch et al. (2020) developed a high-quality proxy for bank fraud based on CFPB complaint data. Additionally, to assess CFPB customer complaints, Bastani et al. (2019) suggested an intellectual methodology based on Latent Dirichlet Allocation (LDA). Their suggested method extracts latent topics from CFPB complaint narratives and investigates their patterns over time. Hayes et al. (2021) used the CFPB's information to discover that a greater degree of trust in a specific place is linked to a lower number of complaints made against financial institutions in that place. They also discovered that, following the introduction of the CFPB, banks in low-trust areas reduced fees charged to consumers more than banks in high-trust regions, using a difference-in-differences method. They also stated that the prospect of consumer complaints to a government agency influences how banks handle their clients, and they provided insight into the relationship between informal culture and formal institutions, as well as the effect of stakeholders on corporate policy.

Despite the fact that the CFPB's complaint data has been investigated in a number of studies, consumers' complaint retention behavior against businesses is still unknown. Moreover, despite the growing interest in CCB, the complaint retention rate has received little attention. The goal of this study is to show how behavioral analytics may be used to analyze textual data from CFPB consumer complaint narratives. To the best of the author's knowledge, no earlier study has been published that uses behavioral analytics to analyze consumers' complaints. Thus, the current study employed cohort analysis to determine the rate of complaints retention against businesses in this study.

Consumer Complaining Behavior (CCB)

CCB is a broad notion that covers a variety of possible responses to unsatisfactory consumer experiences (Arora and Chakraborty, 2021; Istanbulluoglu et al., 2017). Customer discontent is defined as the gap between pre-purchase expectations and actual product or service performance (Hu et al., 2019). Basically, consumer complaints have been regarded as a behavioral manifestation of displeasure (Jung et al., 2017). Customers that are dissatisfied with a service provider will switch providers, complain, and spread bad word-of-mouth (Bolton, 1998; Cheng et al., 2005; Berry et al., 2018). Additionally, Ferguson and Johnston (2011) describe how customers who are unhappy with services or products can express their dissatisfaction by making complaints, exiting transaction relationships, spreading negative word-of-mouth (WOM) about their perceptions, and/or continuing transactional relationships as they are.

Sing (1989) characterized CCB as a three-faceted phenomenon consisting of speech (directly talking to the service provider), third party complaining (word-of-mouth), and private activities (taking legal actions). Sing (1988) found a link between the intention to complain and the actual action of complaining. The aspects have been separated in more recent consumer complaint investigations. In a number of studies (e.g., Lacey, 2012; Fan et al., 2016), customer voice has been used as a proxy for customer complaints. Others went on to say that customer negative voice (e.g., Luo, 2007) is an expression of customer dissatisfaction as opposed to customer positive voice, like expressing compliments and sharing great experiences with services and products (Min et al., 2019; Van Doorn et al., 2010). According to cognitive appraisal theory, consumers' interpretations of service failures impact emotional reactions (e.g., rage), which are a key predictor of customer complaints (Min et al., 2019; Joireman et al., 2015).

Cohort Analysis

Cohort analysis is a common method for businesses to acquire a deeper understanding of their consumers' behavior. It provides priceless insight into consumer behavior, which we can use to develop successful growth plans and enhance decision-making. The consumption trends of various cohorts are frequently varied. People born during the same epoch have shared many of the same historical events, as well as many of the possibilities and limits imposed by society at the time (Gustavsen, 2014). As a result, cohort analysis is critical for making decisions based on time periods.

Many studies have employed cohort analysis to estimate the retention rate over time, but there is as yet no cohort analytic research on consumer complaints or reviews. As a result, we'll discuss research that employed cohort analysis in domains other than complaints in this sub-section. Cohort analysis is an investigation approach for studying changes in group members using a collection of statistical tools. It is frequently used in domains such as social health care, science, ecology, and bioinformatics (Glenn, 2005). Cohort investigations are frequently conducted prospectively. Cohorts of interest are pre-defined based on an expert's initial hypothesis (for example, identifying cohorts with and without a certain pharmaceutical exposure, with different controls over the population's appearances). Following that, a specified set of data for the individuals in these cohorts is acquired over time and evaluated to find meaningful relationships. While this method can yield extremely useful information, prospective studies of this type often need costly data collection activities and take a long time to plan and conduct (Zhang et al., 2014).

Porta (2008) mentioned that in clinical investigations, one of the most popular applications of cohort analysis is to examine medical risk factors. Moreover, birth cohort analysis was performed by Fanslow et al. (2021) to assess prevalence rates for various age groups using data from single surveys. Cayuela et al. (2020) examined the impact of age, death period, and birth cohort on the evolution of suicide mortality from 1984 to 2018. They used a web tool supplied by the NCI (National Cancer Institute)'s Division of Cancer Epidemiology and Genetics for age-period-cohort analysis. Gustavsen (2014) estimates intercepts, price, and spending elasticities for vegetables, meat, and fish in different cohorts using a mixed-effects model. He discovered that older cohorts had larger fish intercepts than younger cohorts, and that meat spending elasticities were greater for older cohorts than for younger cohorts. To gain a deeper understanding of the CCB, we used cohort analysis to determine the complaint retention rate toward businesses, because only a few disgruntled customers voice their displeasure; the others remain silent (Morgeson et al., 2020; Dowding et al., 2000). CCB can be described using the Exit, Voice, and Loyalty (EVL) theory.

EVL Theory

The EVL theory (Hirschman, 1970) was originally explored in the context of political science. After a few decades, the idea has been generally accepted in management science to examine customer reaction behavior (Peeters et al., 2020; Kingshott et al., 2020; Hult and Morgeson, 2020; Morgeson et al., 2020; Thompson, 2018; Vidal et al., 2016; Singh, 1990). According to EVL theory, a customer who is dissatisfied with a company's products or services has three primary options: (i) show disloyalty and defect from the company (i.e., "exit") to an alternative supplier; (ii) complain and express dissatisfaction to the company (i.e., "voice"); (iii) do neither, accept the problems causing the displeasure, and stay "silently loyal" (Hult and Morgeson, 2020; Morgeson et al., 2020; Dowding et al., 2000). Classical economics argued that when customers are presented with providers of low-quality products or services, they have the option of buying or not buying, with the market's "invisible hand" (Thompson, 2018) re-ordering supply and demand as a consequence. In the event of repairable lapses, the theory of exit, voice, and loyalty proposes a third option of voice, which is used either as a residual of exit in instances when exit is not feasible (typically due to location or restricted availability) or as an alternative to it (Hirschman, 1970). Scholars have further expanded the EVL seminal paradigm to include neglect as part of the exit, voice, loyalty, and neglect (EVLN) typology, since neglect better depicts a more passive type of damaging relational behavior that is also present in partnerships (e.g. Rai & Agarwal, 2019; Turnley and Feldman, 1999; Zagenczyk et al., 2015). Neglect occurs when an offended person, such as in many collectivist societies, wants to avoid relational conflict by allowing the relationship to degrade passively (Kingshott et al., 2020). Moreover, according to the EVL or EVLN theories, customers do not wish to raise complaints. Only a handful of them have expressed dissatisfaction because of their internal CCB, which is a major concern in the current investigation because the current study wants to examine the complaint retention rate by the same consumers against businesses, which is yet unknown in the earlier CCB literature.

Hypotheses Development

Consumers' Complaints and Complain Retention Rate

CCB relates to consumers' behaviors aimed at resolving their unhappiness by complaining to merchants or service providers about their unpleasant experiences (Blodgett et al., 2018; Berry et al., 2018; Singh, 1988). The perceived low cost of complaining (Chebat et al., 2005), positive feelings toward complaining (Thøgersen et al., 2009; Bodey & Grace, 2007), increased levels of confidence (Richins, 1982), and the perceived chances of success (Chebat et al., 2005) are all well-established significant predictors of customer complaint behavior (Blodgett et al., 2018).

According to EVL and EVLN theories, only a few disgruntled customers voice their displeasure; the others remain silent (Morgeson et al., 2020; Dowding et al., 2000). According to Hansen et al. (2010), more than 55% of unsatisfied consumers only complain sometimes or never. These findings are consistent with early reviews of the (dis)satisfaction literature, which showed that the majority of unhappy consumers do not complain (Berg et al., 2020; TARP, 1986). Other studies (e.g., Warland et al., 1975; Best and Andreasen, 1977; Day et al., 1981; Francken, 1983; Andreassen, 1999) found that between 29 and 68 percent of respondents preferred to do nothing rather than complain (Andreassen, 1999; Hansen et al., 2010). As a result, despite the rise in consumer rights and power over the last few decades, most unsatisfied customers do not appear to complain very often. Even with customer-centric businesses, not all unsatisfied customers see complaining as a realistic choice, because one of the factors driving this decision is a chronic lack of personal power (Popelnukha et al., 2021). From the explanation above, it is obvious that only a small percentage of customers make complaints. Although no study exists to determine the consumers' complaint retention rate, we assumed that a small number of customers make recurrent complaints owing to their internal complaint behavior. As a result, the current study proposed the following hypothesis.

H1: The rate of complaint retention from the same customers to organizations will be higher.

METHOD

Few organizations collect data on consumer complaints in the digital age. The Consumer Financial Protection Bureau (CFPB) is one of them, which is a US federal organization in charge of financial consumer protection (Jung et al., 2017). Banks, securities firms, credit unions, mortgage-servicing operations, payday lenders, debt collectors, foreclosure relief services, and other monetary enterprises operating in the United States are all within the CFPB's supervision. Since its inception, the Consumer Financial Protection Bureau has "involved the twenty-first century" by employing digital tools to track how financial institutions utilize social media and procedures to target customers (Van Loo, 2018). The CFPB's objective is to make consumer financial goods and services marketplaces work for consumers by making regulations more effective, enforcing those rules consistently and equitably, and empowering people to take greater control over their financial lives. The Consumer Complaint Database of the CFPB is a compilation of complaints regarding consumer financial goods and services that the bureau has submitted to businesses for a response. After the company answers, verifying a business relationship with the customer, or after 15 days, whichever happens first, complaints are publicized. The Consumer Complaint Database does not publish complaints submitted to depository institutions with less than $10 billion in assets. The database is updated daily.

The CFPB's consumer complaint database is open to the public and can be downloaded from the organization's website. This database contained 2,090,327

Table 1. Yearly number of complaints towards products

Product	year_received Consumers' Complaint		
	2018	2019	2020
Debt collection	26155	23978	25704
Credit card or prepaid card	11856	12530	16986
Checking or savings account	6999	7353	9456
Credit reporting, credit repair services, or other personal consumer reports	48992	58527	95287
Student loan	5291	4282	2449
Money transfer, virtual currency, or money service	3242	2835	4790
Mortgage	10272	10035	12381
Vehicle loan or lease	3268	2930	3786
Payday loan, title loan, or personal loan	2399	2429	2347
Total	**118474**	**124899**	**173186**

complaint records toward 3930 companies when the author downloaded the required data set on May 20, 2021, each of which included information such as the date of submission, the product and issue under discussion, the firm to whom the complaint was forwarded for the response, and so on. In addition, a consumer complaint narrative has been submitted to the database, which includes the customer's account of what occurred. This field, however, is not filled with all of the entries because it is only available if the customer chooses to share. The author downloaded data for three years, from January 1, 2018, to December 31, 2020, totaling 975,932 complaint records. The focus of this article is solely on customer complaint narratives. After deleting the records that had no consumer complaint narratives and removing all punctuation and stopwords, there were 416559 records left in the filtered dataset. The current study used a Jupyter notebook to implement all of the machine-learning Python scripts in this study. The current study also calculated the yearly number of complaints towards products (presented in table 1), company public response toward products (table 2), the top 10 companies based on the total complaints (table-3), and complaints received on a monthly basis over a three-year period (figure 1).

Then, using Python and Seaborn, the author used cohort analysis to calculate the behavioral analytics of consumers' complaints retention rates toward the companies. The current study created a new column called "cohort index" for cohort analysis, which is based on the date of receiving customer complaints and the complaint ID. To begin, the author estimated the difference in dates between the first and subsequent complaints based on the same complaint ID. As a result, the author wrote

Table 2. Company public response toward products

Product	company_public_response										
	Company Believes Complaint Caused Principally by Actions of Third Party Outside the Control or Direction of the Company	Company Believes Complaint Is the Result of an Isolated Error	Company Believes Complaint Relates to a Discontinued Policy or Procedure	Company Believes Complaint Represents an Opportunity for Improvement to Better Serve Consumers	Company Believes It Acted Appropriately As Authorized By Contract Or Law	Company Believes the Complaint Is the Result of a Misunderstanding	Company Believes the Complaint Provided an Opportunity to Answer Consumer's Questions	Company Can't Verify or Dispute the Facts in the Complaint	Company Disputes the Facts Presented in the Complaint	Company Has Responded to the Consumer and the CFPB and Chooses Not to Provide a Public Response	None
Checking or savings account	5	59	2	39	1152	8	7	6	4	**11297**	11229
Credit card or prepaid card	10	50	0	15	962	16	4	8	4	18524	**21779**
Credit reporting, credit repair services, or other personal consumer reports	126	114	8	96	3073	221	30	104	210	**116969**	81855
Debt collection	571	200	6	529	9255	1069	71	376	1114	16408	**46238**
Money transfer, virtual currency, or money service	14	39	0	3	186	17	0	3	11	2062	**8532**
Mortgage	127	483	3	351	3810	419	102	20	153	11447	**15773**
Payday loan, title loan, or personal loan	52	24	0	17	687	57	2	14	153	1271	4898
Student loan	19	71	1	10	838	24	1	4	21	554	**10479**
Vehicle loan or lease	18	19	0	16	455	34	5	7	29	2750	**6651**

Table 3. Top 10 companies based on the total complaints

Company	Total Complaints
Experian Information Solutions Inc.	**54767**
EQUIFAX, INC.	54222
TRANSUNION INTERMEDIATE HOLDINGS, INC.	50939
CAPITAL ONE FINANCIAL CORPORATION	12438
CITIBANK, N.A.	11327
JPMORGAN CHASE & CO.	11282
BANK OF AMERICA, NATIONAL ASSOCIATION	10390
WELLS FARGO & COMPANY	9493
SYNCHRONY FINANCIAL	7214
Navient Solutions, LLC.	6451

Figure 1. Complaints received on a monthly basis over a three-year period.

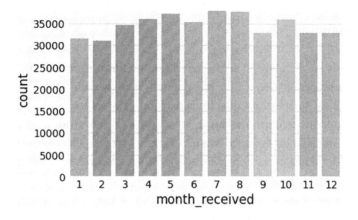

a python function and used it to extract the value of the year and month difference in consumer complaints from the data frame. Finally, using the formulas below, the author created a cohort index for each complaint depending on the number of years and months since the first complaint.

$$YD = CY - CoY \tag{1}$$

$$MD = CM - CoM \tag{2}$$

$$CI = YD \times 12 + MD + 1 \tag{3}$$

Here

CY= year of first complaint
CoY= year of selected complaint
CM= month of first complaint
CoM = month of selected complaint
YD= difference of year between the first complaints and selected complaints
MD= difference of month between the first complaints and selected complaints
CI= Cohort Index

RESULT AND DISCUSSION

Cohort Analysis

Cohort analysis is a behavioral analytics technique for tracking consumer activities over time. It's helpful to see if user engagement is improving over time or whether it's only seeming to increase due to expansion. The current study assessed the customer complaint retention rate for 36 months (3 years) for companies in the cohort table. The first day of each month of each year was shown in column 1. The proportion of total customer complaints was shown in column 2, which was 100%. Based on this information, the proportion of complaints from the same customers that were retained was calculated. A cohort table on customer complaint response (Figure 2) reveals that a significant portion of the same customers are complaining in subsequent months. Each row horizontally to the right of the table represents the complaint retention rate of the same customers based on the first month. For example, row-1 of Figure 2 showed that customers who had complained in January 2018 had 60 percent of them complaining again in February 2018 and 61 percent of those complaining again in March 2018. Similarly, in December 2020, 49 percent of the same customers who complained in January 2018 are still complaining. Thus, the H1 hypothesis, indicating that the percentage of complaints retained by the same customers to organizations will be greater, is supported by the current study's findings, which reveal that a large number of these same customers complained in the months after the initial complaint.

On the other hand, each column vertically down in Figure 2 showed the complaint retention rate for the same company from the same customers. For example, 34 percent of customers who complained to the same company in January 2018 complained again in February 2018, and 24 percent complained again in March 2018. Similarly, in November 2020, 10% of the same customers were still complaining.

CONCLUSION

Companies deal with customer concerns regularly. Apart from customer happiness, the number of new customers, and gratitude letters, it is also one of the success metrics for businesses (Abdul Rahim et al., 2019). Complaint analysis is very important for any type of organization, which involves not just analyzing and interpreting complaint data, but also putting it to good use for present and future generations. For the purpose of preventing failures and developing new products and processes, a methodical implementation of this activity is essential. Several studies (Abdul

Figure 2. Consumers' complaints retention rate through cohort analysis.

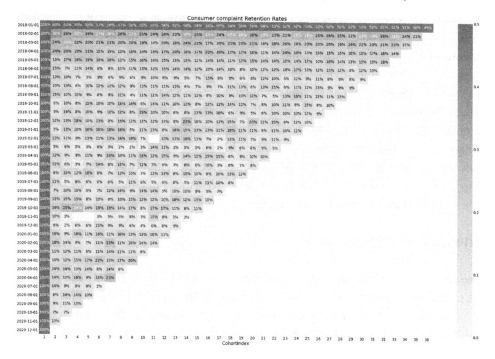

Rahim et al., 2019; Shooshtari et al., 2018; Effey and Schmitt, 2012) suggest that this is precisely where there is a significant demand for research and practice activities.

The current study used unsupervised machine learning-based behavioral analytics to learn about financial consumers' complaint behaviors. Using cohort analysis, the author discovered that a significant number of consumers complain on a regular basis, despite the fact that the number of complaints from the same organizations and customers was decreasing.

Implications for Practice

By creating and deploying an unsupervised machine learning-based technique to conceptualize consumers' complaint behavior in the financial service providers industry, this work contributes to the body of knowledge. Moreover, professionals will benefit greatly from this research. First, the current study analyzed consumer complaint retention rate using an unsupervised machine learning algorithm, which might help firms better understand comprehend their consumers' CCB. Second, using cohort analysis of customer complaint responses, the author discovered that a significant number of the same customers continue to complain in the months following the initial complaint. Thus, companies are able to know the complaints' retention behavior of consumers. Third, the offered approaches are not confined to the CFPB use case alone. Similar methodologies, such as estimating the complaint retention rate, might be used to evaluate customer narratives in a variety of applications or sectors, such as hotel reviews, movie reviews, product reviews, and so on. Fourth, it is widely accepted that analyzing complaint data is an important duty because it leads to a better understanding of procedures, flaws, and methods for improvement. Consumer complaints data from the Consumer Financial Protection Bureau is critical for identifying the root reasons for CCB. This paper's analytic tasks demonstrate how intelligent computing may be utilized to better understand and serve customers. Also, consumers will be able to comprehend their own complaints about the behavior towards financial firms after studying the current findings.

Theoretical Implications

The current research also has significant theoretical implications in the fields of CCB. As a result of the current study , we will have a better understanding of those fields because the research uncovered fresh insights into customer complaint behavior, which is a significant contribution to the theoretical disciplines.

Additionally, according to the EVL and EVLN theories, only a few unsatisfied consumers file complaints, and the study's findings indicate that a significant portion of the same consumers complained in the following months due to their internal CCB. This revealed that a few consumers constantly complain, while others remain silent.

Furthermore, in the social science literature, the use of machine learning algorithms to determine consumer complaint retention is not yet clear. The current study used unsupervised machine learning techniques to assess customer complaint behavior using a cohort analysis methodology of ML to assess the rate of consumer complaint retention behavior toward firms, which could be a worthy addition to the theoretical domain of social science, such as marketing, psychology, and consumer behavior.

Finally, aside from that, while customer complaints and the repercussions of a company's bad complaint management are as ancient as the company itself, most marketers believe that the financial stakes are higher in today's competitive marketing environment. The speed and flexibility with which information and communication technologies may be employed raises the negative risks of consumer complaints and emphasizes the necessity of good business complaint recovery. For example, social media has created an atmosphere where a customer's negative feedback is frequently amplified substantially. A dissatisfied consumer may complain to a company and possibly millions of other stakeholders at the same time (Morgeson et al., 2020). Every business must be aware of how consumers behave when they complain (Bell et al., 2004). The study revealed that the cohort analysis approaches of machine learning are the most effective methods for deciphering the behavior of complaining consumers. As a result, the current study enhanced the theoretical area of consumer complaint behavior.

Limitations

While the current research is focused on the CFPB's complaints database, it is restricted to a specific geographical financial area. It would be necessary to collect more data from a wider region and more different sorts of cultures. Second, despite the clear and reliable results obtained, the application of the study findings to other service sectors and firms must be done with caution owing to the unique characteristics of consumers' complaint behavior and the usage of a single database. Further study in other industries is needed to analyze and confirm our findings. Finally, according to the current research, a portion of dissatisfied customers might complain to businesses as a result of their internal CCB. Future research might investigate the sentiments of complaining consumers based on their level of satisfaction (i.e., high, moderate, or low).

REFERENCES

Abdul Rahim, N. F., Ahmed, E. R., Sarkawi, M. N., Jaaffar, A. R., & Shamsuddin, J. (2019). Operational risk management and customer complaints: The role of product complexity as a moderator. *Benchmarking*, *26*(8), 2486–2513. doi:10.1108/BIJ-04-2018-0089

Agag, G., & Eid, R. (2020). Which consumer feedback metrics are the most valuable in driving consumer expenditure in the tourism industries? A view from macroeconomic perspective. *Tourism Management*, *80*, 104109. doi:10.1016/j.tourman.2020.104109

Andreassen, T. W. (1999). What drives customer loyalty with complaint resolution? *Journal of Service Research*, *1*(4), 324–332. doi:10.1177/109467059914004

Armstrong, C., Kulczynski, A., & Brennan, S. (2021). Cue the complaint: The visual cues of Facebook business pages and their influence on consumer complaint behaviour. *Journal of Marketing Management*, *37*(11–12), 1027–1057. doi:10.1080/0267257X.2021.1934085

Arora, S. D., & Chakraborty, A. (2020). Legitimate and illegitimate consumer complaining behavior: a review and taxonomy. *Journal of Services Marketing*, Emerald Group Holdings Ltd. doi:10.1108/JSM-12-2019-0490

Arora, S. D., & Chakraborty, A. (2021). Intellectual structure of consumer complaining behavior (CCB) research: A bibliometric analysis. *Journal of Business Research, 122*, 60–74. doi:10.1016/j.jbusres.2020.08.043

Ayres, I., Lingwall, J., & Steinway, S. (2013). *Skeletons in the Database: An Early Analysis of the CFPB's Consumer Complaints*. SSRN Electronic Journal. doi:10.2139srn.2295157

Bastani, K., Namavari, H., & Shaffer, J. (2019). Latent Dirichlet allocation (LDA) for topic modeling of the CFPB consumer complaints. *Expert Systems with Applications, 127*, 256–271. doi:10.1016/j.eswa.2019.03.001

Bell, S. J., & Luddington, J. A. (2006). Coping with Customer Complaints. *Journal of Service Research, 8*(3), 221–233. doi:10.1177/1094670505283785

Bell, S. J., Mengüç, B., & Stefani, S. L. (2004). When Customers Disappoint: A Model of Relational Internal Marketing and Customer Complaints. *Journal of the Academy of Marketing Science, 32*(2), 112–126. doi:10.1177/0092070303261467

Berg, L., Slettemeås, D., Kjørstad, I., & Rosenberg, T. G. (2020). Trust and the don't-want-to-complain bias in peer-to-peer platform markets. *International Journal of Consumer Studies, 44*(3), 220–231. doi:10.1111/ijcs.12561

Berry, R., Tanford, S., Montgomery, R., & Green, A. J. (2018). How we complain: The effect of personality on consumer complaint channels. *Journal of Hospitality & Tourism Research (Washington, D.C.), 42*(1), 74–101. doi:10.1177/1096348014550921

Bertsch, C., Hull, I., Qi, Y., & Zhang, X. (2020). Bank misconduct and online lending. *Journal of Banking & Finance, 116*, 105822. doi:10.1016/j.jbankfin.2020.105822

Best, A., & Andreasen, A. R. (1977). Consumer Response to Unsatisfactory Purchases: A Survey of Perceiving Defects, Voicing Complaints, and Obtaining Redress. *Law & Society Review, 11*(4), 701. doi:10.2307/3053179

Blodgett, J. G., Bakir, A., Mattila, A. S., Trujillo, A., Quintanilla, C., & Elmadağ, A. B. (2018). Cross-national differences in complaint behavior: Cultural or situational? *Journal of Services Marketing, 32*(7), 913–924. doi:10.1108/JSM-12-2017-0413

Bodey, K., & Grace, D. (2007). Contrasting "complainers" with "non-complainers" on attitude toward complaining, propensity to complain, and key personality characteristics: A nomological look. *Psychology and Marketing, 24*(7), 579–594. doi:10.1002/mar.20174

Bolton, R. N. (1998). A dynamic model of the duration of the customer's relationship with a continuous service provider: The role of satisfaction. *Marketing Science*, *17*(1), 45–65. doi:10.1287/mksc.17.1.45

Brennan, C., Sourdin, T., Williams, J., Burstyner, N., & Gill, C. (2017). Consumer vulnerability and complaint handling: Challenges, opportunities and dispute system design. *International Journal of Consumer Studies*, *41*(6), 638–646. doi:10.1111/ijcs.12377

Buonincontri, P., Morvillo, A., Okumus, F., & van Niekerk, M. (2017). Managing the experience co-creation process in tourism destinations: Empirical findings from Naples. *Tourism Management*, *62*, 264–277. doi:10.1016/j.tourman.2017.04.014

Cambra-Fierro, J., Melero-Polo, I., & Javier Sese, F. (2016). Can complaint-handling efforts promote customer engagement? *Service Business*, *10*(4), 847–866. doi:10.100711628-015-0295-9

Cayuela, L., Sánchez Gayango, A., Sánchez-Trincado, P. A., Rodríguez-Domínguez, S., Velasco Quiles, A. A., & Cayuela, A. (2020). Suicide mortality in Spain (1984-2018): Age-period-cohort analysis. *Revista de Psiquiatría y Salud Mental.* doi:10.1016/j.rpsm.2020.05.010 PMID:32674993

Chebat, J.-C., Davidow, M., & Codjovi, I. (2005). Silent Voices. *Journal of Service Research*, *7*(4), 328–342. doi:10.1177/1094670504273965

Cheng, S., Lam, T., & Hsu, C. H. C. (2005). Testing the sufficiency of the theory of planned behavior: A case of customer dissatisfaction responses in restaurants. *International Journal of Hospitality Management*, *24*(4), 475–492. doi:10.1016/j.ijhm.2004.10.006

Crié, D. (2003). Consumers' complaint behaviour. Taxonomy, typology and determinants: Towards a unified ontology. *Journal of Database Marketing & Customer Strategy Management*, *11*(1), 60–79. doi:10.1057/palgrave.dbm.3240206

Day, R. L. (1980). Research perspectives on consumer complaining behavior. In C. Lamb and P. Dunne (eds). Theoretical Developments in Marketing. American Marketing Association Press, 211–215.

Day, R. L., Grabicke, K., Schaetzle, T., & Staubach, F. (1981). The Hidden Agenda of Consumer Complaining. *Journal of Retailing*, *57*(3), 86–106.

de Haan, E., Verhoef, P. C., & Wiesel, T. (2015). The predictive ability of different customer feedback metrics for retention. *International Journal of Research in Marketing*, *32*(2), 195–206. doi:10.1016/j.ijresmar.2015.02.004

Dowding, K., John, P., Mergoupis, T., & Van Vugt, M. (2000). Exit, voice and loyalty: Analytic and empirical developments. *European Journal of Political Research, 37*(4), 469–495. doi:10.1111/1475-6765.00522

Effey, T., & Schmitt, R. (2012). Efficient analysis, handling and use of customer complaints. In *Enabling Manufacturing Competitiveness and Economic Sustainability,* (pp. 476–481). Springer Berlin Heidelberg., doi:10.1007/978-3-642-23860-4_78

Fan, A., Wu, L., & Mattila, A. S. (2016). Gender differences in the intentions to voice complaints across different service failure modes. *Journal of Foodservice Business Research, 21*(1)–11.

Fanslow, J., Hashemi, L., Gulliver, P., & McIntosh, T. (2021). A century of sexual abuse victimisation: A birth cohort analysis. *Social Science & Medicine, 270,* 113574. doi:10.1016/j.socscimed.2020.113574 PMID:33445116

Ferguson, J. L., & Johnston, W. J. (2011). Customer response to dissatisfaction: A synthesis of literature and conceptual framework. *Industrial Marketing Management, 40*(1), 118–127. doi:10.1016/j.indmarman.2010.05.002

Francken, D. A. (1983). Postpurchase consumer evaluations, complaint actions and repurchase behavior. *Journal of Economic Psychology, 4*(3), 273–290. doi:10.1016/0167-4870(83)90031-4

Garay, J., Yap, R., & Sabellano, M. J. (2019). An analysis on the insights of the anti-vaccine movement from social media posts using k-means clustering algorithm and VADER sentiment analyzer. *IOP Conference Series. Materials Science and Engineering, 482,* 012043. doi:10.1088/1757-899X/482/1/012043

Glenn, N. D. (2005). *Cohort analysis,* (2nd ed.). SAGE Publications, Inc. https://www.doi.org/10.4135/9781412983662 doi:10.4135/9781412983662

Gustavsen, G. W. (2014). Consumer cohorts and demand elasticities. *European Review of Agriculture Economics, 44*(2), 217–237. doi:10.1093/erae/jbu020

Hansen, H., Samuelsen, B. M., & Andreassen, T. W. (2010). Trying to complain: The impact of self-referencing on complaining intentions. *International Journal of Consumer Studies, 35*(4), 375–382. doi:10.1111/j.1470-6431.2010.00948.x

Hayes, R. M., Jiang, F., & Pan, Y. (2021). Voice of the Customers: Local Trust Culture and Consumer Complaints to the CFPB. *Journal of Accounting Research, 59*(3), 1077–1121. doi:10.1111/1475-679X.12364

Hirschman, A. O. (1970). *Exit, Voice, and Loyalty.* Harvard University Press.

Hossain, M. S., & Rahman, M. F. (2021). Website quality, perceived flow, trust, and commitment: developing a customer relationship management model. In *Impact of Globalization and Advanced Technologies on Online Business Models,* (pp. 202–226). IGI Global. doi:10.4018/978-1-7998-7603-8.ch013

Hossain, M. S., & Rahman, M. F. (2022a). Machine Learning and Artificial Intelligence: The New Move for Marketers. In Kaur, J., Jindal, P., & Singh, A. (Eds.). Developing Relationships, Personalization, and Data Herald in Marketing 5.0. IGI Global.

Hossain, M. S., & Rahman, M. F. (2022b). Detection of potential customers' empathy behavior towards customers' reviews. *Journal of Retailing and Consumer Services*, *65*, 102881. doi:10.1016/j.jretconser.2021.102881

Hossain, M. S., Rahman, M. F., & Uddin, M. K. (2022). Analyzing and Predicting Learner Sentiment Toward Specialty Schools Using Machine Learning Techniques. In G. Trajkovski, M. Demeter, & H. Hayes (Eds.), *Applying Data Science and Learning Analytics Throughout a Learner's Lifespan,* (pp. 133–158). IGI Global., doi:10.4018/978-1-7998-9644-9.ch007

Hossain, M. S., Rahman, M. F., & Zhou, X. (2021). Impact of customers' interpersonal interactions in social commerce on customer relationship management performance. *Journal of Contemporary Marketing Science*, *4*(1), 161–181. doi:10.1108/JCMARS-12-2020-0050

Hsiao, Y.-H., Chen, L.-F., Choy, Y. L., & Su, C.-T. (2016). A novel framework for customer complaint management. *Service Industries Journal*, *36*(13/14), 675–698. doi:10.1080/02642069.2016.1272592

Hu, N., Zhang, T., Gao, B., & Bose, I. (2019). What do hotel customers complain about? Text analysis using structural topic model. *Tourism Management*, *72*, 417–426. doi:10.1016/j.tourman.2019.01.002

Hult, G. T. M., & Morgeson, F. V. (2020). *Marketing's value propositions: a focus on exit, voice, and loyalty.* AMS Review. doi:10.100713162-020-00187-4

Istanbulluoglu, D., Leek, S., & Szmigin, I. T. (2017). Beyond exit and voice: Developing an integrated taxonomy of consumer complaining behaviour. *European Journal of Marketing*, *51*(5/6), 1109–1128. doi:10.1108/EJM-04-2016-0204

Jeanpert, S., Jacquemier-Paquin, L., & Claye-Puaux, S. (2021). The role of human interaction in complaint handling. *Journal of Retailing and Consumer Services*, *62*, 102670. doi:10.1016/j.jretconser.2021.102670

Jiang, D., Cai, Q., Chen, G., Jagadish, H. V., Ooi, B. C., Tan, K. L., & Tung, A. K. H. (2016). Cohort query processing. In *Proceedings of the VLDB Endowment*, (Vol. 10, pp. 1–12). Association for Computing Machinery. 10.14778/3015270.3015271

Joireman, J., Smith, D., Liu, R. L., & Arthurs, J. (2015). It's all Good: Corporate social responsibility reduces negative and promotes positive responses to service failures among value-aligned customers. *Journal of Public Policy & Marketing*, *34*(1), 32–49. doi:10.1509/jppm.13.065

Jung, K., Garbarino, E., Briley, D., & Wynhausen, J. (2017). Blue and Red Voices: Effects of Political Ideology on Consumers' Complaining and Disputing Behavior. *The Journal of Consumer Research*, *44*(3), 477–499. doi:10.1093/jcr/ucx037

Khattak, A., Asghar, M. Z., Ishaq, Z., Bangyal, W. H., & Hameed, I. A. (2021). *Enhanced concept-level sentiment analysis system with expanded ontological relations for efficient classification of user reviews*. Egyptian Informatics Journal. doi:10.1016/j.eij.2021.03.001

Kim, B., Kim, S., & Heo, C. Y. (2019). Consequences of Customer Dissatisfaction in Upscale and Budget Hotels: Focusing on Dissatisfied Customers' Attitude Toward a Hotel. *International Journal of Hospitality & Tourism Administration*, *20*(1), 15–46. doi:10.1080/15256480.2017.1359728

Kingshott, R. P. J., Sharma, P., Sima, H., & Wong, D. (2020). The impact of psychological contract breaches within east-west buyer-supplier relationships. *Industrial Marketing Management*, *89*, 220–231. doi:10.1016/j.indmarman.2020.03.008

Kuster-Boluda, A., Vila, N. V., & Kuster, I. (2020). Managing international distributors' complaints: An exploratory study. *Journal of Business and Industrial Marketing*, *35*(11), 1817–1829. doi:10.1108/JBIM-11-2018-0336

Lacey, R. (2012). How customer voice contributes to stronger service provider relationships. *Journal of Services Marketing*, *26*(2), 137–144. doi:10.1108/08876041211215293

Landon, E. L. (1980). The direction of consumer complaint research. *Advances in Consumer Research. Association for Consumer Research (U. S.)*, *7*(1), 335–338. https://www.acrwebsite.org/volumes/9693/volumes/v07/NA-07

Lee, C. G., & How, S. M. (2019, August 27). Long-run causality between customer satisfaction and financial performance: the case of Marriott. *Current Issues in Tourism*. Routledge. doi:10.1080/13683500.2018.1453788

Liu, W., & Atuahene-Gima, K. (2018). Enhancing product innovation performance in a dysfunctional competitive environment: The roles of competitive strategies and market-based assets. *Industrial Marketing Management, 73*, 7–20. doi:10.1016/j.indmarman.2018.01.006

Luo, X. (2007). Consumer negative voice and firm-idiosyncratic stock returns. *Journal of Marketing, 71*(3), 75–88. doi:10.1509/jmkg.71.3.075

Min, H., Joireman, J., & Kim, H. J. (2019). Understanding why anger predicts intention to complain among high but not low power customers: A test of competing models. *Journal of Business Research, 95*, 93–102. doi:10.1016/j.jbusres.2018.10.017

Mogaji, E., Soetan, T. O., & Kieu, T. A. (2020). The implications of artificial intelligence on the digital marketing of financial services to vulnerable customers. *Australasian Marketing Journal.* doi:10.1016/j.ausmj.2020.05.003

Morgeson, F. V. III, Hult, G. T. M., Mithas, S., Keiningham, T., & Fornell, C. (2020). Turning Complaining Customers into Loyal Customers: Moderators of the Complaint Handling–Customer Loyalty Relationship. *Journal of Marketing, 002224292092902*(5), 79–99. doi:10.1177/0022242920929029

Pashchenko, Y., Rahman, M. F., Hossain, M. S., Uddin, M. K., & Islam, T. (2022). Emotional and the normative aspects of customers' reviews. *Journal of Retailing and Consumer Services, 68*, 103011. doi:10.1016/j.jretconser.2022.103011

Peeters, R., Gofen, A., & Meza, O. (2020). Gaming the system: Responses to dissatisfaction with public services beyond exit and voice. *Public Administration, 98*(4), 824–839. doi:10.1111/padm.12680

Popelnukha, A., Weng, Q., Ali, A., & Atamba, C. (2021). When do low-power customers complain? The joint effects of chronic sense of personal power and complaint success on complaining intentions. *Journal of Consumer Behaviour, 20*(1), 101–118. doi:10.1002/cb.1859

Porta, M. (2008). *A dictionary of epidemiology,* (5th ed.). Oxford University Press.

Rai, A., & Agarwal, U. A. (2019). Linking workplace bullying and EVLN outcomes: Role of psychological contract violation and workplace friendship. *International Journal of Manpower, 40*(2), 211–227. doi:10.1108/IJM-05-2017-0091

Richins, M. L. (1982). An investigation of consumers' attitudes toward complaining. *ACR North American Advances,* NA-09. https://www.acrwebsite.org/volumes/6055/volumes/v09/NA-09

Rosenberg, L. J., & Czepiel, J. A. (1984). A marketing approach for customer retention. *Journal of Consumer Marketing*, *1*(2), 45–51. doi:10.1108/eb008094

Schwartz, L. B., & Hirschman, A. O. (1972). Exit, Voice, and Loyalty: Responses to Decline in Firms, Organizations, and States. *University of Pennsylvania Law Review*, *120*(6), 1210. doi:10.2307/3311348

Shooshtari, N. H., Stan, S., & Clouse, S. F. (2018). Receiving, Recording, and Responding to Customer Complaints: The Effects of Formalizing Customer Complaint Handling Policies in Retail Firms. *Services Marketing Quarterly*, *39*(3), 225–239. doi:10.1080/15332969.2018.1472982

Singh, A., Saha, S., Hasanuzzaman, M., & Dey, K. (2021). Multitask Learning for Complaint Identification and Sentiment Analysis. *Cognitive Computation*. doi:10.100712559-021-09844-7

Singh, J. (1988). Consumer complaint intentions and behavior: Definitional and taxonomical issues. *Journal of Marketing*, *52*(1), 93–107. doi:10.1177/002224298805200108

Singh, J. (1989). Determinants of consumers' decisions to seek third party redress: An empirical study of dissatisfied patients. *The Journal of Consumer Affairs*, *23*(2), 329–363. doi:10.1111/j.1745-6606.1989.tb00251.x

TARP. (1986). *Consumer complaint Handling in America: an update study. Report.* US Office of Consumer Affairs.

Tax, S. S., Brown, S. W., & Chandrashekaran, M. (1998). Customer evaluations of service complaint experiences: Implications for relationship marketing. *Journal of Marketing*, *62*(2), 60–76. doi:10.1177/002224299806200205

Thøgersen, J., Juhl, H. J., & Poulsen, C. S. (2009). Complaining: A function of attitude, personality, and situation. *Psychology and Marketing*, *26*(8), 760–777. doi:10.1002/mar.20298

Thompson, G. (2018). Social gains from the public relations voice of activist investors: The case of Herbalife and Pershing Square Capital Management. *Public Relations Review*, *44*(4), 481–489. doi:10.1016/j.pubrev.2018.04.003

Thompson, G. (2018). Social gains from the public relations voice of activist investors: The case of Herbalife and Pershing Square Capital Management. *Public Relations Review*, *44*(4), 481–489. doi:10.1016/j.pubrev.2018.04.003

Turnley, W. H., & Feldman, D. C. (1999). The impact of psychological contract violations on exit, voice, loyalty, and neglect. *Human Relations*, *52*(7), 895–922. doi:10.1177/001872679905200703

Van Doorn, J., Lemon, K. N., Mittal, V., Nass, S., Pick, D., Pirner, P., & Verhoef, P. C. (2010). Customer engagement behavior: Theoretical foundations and research directions. *Journal of Service Research*, *13*(3), 253–266. doi:10.1177/1094670510375599

Van Loo, R. (2018). Technology Regulation by Default: Platforms, Privacy, and the CFPB. *Georgetown Law Technology Review*, *2*(2), 531.

Venkatesan, R., Shao, Y. S., Zimmer, B., Clemons, J., Fojtik, M., & Jiang, N. & Khailany, B. (2019). A 0.11 PJ/OP, 0.32-128 Tops, Scalable Multi-Chip-Module-Based Deep Neural Network Accelerator Designed with A High-Productivity VLSI Methodology. In *IEEE Hot Chips 31 Symposium, HCS 2019*. Institute of Electrical and Electronics Engineers Inc. doi:10.1109/HOTCHIPS.2019.8875657

Vidal, D., Fenneteau, H., & Paché, G. (2016). Should I stay or should I go? Customers' reactions faced with the deterioration of a business relationship. *Journal of Business and Industrial Marketing*, *31*(1), 47–58. doi:10.1108/JBIM-06-2014-0124

von Janda, S., Polthier, A., & Kuester, S. (2021). Do they see the signs? Organizational response behavior to customer complaint messages. *Journal of Business Research*, *137*, 116–127. doi:10.1016/j.jbusres.2021.08.017

Warland, R. H., Herrmann, R. O., & Willits, J. (1975). Dissatisfied consumers: Who gets upset and what they do about it. *The Journal of Consumer Affairs*, *9*(2), 152–162. doi:10.1111/j.1745-6606.1975.tb00559.x

Wirtz, J., Patterson, P. G., Kunz, W. H., Gruber, T., Lu, V. N., Paluch, S., & Martins, A. (2018). Brave new world: Service robots in the frontline. *Journal of Service Management*, *29*(5), 907–931. doi:10.1108/JOSM-04-2018-0119

Wirtz, J. and Zeithaml, V. (2018). Cost-effective service excellence. *Journal of the Academy of Marketing Science, 46*(1), 59-80.

Xie, Z., Cai, Q., He, F., Ooi, G. Y., Huang, W., & Ooi, B. C. (2018). Cohort analysis with ease. In *Proceedings of the ACM SIGMOD International Conference on Management of Data,* (pp. 1737–1740). Association for Computing Machinery. doi:10.1145/3183713.3193540

Xu, Y., Shieh, C. H., van Esch, P., & Ling, I. L. (2020). AI customer service: Task complexity, problem-solving ability, and usage intention. *Australasian Marketing Journal*, *28*(4), 189–199. doi:10.1016/j.ausmj.2020.03.005

Yan, N., Xu, X., Tong, T., & Huang, L. (2021). Examining consumer complaints from an on-demand service platform. *International Journal of Production Economics*, *237*, 108153. doi:10.1016/j.ijpe.2021.108153

Yang, Y., Xu, D.-L., Yang, J.-B., & Chen, Y.-W. (2018). An evidential reasoning-based decision support system for handling customer complaints in mobile telecommunications. *Knowledge-Based Systems*, *162*, 202–210. doi:10.1016/j.knosys.2018.09.029

Zagenczyk, T. J., Cruz, K. S., Cheung, J. H., Scott, K. L., Kiewitz, C., & Galloway, B. (2015). The moderating effect of power distance on employee responses to psychological contract breach. *European Journal of Work and Organizational Psychology*, *24*(6), 853–865. doi:10.1080/1359432X.2014.961432

Zhang, Z., Gotz, D., & Perer, A. (2014). Iterative cohort analysis and exploration. *Information Visualization*, *14*(4), 289–307. doi:10.1177/1473871614526077

ADDITIONAL READING

Armstrong, C., Kulczynski, A., & Brennan, S. (2021). Cue the complaint: The visual cues of Facebook business pages and their influence on consumer complaint behaviour. *Journal of Marketing Management*, *37*(11–12), 1027–1057. doi:10.1080/0267257X.2021.1934085

Grasso, M. T., Farrall, S., Gray, E., Hay, C., & Jennings, W. (2019, January 1). Thatcher's children, blair's babies, political socialization and trickle-down value change: An age, period and cohort analysis. *British Journal of Political Science*. Cambridge University Press. doi:10.1017/S0007123416000375

Ligthart, A., Catal, C., & Tekinerdogan, B. (2021). Systematic reviews in sentiment analysis: A tertiary study. *Artificial Intelligence Review*, *54*(7), 4997–5053. doi:10.100710462-021-09973-3

Nasreen Taj, M. B., & Girisha, G. S. (2021). Insights of strength and weakness of evolving methodologies of sentiment analysis. *Global Transitions Proceedings*, *2*(2), 157–162. doi:10.1016/j.gltp.2021.08.059

Taboada, M., Brooke, J., Tofiloski, M., Voll, K., & Stede, M. (2011). Lexicon-basedmethods for sentiment analysis. *Computational Linguistics*, *37*(2), 267–307. doi:10.1162/COLI_a_00049

Yan, N., Xu, X., Tong, T., & Huang, L. (2021). Examining consumer complaints from an on-demand service platform. *International Journal of Production Economics*, *237*, 108153. doi:10.1016/j.ijpe.2021.108153

Yang, L., Li, Y., Wang, J., & Sherratt, R. S. (2020). Sentiment Analysis for E-Commerce Product Reviews in Chinese Based on Sentiment Lexicon and Deep Learning. *IEEE Access: Practical Innovations, Open Solutions*, *8*, 23522–23530. doi:10.1109/ACCESS.2020.2969854

KEY TERMS AND DEFINITIONS

Consumer Complaint: A consumer complaint, also known as a customer complaint, is a statement of discontent directed towards a responsible party on behalf of a customer. A customer complaint is any written, electronic, or oral message alleging deficiencies in the identity, quality, longevity, dependability, safety, or performance of a product or service that has been placed on the market.

Cohort Analysis: is a common method for businesses to acquire a deeper understanding of their consumers' behavior. It provides priceless insight into consumer behavior, which we can use to develop successful growth plans and enhance decision-making

Machine Learning: is a sort of data analysis that uses artificial intelligence to automate the process of developing analytical models. It's a branch of AI based on the premise that robots can learn from data, discover patterns, and make judgments with little or no human involvement.

Consumer Complaint Behavior (CCB): A collection of consumer dissatisfaction responses is known as complaint behavior. It is an outward display of unhappiness, but it is only one factor that influences this behavior. Complaint behavior may be broken down into several sorts of responses, as well as a process.

Chapter 4
Business Analysis During the Pandemic Crisis Using Deep Learning Models

Sudheer Devulapalli

iD https://orcid.org/0000-0001-7056-5195

Vallurupalli Nageswara Rao Vignana Jyothi Institute of Engineering and Technology, India

Venkatesh B.

Vignan Foundation for Science Technology and Research, India

Ramasubbareddy Somula

Vallurupalli Nageswara Rao Vignana Jyothi Institute of Engineering and Technology, India

ABSTRACT

This chapter aims to investigate pandemic crisis in the various business fields like real estate, restaurants, gold, and the stock market. The importance of deep learning models is to analyse the business data for future predictions to overcome the crisis. Most of the recent research articles are published on intelligent business models in sustainable development and predicting the growth rate after the pandemic crisis. This clear study will be presented based on all reputed journal articles and information from business magazines on the various business domains. Comparison of best intelligent models in business data analysis will be done to transform the business operations and the global economy. Different deep learning applications in business data analysis will be addressed. The deep learning models are investigated which are applied on descriptive, predictive, and prescriptive business analytics.

DOI: 10.4018/978-1-6684-4246-3.ch004

INTRODUCTION

Artificial Intelligence (AI) has been emerging technology for the past two decades in business intelligence. Researchers and engineers have contributed a lot of innovations for developing smarter and cognitive applications. The vast volume of data is produced through the internet by many e-commerce websites, and the processing and storage challenges are addressed and resolved using the Bigdata concepts explained in Rajkumar and Sudheer (2016), Sudheer, Devulapalli, and Krishnan (2019), Sudheer and Lakshmi (2015). The processing advancements that evolved in recent years led to the use of more AI-based methods to apply predictive and descriptive analytics. The primary issue in improving the accuracy of predictions using AI algorithms is the availability of training data. Since the technologies such as the cloud and Internet Of things (IOT) are connected to all fields, more data can be gathered and accessed faster. However, labeling and grouping the unstructured data still become a tedious task Sankar et al. (2021), Sankar et al. (2022). Knowledge representation and pattern recognition tools had used to resolve these issues. Especially in the business field, decision-making and recommendation systems play a vital role based on previous experiences. The literature of the chapter had discussed various AI-based techniques applied in different business applications and their impact during the COVID-19 pandemic. Figure 1 Explains that recent tools available for data extraction, data pre-processing, data analysis and pattern recognition and data visualization steps.

The rest of chapter is organized as section 1 explained introduction, section 2 is about literature survey, section 3 explains comparison of AI models and section 4 is conclusions.

LITERATURE SURVEY

The literature study section investigated the recent techniques developed in various business sectors such as restaurants, real estate, banking, stock market and e-learning. It will discuss about different AI methods applied on various data sources and their advantages.

Food Processing Industry

Luo, Yi, and Xu have studied deep learning models to analyze the reviews of the restaurant industry in the period of the COVID-19 pandemic. Total 1,12,412 reviews from January to June of the year 2020 are considered as a dataset to develop prediction models. The features such as service, food, place, and experience are analyzed to find the sentiment of the reviews Luo, Yi, and Xu (2021).

Figure 1. Data analytics steps and popular tools.

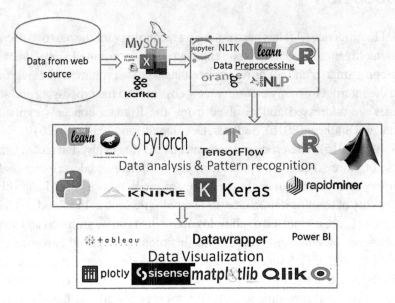

Hossain et al. (2020) have collected a dataset using the web scrapping method to extract reviews from websites associated with restaurants such as Food pandas and Shohoz. The significant contribution of this work is to prepare a dataset with 1000 reviews in that half of the data was labeled as positive and the remaining was negative.

Zahoor et al. (2020) have investigated sentiment analysis on Pakistani restaurant reviews collected by the Facebook community. The features of restaurants nearby Karachi city are analyzed with taste, service, money, and Ambience.

Kumar et al (2021). have explained all possible opportunities for automation in the food industry. Product ordering, packaging, customer satisfaction, maintenance, launching new products, and supply chain management are the best ways to implement AI to improve the food processing industry .

Rafay et al (2020). have developed deep learning-based feature extraction models and pre-processing of customer reviews using NLP. Instead of binary classification of positive and negative labels of the data, it is recommended to apply multiclass classification based on rating factors.

Real Estate

Heidari et al (2021). The authors have developed a house rent prediction model using house type and zip code, and Zipcodes are not precise data to predict the rent of the house. Other factors such as the development of the area and facing of the house, etc., affect the rental price.

Treleaven et al. (2021) had discussed marketing strategies in various levels of real estate applications. The usage of developing AI-based applications will be helpful to different users such as cost consultants, contractors, maintainers, etc,.

Niu and Peiqing (2019) have designed a real estate valuation system using machine learning to recognize the record from the collection of house records from the crawlers. This method aims to predict the prices of the houses of the community, building, and house-level features using ensemble neural network classifiers.

Banking

The goal of Paule-Vianez and colleagues (2020) is to create a short-term financial crisis prediction model for the Spanish banking sector. According to the findings, Artificial Neural Networks (ANN) are an outstanding tool for analyzing financial difficulty in Spanish financial institutions and anticipating all occurrences of short-term financial troubles.

ANN approaches are used by Elzamly (2017), and others to discover severe cloud computing security problems. To measure cloud security level performance, we suggested Levenberg–Marquardt-based Back Propagation (LMBP) Algorithms. The accuracy of cloud security level prediction may also be measured using LMBP methodologies. ANNs are more effective at improving performance and learning membership functions. In this work, the scientists also used the cloud Delphi technique for data collecting and analysis. Based on their cloud computing experience, 40 panelists were selected from both inside and outside Malaysian banking businesses for this study.

Retail investors' financial behaviour is influenced by their financial attitudes. Despite the fact that existing research has recognised and investigated this link, financial attitude and behaviour assessments still vary greatly and are often asked as a series of questions rather than statements. Furthermore, there is a lack of evidence about the conduct of retail investors in the face of a health catastrophe, such as the present COVID-19 epidemic. Talwar et al. (2020) studied fills in the gaps in the prior literature by examining the relative impact of six financial attitude dimensions on retail investor trading activity during the pandemic, including optimism, financial anxiety, financial security, interest in financial issues, deliberative thinking and the need for precautionary savings. The ANN approach was used to evaluate data from 404 respondents. The findings found that all six aspects had a beneficial impact on trading behaviour, with financial interest having the most impact, followed by deliberative thinking. As a result, the study provides vital conclusions for academics and management.

Stock Market

The ongoing COVID-19 epidemic had worldwide health consequences, and countries have imposed certain restrictions on migration. Economic activity has been disrupted as a result of these limitations. The GDP estimates for eight nations, including the United States, Mexico, Germany, Italy, Spain, France, India, and Japan, are anticipated in this article for the April–June quarter of 2020. Jena et al. (2021) had develops a multilayer ANN model because they have superior forecasting accuracy to statistical approaches. This model divides the dataset into two halves, the first containing 80% of the observations and the second containing 20%. The model then applies the improved parameters to the second half of the dataset to evaluate the model's performance. The model achieves a predicting error of less than 2% during the testing phase. According to predicted GDP data, the April–June quarter of this year saw severe reductions in GDP for all nations. Furthermore, yearly GDP growth is predicted to be in the negative double digits. Such ominous implications necessitate immediate government intervention.

After the Great Depression of the 1930s, the COVID-19 pandemic was the most devastating worldwide economic disaster. Most countries worldwide are confronting declining economic growth, decelerating trade, rising global imbalances, and crippling financial markets, all of which are contributing to the freezing of the monetary system. If the international commerce and financial markets were hit hard by the 2008 crisis, the present pandemic issue might cause demand and supply disruptions. According to the World Bank's projections for 2020, the global Gross Domestic Product (GDP) will drop significantly because of the COVID-19 pandemic. In 2020, advanced economies were expected to fall by 7%, while emerging and underdeveloped economies will shrink by 2.5 percent.

Similarly, global commerce is anticipated to drop by 13% in 2020, higher than the fall seen during World War II. according to these estimates, the COVID-19 epidemic has caused a considerable drop in worldwide trade. In March 2020, COVID-19 instances increased significantly in China, Korea, Italy, Japan, the United States, and Germany. To stop the illness from spreading, a lockdown was put in place. Because of the lockdown, all manufacturing in these economies stopped Vidya et al. (2020).

To stop the spreading virus, a lockdown was chosen as an option. Because of this, production in these economies came to a complete stop. The COVID-19 health and economic crisis have impacted every aspect of global society, including the economy. The global economy has suffered due to the loss of purchasing power of those forced to stay at home and cannot work. Due to the restrictions imposed to prevent the spread of SARS-Cov-2, electronic commerce, and mobile commerce have become more popular as instruments for obtaining goods and services. Vărzaru and Bocean (2021) conducted a longitudinal analysis of the mobile business as an essential component of electronic commerce, identifying the primary drivers of the mobile industry and the extent to which they impact the market. The study concentrates on mobile business in the US (U.S.). It spans the years 2010 through 2020, with the last year reflecting the background of the COVID-19 epidemic and its influence on electronic commerce (e-commerce) and mobile commerce (m-commerce). Using artificial neural networks and structural equation modeling, we identified the key drivers of m-commerce and the mediation effects observed between the variables that define m-commerce, e-commerce, and total sales in the macroeconomic study of competitiveness. In the background of driving limitations and social distance limits imposed owing to the COVID-19 epidemic, the study findings show an increase in the percentage of e-commerce in total sales and a majority of the m-commerce share in e-commerce. Stakeholders should consider increased internet speed, expanded 5G and Wi-Fi networks, and increased accessibility and confidence in mobile devices and apps should all be considered by stakeholders in the m-commerce space.

Financial time series prediction is a difficult task for statistical models. Because of its vulnerability to economic and political circumstances, the stock market period series has a high level of volatility. Furthermore, the covid-19 epidemic has lately created a significant shift in the stock exchange time series. Several computational strategies have been presented to improve the performance of forecasting such time series in this challenging situation. de Pauli et al. (2020) major's purpose is to assess the performance of five neural network architectures in forecasting the six most traded equities on the official Brazilian stock market B3 from March 2019 to April 2020. We used prior values as inputs to train the algorithms to forecast the next day's closing price. Based on the root of the mean square error, we examined the predictive performance of multiple linear regression, Elman, Jordan, radial basis function, and multilayer perceptron designs. The training set was used to train all models, while the testing set was used to choose hyper-parameters such as the number of input variables and hidden layers.

Furthermore, prediction was based on the trimmed average of 100 bootstrap samples. As a result, our method may assess the uncertainty associated with the anticipated values. The findings indicated that network-tuning provides appropriate fit, realistic forecasts, and confidence intervals for all-time series, considering all architectures except the radial basis function.

e-Learning

The COVID-19 pandemic has recently prompted many educational activities, particularly during lockdowns, to control the global viral outbreak. As a result, educational institutions worldwide are now relying on online learning platforms to keep their educational presence alive. This study introduces and evaluates the

E-Learning DJUST dataset, which comprises a sample of Jordan University of Science and Technology students' academic progress throughout the epidemic (JUST). The dataset is a representative sample of the university's students, as it contains 9,246 students from 11 faculties enrolled in four courses during the spring, summer, and autumn 2020 semesters. This is the first dataset that uses e-learning system records to show students' study progress inside a Jordanian institute. One of the essential conclusions of this study is that there is a strong link between e-learning events and final grades out of 100. To predict student performance, the E-Learning DJUST dataset was used to test two robust machine learning models (Random Forest and XGBoost) and one basic deep learning model (Feed Forward Neural Network). The RMSE scores vary from 7 to 17 when using RMSE as the significant assessment factor. Among the other key findings, using feature selection with the random forest improves prediction performance for all courses, with the RMSE difference ranging from 0 to 0.20. Finally, comparative research looked at how the Corona virus pandemic affected students' grades before and after the outbreak. Because the tests were online, a high success rate was found during the pandemic compared to what it had been previously. However, the percentage of students receiving good grades remained consistent with pre-pandemic courses examined by Abdullah et al. (2021).

The COVID-19 epidemic has disturbed regular life and work in practically every corner of the planet. The education industry, among others, has been heavily damaged. The learning process should continue, and e-learning is the most excellent option for replacing traditional classrooms. eLearning programs and courses were already accessible for those psychologically and financially prepared. Students have been forced to learn this method because of how bad the pandemic is since their willingness to use it is considered secondary. The research involved 375 students enrolled in undergraduate and graduate management programs at South Korean institutions. This research investigated the influence of student characteristics (motivation, mindset, and collaboration) and the technology acceptance model (perceived ease of use and perceived usefulness) on students' behavioural intention to embrace and utilize e-learning in the future. The external factor 'perceived severity of pandemic COVID-19' was investigated for its moderating effect. The findings revealed that all elements favourably impacted the learners' behavioural intention to use and embrace the e-learning system throughout the pandemic. The data were looked at with the partial least square structural equation modelling (PLS-SEM) method. This study will help all education stakeholders who are switching to e-learning or have already made the switch. The research focuses on the numerous aspects that are important for students and instructors to adopt and apply this method in this unavoidable circumstance Baber (2021).

The impact of fear on students' and teachers' technology adoption during the COVID-19 pandemic is investigated in this study. The study used Mobile Learning

(ML) as an educational, social platform at public and private higher education institutions. COVID-19 has impacted mobile learning (ML) since the pandemic and has caused an upsurge in many sorts of anxiety. Students and teachers/instructors face a wide range of fears, including the dread of a total lockdown, the fear of the collapse of education, and the anxiety of giving up social interactions. It was found that the proposed model worked well when administered to 280 students at Zayed University's Abu Dhabi campus, which is located in the United Arab Emirates (UAE). SEM and deep learning-based artificial neural networks (ANN) are used in this study to create a new hybrid analytic approach (ANN). Additionally, the importance-performance map analysis is used to discover the relevance and performance of each element. Attitude (ATD) was the most important predictor of intention to use mobile learning in both ANN and IPMA investigations. Perceived ease of use, usefulness, satisfaction, attitude, behavioral control, and subjective norm were all shown to significantly impact whether or not people continued to use Mobile Learning. It was shown that the motivation to use mobile learning was strongly influenced by how anxious participants felt and how confident they felt about the results. It is possible that mobile learning might boost teaching and understanding during a pandemic, but this may be diminished by the dread of losing friends and the stress of a difficult home situation, as well a student's concern for their future academic success. Therefore, a pandemic examination of pupils is essential to equip them to cope emotionally with the circumstance. The suggested model has theoretically supplied adequate information about what determines an individual's intention to use ML from internet service characteristics. Decision-makers in higher education may use the data to better structure their policies by selecting which criteria should be prioritized. Methodologically, this study investigates the deep ANN model's ability to determine non-linear relationships among the variables in the theoretical model Alhumaid et al. (2021).

BUSINESS ANALYSIS DATASETS FOR AI APPLICATIONS

Yelp Dataset

Yelp is the company to publish the review of local business and online services in USA and Canada. It was founded by former PayPal employees in the year 2004 to train the business predictions including health scores. The dataset will be used to analyse the market predictions using various deep learning techniques and ANN models Asghar et al. (2016).

Africa Economic, Banking and Systemic Crisis Data

The dataset includes the banking transactions during the inflation raised in African countries in the period of 1860 to 2014. It will be used to estimate the gradual drop in the financial crisis using neural network models.

e-Learning DJUST

The Jordan university students has survey on progress of the education during pandemic through online. The aim of the survey is to find out the correlation between e-learning events and final grade obtained by the students. Many researchers have used to apply classification models on this datasets.

Yahoo Finance Data

The stock market growth will be given in Yahoo finance official website. It will be useful to predict the stock growth in pandemic by applying the regression analysis between stock data and COVID-19 data released by World Health Organization, Mottaghi et al. (2021).

COMPARISON OF AI MODELS IN BUSINESS APPLICATIONS

Table 1 shows various AI based models to analyse the business applications during the pandemic. The industries such as food, banking, stock market and e-learning have vastly applied neural networks for predicting the causes of downfall or growth in the particular industry during the pandemic period using deep learning models. The LSTM, CNN has got more precision than the machine learning models such as random forest or SVM. The business data represented in the above literature is text related. So LSTM has combined with CNN obtained more importance for predicting in the food processing industry.

CONCLUSION

This chapter aims to study the AI based models on various business applications during pandemic. The literature section has discussed different applications such as Food, Banking, Stock market and e-learning. The datasets available open source and used by researchers has been discussed. In the section 4 comparison of the AI models on various applications and their findings are discussed. The chapter has fulfilled the justification of the title by discussing the related literature published in the recent researchers during the pandemic.

Table 1. AI models developed on business applications and findings.

S. No.	Author and Year	Industry	Models	Findings
1	Luo, Yi et al. (2021)	Food	Bidirectional LSTM	90.8 accuracy, Service, food, place and experience parameters considered.
2	Naimul Hossain, et al. (2020)	Food	Combined CNN-LSTM	94.22 training accuracy and 75.01 validation accuracy.
3	Kanwal Zahoor, et al. (2020)	Food	Random forest	95% accuracy obtained. Taste, money, ambience and service parameters considered.
4	Manish Talwar, et al. (2020)	Banking	ANN	Relative influence of various financial attitude dimensions are analysed
5	Pradyot Ranjan Jena, et al. (2021)	Stock market	ANN	GDP growth of various countries during pandemic.
6	C. T. Vidyaa and K. P. Prabheesh (2020)	Stock market	LSTM	GDP growth of various countries during pandemic.
7	Anca Antoaneta Varzaru and Claudiu George Bocean (2021)	Stock market	SEM and ANN	Comparative evolution of m-commerce and other tools of commerce. Source: developed by authors
8	Malak Abdullah, et al. (2021)	e-learning	Feed Forward Neural Networks	Students grade analysed in all semesters of Jordan university data during pandemic.

REFERENCES

Abdullah, M., Al-Ayyoub, M., AlRawashdeh, S., & Shatnawi, F. (2021). E-learningDJUST: E-learning dataset from Jordan university of science and technology toward investigating the impact of COVID-19 pandemic on education. *Neural Computing & Applications*, 1–15. doi:10.100700521-021-06712-1 PMID:34803236

Alhumaid, K., Habes, M., & Salloum, S. A. (2021). Examining the factors influencing the mobile learning usage during COVID-19 Pandemic: An Integrated SEM-ANN Method. *IEEE Access: Practical Innovations, Open Solutions*, 9, 102567–102578. doi:10.1109/ACCESS.2021.3097753

Asghar, N. (2016). Yelp dataset challenge: Review rating prediction doi:10.48550/arXiv.1605.05362

Baber, H. (2021). Modelling the acceptance of e-learning during the pandemic of COVID-19-A study of South Korea. *The International Journal of Management Education*. doi:. doi:10.1016/j.ijme.2021.100503

de Pauli, Z. T., Suellen, M. K., & Bonat, W. H. (2020). Comparing artificial neural network architectures for Brazilian stock market prediction. *Annals of Data Science*, 7(4), 613–628. doi:10.100740745-020-00305-w

Elzamly, A. (2017). Predicting critical cloud computing security issues using Artificial Neural Network (ANNs) algorithms in banking organizations. http://dstore.alazhar.edu.ps/xmlui/handle/123456789/445

Heidari, M., Zad, S., & Rafatirad, S. (2021). Ensemble of supervised and unsupervised learning models to predict a profitable business decision. *IEEE International IOT, Electronics and Mechatronics Conference (IEMTRONICS)*, IEEE. 10.1109/IEMTRONICS52119.2021.9422649

Hossain, N. (2020). Sentiment analysis of restaurant reviews using combined CNN-LSTM. *11th International Conference on Computing, Communication and Networking Technologies (ICCCNT)*, IEEE. 10.1109/ICCCNT49239.2020.9225328

Jena, P. R., Majhi, R., Kalli, R., Managi, S., & Majhi, B. (2021). Impact of COVID-19 on GDP of major economies: Application of the artificial neural network forecaster. *Economic Analysis and Policy*, 69, 324–339. doi:10.1016/j.eap.2020.12.013

Kumar, I., Rawat, J., Mohd, N., & Husain, S. (2021). Opportunities of artificial intelligence and machine learning in the food industry. *Journal of Food Quality*, 2021, 1–10. doi:10.1155/2021/4535567

Luo, Y., & Xu, X. (2021). Comparative study of deep learning models for analyzing online restaurant reviews in the era of the COVID-19 pandemic. *International Journal of Hospitality Management*, *94*, 102849. doi:10.1016/j.ijhm.2020.102849 PMID:34785843

Mottaghi, N., & Farhangdoost, S. (2021). Stock Price Forecasting in Presence of Covid-19 Pandemic and Evaluating Performances of Machine Learning Models for Time-Series Forecasting. https://arxiv.org/abs/2105.02785

Niu, J., & Niu, P. (2019). An intelligent automatic valuation system for real estate based on machine learning. *Proceedings of the International Conference on Artificial Intelligence, Information Processing and Cloud Computing*. 10.1145/3371425.3371454

Paule-Vianez, J., Gutiérrez-Fernández, M., & Coca-Pérez, J. L. (2019). *Prediction of financial distress in the Spanish banking system: An application using artificial neural networks*. Applied Economic Analysis. doi:10.1108/AEA-10-2019-0039

Rafay, A., Suleman, M., & Alim, A. (2020). Robust review rating prediction model based on machine and deep learning: Yelp dataset. *International Conference on Emerging Trends in Smart Technologies (ICETST)*, IEEE. 10.1109/ICETST49965.2020.9080713

Rajkumar, K., & Sudheer, D. (2016). A review of visual information retrieval on massive image data using hadoop. *Int. J. Control Theor. Appl*, *9*, 425–430.

Sankar, S., Ramasubbareddy, S., Luhach, A. K., & Chatterjee, P. (2022). NCCLA: New caledonian crow learning algorithm based cluster head selection for Internet of Things in smart cities. *Journal of Ambient Intelligence and Humanized Computing*, *13*(10), 1–11. doi:10.100712652-021-03503-3

Sankar, S., Somula, R., Parvathala, B., Kolli, S., & Pulipati, S. (2022). SOA-EACR: Seagull optimization algorithm based energy aware cluster routing protocol for wireless sensor networks in the livestock industry. *Sustainable Computing: Informatics and Systems*, *33*, 100645.

Sudheer, D., & Krishnan, R. (2019). Multiscale texture analysis and color coherence vector based feature descriptor for multispectral image retrieval. *Advances in Science, Technology and Engineering Systems Journal*, *4*(6), 270–279. doi:10.25046/aj040634

Sudheer, D., & Lakshmi, A. R. (2015). Performance evaluation of Hadoop distributed file system. *Pseudo Distrib Mode Fully Distrib Mode*, (9), 81-86.

Talwar, M., Talwar, S., Kaur, P., Tripathy, N., & Dhir, A. (2021). Has financial attitude impacted the trading activity of retail investors during the COVID-19 pandemic? *Journal of Retailing and Consumer Services*, *58*, 102341. doi:10.1016/j. jretconser.2020.102341

Treleaven, P., Barnett, J., Knight, A., & Serrano, W. (2021). Real estate data marketplace. *AI and Ethics*, *1*(4), 445–462. doi:10.100743681-021-00053-4

Vărzaru, A. A., & Bocean, C. G. (2021). A two-stage SEM–artificial neural network analysis of mobile commerce and its drivers. *Journal of Theoretical and Applied Electronic Commerce Research*, *16*(6), 2304–2318. doi:10.3390/jtaer16060127

Vidya, C. T., & Prabheesh, K. P. (2020). Implications of COVID-19 pandemic on the global trade networks. *Emerging Markets Finance & Trade*, *56*(10), 2408–2421. doi:10.1080/1540496X.2020.1785426

Zahoor, K., Bawany, N. Z., & Hamid, S. (2020). Sentiment analysis and classification of restaurant reviews using machine learning. *21st International Arab Conference on Information Technology (ACIT)*, IEEE. 10.1109/ACIT50332.2020.9300098

Chapter 5
Business Tech in Media and Entertainment

Sapna Chopra
Woxsen University, India

Samala Nagaraj
ⓘD https://orcid.org/0000-0002-1182-115X
Woxsen University, India

ABSTRACT

Businesses are using innovation to communicate their story online so they can reach hundreds of thousands of users at once. The technology trend is probably here to stay. This means that innovation is still in its infancy and that new types of technical advances are appearing every day. Video content is becoming more popular as a result of the use of cutting-edge technologies in the media and entertainment industries. However, the creation of novel technical ideas may result in a wide range of previously unheard-of digitalized tools and functionalities. Films, print, television, and radio were the key components of media and entertainment. The usage of gesture recognition technology, picture analysis in journalism, film screenplay analysis, and music composition and generation are a few of the new components that make up the media and entertainment environment. Due to the incorporation of innovation and technology, the media and entertainment sector has seen dramatic changes in recent years.

INTRODUCTION

In the former times, media and entertainment mainly encompassed films, print,

DOI: 10.4018/978-1-6684-4246-3.ch005

television, and radio. But in the 21st century, it has undergone a transformational change, especially in the past few years. One of the key factors that have led to dramatic change is the high application of advanced technology and innovative elements. In fact, it can be said that due to the integration of technology in the media and entertainment setting, there has been a consistent upward growth in the domain. Various business undertakings that have succeeded to exploit the ever-evolving technological landscape have grown from strength to strength and established their name when it comes to the media and entertainment setting. Technology has opened up new opportunities for organizations that enable them to creatively work in the evolving domain (Media and Entertainment|Vault.com, 2020).

It can be said that the media and entertainment realm is in a transformational phase right now. This is because both new and old elements coexist with each other. Some of the new elements that make up the media and entertainment setting include the use of gesture recognition technology, image analysis in the field of journalism, film script analysis, music production and generation, and many more (Mukherji & Sengupta, 2020). Each of the elements of the media and entertainment backdrop plays a critical role in its own way.

ALGORITHMIC NEWS STORIES

The field of journalism basically revolves around the production and distribution or sharing of news stories. Due to the use of advanced technology in this field, the process has undergone substantial alteration lately. Technology has opened up new opportunities for journalists to share their stories in unique and creative ways with the target audience. In the age of digitalization, one of the concepts that have gained high popularity is 'the algorithm method (The Algorithm Method, 2020).' The use of algorithms for the purpose of sharing news stories has the potential to redefine the existing journalism and audience relationship. One of the simple examples that can be used to understand this in a better way is that today it is much easier for people to make comments on news stories. Moreover, people can do so in a fast and public way as well. Due to the use of algorithms when it comes to sharing news stories, it is easier to relate with the audience in aggregate as well as big data sort of way (The Algorithm Method, 2020). Hammond has stated in his research study that the use of technology-driven elements such as huge volumes of data has revolutionized how news stories are stared (Hammond, 2017). Since it is not possible for human beings to process such humongous quantity of data, the role of algorithms has gained a lot of popularity these days. According to Linden, the use of algorithms or robots in the journalism scene has captured the attention of organizations and individuals who are involved in the field (Lindén, 2017, p 1).

The concept of algorithmic news stories has been bringing about gradual changes in how the journalism process takes place. The use of algorithm plays a vital role as they can choose relevant information for the users. In addition to this, the use of algorithms can also mold the overall construct relating to social processes as well as practices. The integration of technology in the field of journalism has not just empowered organizations but it has also empowered the users of the current times. The impact of algorithmic turn in the news production process and the news stories sharing cannot be ignored. This method of automation has given rise to a number of positive changes in the form of better efficiency in the news story sharing process, elimination of error-prone routine activities and processes and the introduction of new kinds of work that requires computational thinking (Lindén, 2017,p 1).

FILM SCRIPT ANALYSIS

Film script analysis is an important function in the media and entertainment arena. In fact, the process significantly molds the quality of a film. The evolution of technology and innovation has had a major impact on how the analytical process is carried out when relating to a film script. Gillick and Bamman have pointed out in their analysis that, in the current times, many filmmakers are trying to integrate the ideal kind of soundtrack that will enable them to share stories with the audience (Gillick & Bamman, 2018).

It is very important to understand the association that exists among various elements such as film story or script, song and the reception by the audience. Due to the development and implementation of technology, it has become easier to assess film scripts. The use of technology is not just restricted to the film script analysis process. In fact, it is also possible to easily and effectively synchronize picture with sound or music (Gillick & Bamman, 2018, p 2).

Conducting a thorough and in-depth analysis of a film script acts as a foundation in the media and entertainment backdrop. Before a screenplay is given the green signal, it is really highly critical to make sure that an accurate and precise film script analysis process is in place. This is because the film script is the key component on which the strength of content is assessed. The involvement of a myriad of participants such as executives, readers, and assistants in the reading as well as evaluation is necessary so that the weaknesses in the film script can be identified and suitable changes can be made (How to Analyse a Film Script, 2020). Due to the application of technology in the film script analysis arena, the process has become simplified to a substantial degree. The use of technological tools in the form of software and applications is creating value to devise high-quality feature films, documentaries, and other television productions (Harman, 2020).

In the 21st century, it is not uncommon to see the merger of technology with the scriptwriting or script analysis process. For example, film scripts are being analyzed by taking into consideration the visual ideas and components that are integrated into the story. Thanks to the application of technology-driven elements, it is possible to comprehend whether certain kinds of scenes should be included in a film script or not (Harman, 2020).

GESTURE RECOGNITION

Gesture Recognition is a subdomain in computer science and language technology that has a significant impact on the media and entertainment scene. In technical language, the term gesture recognition can be defined as the mathematical interpretation of human emotions which is done by using a computing instrument. This component of the perpetual user interface (PUI) helps to get an insight into what the audience or users think of the content that is being shared with them (What is Gesture Recognition? - Definition from Techopedia, 2020). Due to the rapid advancement of technology and innovation, a number of organizations in the media and entertainment arena have been making investments so that they can explore the gesture recognition technology and use it to gain an edge in the competitive setting. This technological model has made revolutionized the gaming world of the 21st century. Many gamers all across the globe are able to have a new kind so gaming experience thanks to the use of gesture recognition technology (Markets, 2020). For instance, some of the most renounced business undertakings including Sony and Microsoft have launched gesture recognition-based gaming products such as Kinect for Xbox one as well as PlayStation Move. Owing to the gesture recognition technology, a large number of game developers, business organizations and third-party application developers have started working on new kinds of products and offerings that support this new and advanced technology.

According to Manoff and Houck, in the prevalent times, the gesture recognition technology is also being used so that content can be manipulated (Manoff et al., 2019). For example, if a user is going through a diverse range of content out of which he is not interested in specific content, the swipe gesture recognition technique is coming into play. Thus this innovative technology is providing reliable guidance so that perfect content packages can be formed for the users that can enhance their level of satisfaction. In the field of media and entertainment, the gesture recognition technology is creating high value as it is enabling content developers and business organizations to present the kind of content that is synced with the interests and preferences of the audience.

IMAGE ANALYSIS FOR JOURNALISM

For journalists, the image analysis process is considered to be extremely critical in nature. As it is known that an image is worth a thousand words, it is necessary to carefully and tactfully select and analyze images that are used while sharing any content with the audience. Image analysis can be defined as the process that involves the extraction of relevant and meaningful information from images. It is necessary to understand the fact that the image analysis process is different as compared to other kinds of image processing methodologies or techniques that are used such as restoration, enhancement, etc. In the field of journalism and media, the role of image analysis gets further intensified. Thanks to social media and the world wide web, the visual aspect of journalism has increased. Thus, it becomes necessary for companies to stop relying on text and start laying emphasis on images as they are one of the most vital visual components.

According to Stumpf and MacFarlane, when it comes to journalism, especially digital journalism, the role of the image analysis process is indispensable. Images have a very strong and impactful presence in the journalism field (Sylwia Frankowska-Takhari, 2020). They can be used as powerful tools that can help to attract readers or users to a specific topic of interest. According to the author, it is necessary to thoroughly analyze an image and make sure that it complements the story that is being shared for the intended target audience. Even though a diverse range of images is available on the online platform that can be used for journalism purposes, it is necessary for journalists to understand the relevance of the image analysis process. In the research study, the authors have stated that content-based image retrieval systems can be used so that images that add value to content can be used while covering stories. A number of research studies that have been carried out on the use of images in the field of journalism such as Garcia and Stark (1991) and Machin and Niblock (2006) have stated that images act as eye-catchers in the journalism domain, But in the 21st century, the significance of images has increased to a substantial extent (Frankowska-Takhari, 2020). In fact, this is evident from the increase in the number of images and a significant decline in the use of a lot of texts. The increased relevance of images in the field of journalism has also increased the overall relevance of the image analysis process.

MUSIC PRODUCTION AND GENERATION (GAN)

GAN can be defined as the state of the mart model that is used for the purpose of generating high quality of music. GAN fundamentally stands for Generative Adversarial Networks that simplifies the process of generating high-fidelity audio content that has high relevance in the field of media and entertainment (Engel et al., 2019). When it comes to the media and entertainment backdrop, the role and relevance of audio elements are equally important like the visual content. In fact, both audio and video components complement each other so that the audience members can read, listen or view the stories and content that they are looking for. GAN is able to produce locally-coherent audio content (Engel et al., 2019). This is possible by modeling the log magnitudes as well as instantaneous frequencies, in the spectral domain, with ample frequency resolution. Authors Engel and Chen have demonstrated in their research study that GAN is a revolutionary concept that can mold the quality of music and overall audio content in the media and entertainment scene for the better. In fact, GANs also has the potential for outperforming robust WaveNet baselines and efficiently produce audio of better quality.

Dong and Yang have stated in their research work that generating high-quality music is a basic necessity for organizations that work in the media and entertainment setting. For instance, if a company is producing a movie, the quality of music that is used can have a direct implication on the overall movie quality. Moreover, it can also have a major implication on the level of satisfaction of the audience members (Engel et al., 2019).

Case study – GAN-based models have gained a lot of popularity in the present times. According to Brunner and Wang, an organization can employ the Generative Adversarial Networks model for creating music. It would primarily consist of a generator and a discriminator (Engel et al., 2019, p 4). The generator would be mainly responsible for generating or producing real looking data from noise. On the other hand, the discriminator would be responsible for differentiating the output of the generator from the actual data. In addition to this, it is necessary to train the model on music in the Musical Instrument Digital Interface (MIDI) format. Such a step would be necessary to ensure that music was being generated as output. The assessment of the GAN model shows that it has helped to carry out effective music genre transfer (Engel et al., 2019, p 2). The state of the art method is here to stay as it has revolutionized the music and entertainment scene. It has become a trending topic as the concept can be configured to generate music for the audience. The algorithm was previously used for generating high-quality image. But today researchers have succeeded to employ the algorithm on more sequential data such as music as well as audio.

NEWS AND FEED CURATION FOR CONSUMERS

The curation of content is a vital aspect in the media and entertainment setting. Since a diverse range of content is available for end-users, the proper curation of news, stories, and other feed is necessary so that customers can be kept engaged. Gray has highlighted in his research study that it is necessary to take into account a number of latent factors such as customer beliefs while curating news feed on Facebook (Rader & Gray, 2015). The awareness of such intangible factors can play an integral role and shape the relationship and association that a user has with a content provider. Due to the rapid evolution of technology, businesses have the ability to use relevant algorithms so that they can make accurate and valuable news and feed curation for their target consumers.

A wide range of research studies has been carried out in the past few years that shed light on how technology can be used to simplify the process relating to the curation of news and other kinds of content for the users. Bandy and Dimakopoulos have stated that conducting the proper auditing of news curation system is necessary in the current times. It can ensure that the end-users can access the information and content that is actually valuable and useful for them (Bandy & Diakopoulos, 2019).

Case study – Bandy and Dimakopoulos have presented a case study in their research work which shows how the curation of Apple news takes place. As Apple Inc. is one of the most renounced business concerns of the 1st century, its news generally captures the attention of a diverse range of audience members (Bandy & Diakopoulos, 2019, p 2). In order to ensure that the news content on the Apple company reaches the intended audience, the brand makes the use of technology-driven algorithms along with human factors to conduct the curation of the news storied for its customers. Some of the key factors that have made Apple Inc. news a prominent and attractive element in the news infrastructure include low entry costs, the massive potential readership, etc. Since the news revolving around apple has always kept customers and overall audience on their toes at all times, Apple has successfully launched the Apple News app which informs the readers or customers about the latest happenings about the brand. Thus the case shows that effective news and feed curation for consumers can strengthen the goodwill of a brand and enhance the level of engagement (Bandy & Diakopoulos, 2019, p 2). The global tech firm has been using technology and communication so that it can forge a deeper connection with the customers and share the information that they are looking for. The business entity is making the optimum use of technology and humongous volume of information that is available with it to engage with the audience by sharing relevant content in the form of news.

SIMULATING CROWDS

The crowd simulation can be defined as the process in which the dynamics of a large number of individuals or entities are simulated. The objective of deploying such a technique is to make sure that these parties are moving in the desired path. This approach has made a mark in a diverse range of settings such as architectural planning, virtual reality, and games and movies (Crowd and Multi-agent Simulation - GAMMA UNC, 2020). In fact, the instances of simulating crowds can also be seen in the media and entertainment arena. The journalism domain is considered to be extremely powerful in nature as it has the power to simulate and influence large masses. According to Boeira and Rockenbach, the content that is produced by journalists can play an integral role when important events take place in the social or community backdrop (Rockenbach et al., 2018). For example, in case some serious incident takes place when a crowded event is being conducted, crowds can be simulated so that safety measures can be taken. Moreover, in the research study, the authors have stated that journalism can make the use of crowd simulation techniques so that the crowd can be relaxed at the time of a stressful situation.

Zhao and Turner have stated in their research study that various forms of content such as video, images and texts can be used so that the behavior of crowds can be influenced to a significant degree. Due to the application of advanced technology in the field of media and entertainment, data-driven approaches can be employed for the purpose of molding the behavior pattern of people in the real-life setting (Zhao, Cai, & Turner, 2018). Thalmann has stated that modern technologies and methods can be employed so that the collective behavior of individuals can be simulated. As per the author, it is necessary to take into consideration a number of aspects such as realism of the behavior aspects as well as achieving the high-quality of visualization. The concept of simulating crowds has gained a high level of popularity in the 21st century. Especially in the media and entertainment arena, the concept is catching up, as quality and relevant content can be used to influence whether people behave in a positive or negative manner to different events and situations.

SOCIAL MEDIA PUBLISHING AND MANAGEMENT

In the current times, the role of social media has skyrocketed in diverse fields and domains. In the media and entertainment setting, social media publication and management can play an integral role. In fact, it can also lead to the success or failure of a business that operates in the specific setting. The content that is published by business undertakings on various social media platforms such as Facebook, Instagram, Twitter, and YouTube can play an integral role. This is because a large section of the market audience members uses social media networking sites for different purposes. The posts and content that are shared on these platforms keep the people updated about the latest events and happenings all across the globe. When it comes to journalism, it is necessary to make sure that relevant, factual and authentic content is shared with the masses on these platforms (Bruns & Nuernbergk, 2019). Due to social media networking sites, it is possible to share information from one corner of the globe to another within a matter of seconds. Thus, responsible journalism is the need of the hour so that social media publishing and management aspects can be taken care of in a professional manner. According to Bruns, the use of social media has become very common in the journalism and communication setting in the 21st century.

The networked platform has the power to ensure that the content that is shared can reach far and wide audience members. Moreover, the manner in which content is shared i.e. in the form of text, images, audio or video could influence how people react and behave to deal with a social event. Thus, it is the responsibility of the participants in the media and entertainment backdrop to behave in a professional and responsible manner (Bruns & Nuernbergk, 2019). Mhamdi has highlighted in his research work that due to the application of social media platforms for content sharing, the media boundaries that existed between conventional and non-conventional models have substantially blurred (Mhamdi, 2016). Since the content that is shared on social media reaches the global audience, it is necessary for journalists and other media and entertainment participants to take care of social media publishing and management aspects.

Case Study – The mushrooming growth of social media has impacted the media and entertainment scene and the journalism backdrop tremendously. Journalism is about witnessing an event in its purest form and recording it for others to read and/ or see. The news media and social media has given a makeover to the concept of journalism as journalists from popular channels such as CNN, etc are able to do their work in an efficient manner. Facebook and Twitter have become some of the most powerful and effective tools that are being used by journalists from all across the globe to disseminate information. Adornato has pointed out that numerous big and small companies that have their own local TV newsrooms have started integrating social media into newscasts as it helps them to gather content or locate story ideas for their newscasts (Adornato, 2016). Social media has given a new dimension to how news is presented in front of people. Moreover, the author has stated that social media has also significantly impacted the editorial as well as production decisions that are taken by local television newsrooms. The case relating to change in how news is made shows the power of social media and its influence on news creation for the masses (Adornato, 2016). One of the main reasons for the high popularity of social media in the journalism context is the ability to generate content, generate conversations which helps to create communities. CNN, the reputed news brand uses social media platform to shape its journalism style. It uses the online communication platform to get an insight into the audience which helps to drive change in its newsroom.

VIDEO COMPRESSION

Video Compression is another latest technology-driven concept that is making a mark in the media and entertainment setting. The term video compression refers to the method that is used for the purpose of reducing the data that has been used so that the encoding of digital video content will be possible. In the digitalized times, content is being shared in various forms and not just text. For example, images and videos are widely being used so that quality content, as well as stories, can be shared with the end-users. Due to the high popularity of the video format to share stories, the technology relating to video compression has gained a lot of popularity in the recent times. The innovative video compression process makes sure that the data that is not very useful or critical for the users can be omitted without compromising the quality of the video content.

According to Wu, in the current times, there has been a substantial increase in how media and entertainment content is being consumed by the audience. Due to the increase in the level of digital communication, the relevance and importance of video compression has increased multifold. The video compression that is possible due to the advanced technology is far superior in nature as compared to the conventional video compression technique. Due to the application of advanced and innovative technology, it is possible to send bulky and lengthy content in a compact manner (Wu, Singhal, & Krahenbuhl, 2018). Sambo has pointed out in his research work that many forms of disruptive technologies have transformed how the media and entertainment processes are carried out in the 21st century. Sophisticated video compression algorithms are one of the most effective disruptive technologies that have the power to bring about dramatic alterations in the domain. The state of the art video compression approach is capable of supporting high-resolution video streams at very low bit rates. Due to this modern technology, the customers are getting the opportunity to have ideal audio and visual experience by using their smartphones or other electronic devices. Since the video compression technology is still evolving, it has the potential to streamline the manner in which video content is shared with the masses across different mediums (Stamos & Ramzan, 2019).

Video Production and Editing

In the media and entertainment domain, the role of video content cannot be negated. In order to share high-quality and impactful video content with the target audience, it is very important to take care of the video production and editing aspects. These functions have the potential to mold how engagement takes place with the audience and how their overall thinking is influenced. Due to the introduction and application of advanced technology in the media and entertainment domain, the video production and editing process have become simple and efficient. In journalism, it is vital to understand how technology-based techniques can be applied while sharing content in the form of video. This is because these digitalized approaches can transform simple content into captivating piece of content. On the other hand, the lack of proper use of technological tools for video generation and editing can adversely affect the quality of decent video content. According to Bock, in the journalism arena, it is necessary for journalists to understand the difference between showing and telling about an event (Bock, 2016). Since video has become a central segment of the journalism of the 21st century, it is necessary to ensure to makes sure that video production and editing help to share a true and authentic picture to the users. In other words, the content that is shared with the audience in the form of the video must not be manipulated or misrepresented (Bock, 2016).

Li and Yang have highlighted in their journal paper that video has always been an important component when it comes to journalism (Li et al., 2018). But due to the use of the latest technology, there is scope in the field of media and entertainment to enhance the effectiveness and attractiveness of video content. For example, subtitles can be introduced so that video journalism can cater to the needs of a broader audience.

CONCLUSION

The media and entertainment domain has undergone revolutionary changes in the past few years due to the integration of innovation and technology. Many business entities and marketers are moving towards digitalization so that the experience of the end-users can be made more real and delightful. Innovation is helping firms to tell their stories digitally so that they can reach hundreds and thousands of users at a time. The technology trend is most likely here to stay. This is because of the fact that technology is still in its nascent stage and with every passing day, new kinds of technological innovations are coming into existence. Thanks to the application of advanced technology in the field of media and entertainment, video content is on the rise. But the development of new technological concepts could give rise to a host of new digitalised tools and features that have not been heard of till now.

REFERENCES

Adornato, A. C. (2016). Forces at the gate: Social media's influence on editorial and production decisions in local television newsrooms. *Electronic News*, *10*(2), 87–104. doi:10.1177/1931243116647768

Bandy, J., & Diakopoulos, N. (2019). Auditing News Curation Systems: A Case Study Examining Algorithmic and Editorial Logic in Apple News.

Bock, M. A. (2016). Showing versus telling: Comparing online video from newspaper and television websites. *Journalism*, *17*(4), 493–510. doi:10.1177/1464884914568076

Bruns, A., & Nuernbergk, C. (2019). Political journalists and their social media audiences: New power relations. *Media and Communication*, *7*(1), 198–212. doi:10.17645/mac.v7i1.1759

Engel, J., Agrawal, K. K., Chen, S., Gulrajani, I., Donahue, C., & Roberts, A. (2019). Gansynth: Adversarial neural audio synthesis.

Fink, K. & Schudson, M. (2020). The Algorithm Method. *Columbia Journalism Review*. https://archives.cjr.org/the_research_report/the_algorithm_method.php

Frankowska-Takhari, S. (2020). Selecting and tailoring of images for visual impact in online journalism. *IR Information Research*. http://informationr.net/ir/22-1/colis/colis1619.html

GAMMA. (2020). Crowd and Multi-agent Simulation. GAMMA. http://gamma.cs.unc.edu/research/crowds/

Gillick, J., & Bamman, D. (2018, June). Telling stories with soundtracks: an empirical analysis of music in film. In *Proceedings of the First Workshop on Storytelling,* (pp. 33-42). 10.18653/v1/W18-1504

Hammond, P. (2017). From computer-assisted to data-driven: Journalism and Big Data. *Journalism*, *18*(4), 408–424. doi:10.1177/1464884915620205

Harman, R. (2020). How technology is changing the Craft of Screenwriting. *Raindance*. https://www.raindance.org/how-technology-is-changing-the-craft-of-screenwriting/

Li, K., Yang, D., Ji, S., & Liu, L. (2018, December). The Impacts of Subtitles on 360-Degree Video Journalism Watching. In *International Joint Conference on Information, Media and Engineering (ICIME),* (pp. 130-134). IEEE. 10.1109/ICIME.2018.00035

Lindén, C. G. (2017). Algorithms for journalism: The future of news work. *The journal of media innovations, 4*(1), 60-76.

Manoff, R. S., Houck, T., & Squire, J. D., & SoMo Audience Corp, (2019). *Content manipulation using swipe gesture recognition technology.* U.S. Patent Application 16/116,459.

Markets, R. (2020). Global Gesture Recognition Market to Reach $23.55 Billion by 2023: Analysis by Technology, Industry and Region. *PR Newswire.* https://www.prnewswire.com/news-releases/global-gesture-reco gnition-market-to-reach-23-55-billion-by-2023-analysis-by-te chnology-industry-and-region-300699427.html

Media and Entertainment|Vault.com. (2020). Overview. *Firsthand.* https://www.vault.com/industries-professions/industries/medi a-and-entertainment

Mhamdi, C. (2016). Transgressing media boundaries: News creation and dissemination in a globalized world. *Mediterranean Journal of Social Sciences*, 7(5), 272–272. doi:10.5901/mjss.2016.v7n5p272

Miles, N. (2020). How to Analyze a Film Script. *Pen and the Pad.* https://penandthepad. com/analyze-film-script-12069589.html

Mukherji, P., & Sengupta, S. (2020). Media & Entertainment Industry: An Overview. https://avasant.com/insights/publications/technology-optimiz ation/media-entertainment-industry-an-overveiw/

Rader, E., & Gray, R. (2015, April). Understanding user beliefs about algorithmic curation in the Facebook news feed. In *Proceedings of the 33rd annual ACM conference on human factors in computing systems,* (pp. 173-182). 10.1145/2702123.2702174

Rockenbach, G., Boeira, C., Schaffer, D., Antonitsch, A., & Musse, S. R. (2018, November). Simulating crowd evacuation: From comfort to panic situations. In *Proceedings of the 18th International Conference on Intelligent Virtual Agents,* (pp. 295-300). 10.1145/3267851.3267872

Stamos Katsigiannis, W. A., & Ramzan, N. (2019). 5G: Disruption in Media and Entertainment. *Enabling 5G Communication Systems to Support Vertical Industries.*

Techopedia. (2020). What is Gesture Recognition? *Techopedia.* https://www.techopedia.com/definition/618/gesture-recognitio n

Wu, C. Y., Singhal, N., & Krahenbuhl, P. (2018). Video compression through image interpolation. In *Proceedings of the European Conference on Computer Vision (ECCV),* (pp. 416-431).

Zhao, M., Cai, W., & Turner, S. J. (2018, February). Clust: Simulating realistic crowd behaviour by mining pattern from crowd videos. *Computer Graphics Forum*, *37*(1), 184–201. doi:10.1111/cgf.13259

Chapter 6

Customer Purchase Prediction and Potential Customer Identification for Digital Marketing Using Machine Learning

Malla Sudhakara
Reva University, India

Bhavya K. R.
Reva University, India

M Rudra Kumar
G. Pullaiah College of Engineering, India

N. Badrinath
Annamacharya Institute of Technology and Sciences, Tirupati, India

K. Rangaswamy
Sai Rajeswari Institute of Technology, India

ABSTRACT

In recent years, digital marketing has surpassed traditional marketing as the preferred technique of reaching customers. Researchers and academics may utilize it for social media marketing and for predicting client buy intent, among other applications. It can boost customer happiness and sales by facilitating a more personalized shopping session, resulting in higher conversion rates and a competitive advantage for the retailer. Advanced analytics technologies are utilized in conjunction with a dynamic and data-driven framework to expect whether or not a customer will make a purchase from the organization within a certain time frame. To increase income and stay ahead of the competition, one must understand customer buying habits. Several sectors offered rules to explore a consumer's potential based on statistics

DOI: 10.4018/978-1-6684-4246-3.ch006

results. A machine learning algorithm for detecting potential customers for a retail superstore is proposed using an engineering approach.

INTRODUCTION

For marketing decision-making, the ability to predict client behaviour is highly prized. For example, retargeting advertisements for online sales retail marketing can be improved by properly predicting which clients are most likely to purchase those who have already visited the site—the more accurate the forecast, the better the marketing investment's return on investment. Machine learning models have recently received attention as a technology capable of forecasting the behaviour of customers Kim & Lee (2022). From 2014 to 2021, the number of digital buyers worldwide (Figure 1). More than 1.66 billion consumers bought digital goods and services in 2016, predicted to rise to over 2.14 billion in 2021.

Machine learning can predict customer behaviour online, and marketing literature establishes numerous models to forecast consumer buying behaviour. Machine learning can forecast customer behaviour online rather than in offline environments by detecting the consumer journey and various clickstream data. The customer journey is a series of stages that a person goes through as they move from recognition to purchase (Chou et al. (2022)). Customer path mapping improves interactions and boosts income using ML models (i.e. Bayesian models, hidden Markov model etc.). Despite its great potential, a little experience utilizing machine learning to forecast online customer behaviour. The findings of the study fill up the following gaps.

1. Forecasting customer attrition has received much attention (Batra, 2016)), but predicting customer buy conversion has received less attention. Online shopping malls' performance depends heavily on their ability to convert visitors into buyers. So it is vital to study the problems of utilizing machine learning to predict online client behaviour.

2. The best machine learning models for forecasting online customer behaviour haven't been discussed sufficiently. All marketing decisions entail predicting certain results. As a result, utilizing machine learning improves forecast accuracy (Agrawal, (2018)). However, prior research has not explained which machine learning model is best used in online consumer behaviour.

3. There was no comparison of the best data sampling approach for converting online customer purchases. Because most marketing data is imbalanced, machine learning is hampered by bias. The asymmetry bias must be overcome to use machine learning in marketing. Currently, there isn't any research comparing two or more different methods of sampling (Migueis, (2017)).

Figure 1. Increasing number of digital buyers globally.

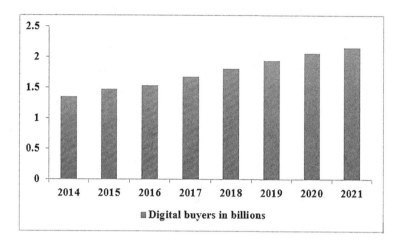

4.   Marketing hasn't given enough attention to the results of machine learning models. It is possible to create accurate predictions using machine learning models; nevertheless, they cannot explain the link between predictors and outcomes. Make sure you communicate the predictive power of machine learning to your target audience so that they can understand. Explainable artificial intelligence is being developed (Rai, (2020)), but studies on the actual commercial environment are limited.

The following sections of this chapter are explained in this order. We'll start by going over a variety of machine learning models, and then we'll go over how these models can be used to make predictions. The current state of predictive science is discussed, followed by an examination of recent research pertinent to the topic at hand. Finally, the SVM-based technique is discussed.

MACHINE LEARNING MODELS

Because large data is readily available and the complex and unpredictable marketing environment, applying machine learning to marketing is a growing trend. Machine learning has been the subject of marketing studies. Prediction, feature extraction, prescriptive analysis, and optimization are all active fields of study. SVM, Topic modelling, Ensemble trees, and deep learning were techniques used in machine learning research (Ma, & Sun, (2020)).

The SVM was initially used in the marketing of machine learning models. Cui (2005) discovered that SVM outperformed the multinomial logit model in marketing. SVM performs better with large amounts of data, whereas the multinomial logit model performs better with implications. While the machine learning model accurately predicts, it cannot explain the relationship between the explanatory variable and the projected result. A machine learning model that analyses text and visual data are deep. For example, Liu et al. (2019) discovered that price and aesthetics influence conversion. Chakraborty et al. (2019) also created a Hybrid CNN-LSTM model to extract emotional traits from text data and demonstrated its ability to classify Yelp reviews. Similarly, Zhang et al. (2018) discovered that Yelp review photos outperform review text when predicting restaurant survival.

For high prediction accuracy, the Ensemble technique combines many individual learners. General strategies include stacking, bagging, and boosting. Bagging obtains each learning tree using bootstrap samples and aggregates individual learning tree predictions to create the final prediction result. Adaptive boosting can also use to compensate for incorrectly classified content. To summarise, bagging learns in parallel, whereas boosting learns sequentially, with weights added after learning. Individual decision trees benefit from increasing, but it is slow and overfits the training data. The Random-Forest algorithm is one of the most commonly used ensemble models; it employs bagging and boosting techniques. To reduce correlation, each divided tree in the random forest receives input variables assigned at random. After considering all of the predictions produced by individual trees, an overall conclusion is drawn. Using GBM, each tree better predicts the future by correcting mistakes in prior trees. X.G.B. has won multiple Kaggle data science challenges.

Machine learning algorithms have been shown to aid marketing decisions. However, there has been little research into which machine learning algorithms are useful in predicting online consumer behaviour (Table 1). Marketing prediction performance suffers when there is a class imbalance. To reduce inequalities, machine learning necessitates comparing methods. According to Cui (2005), the relationship between explanatory factors and prediction outputs is difficult for machine learning algorithms. To properly study retargeting advertising that heavily relies on machine learning, X.A.I. research is required. As a result, this research will bring together machine learning and marketing literature.

PREDICTION PROCESS

Machine learning-related technology was used to analyze and predict the attributes of customers' purchasing behaviours based on past data from customers who had purchased a scooter. Linear regression, time series decomposition, moving average,

Table 1. Comparison between different studies in C.P.P.

Reference	Technique	Observations
Cui, D., & Curry, D. (2005)	SVM	In many marketing prediction contexts, ML-based SVM outperforms conventional prediction models.
Huang, D., & Luo, L. (2016)	Fuzzy SVM	It was suggested that Fuzzy SVM be used to analyze consumer preferences for products with important attributes.
Jacobs et al. (2016)	LDA, MDM	Using LDA and M.D.M., you can predict which products clients will buy based on their preferences.
Migueis et al. (2017)	RF	In the banking industry, there is a distinction between the performance of the conducted sampling method and the prediction of consumer response to direct marketing.
Ballestar et al. (2019)	MLP, ANN	E-commerce social networks' client quality can be estimated using multilayer perceptron ANN.
Hartmann et al. (2019)	5 models	Compare the sentiment classification methods of five machine learning models (SVM, RF, NB, ANN, and K.N.N.).
Lee et.al. (2021)	8 models	The authors use X.A.I. to identify successful customer features for retargeting adverts based on online consumer behaviour. The work also compares ML paradigms and sampling methodologies.

auto-regression, exponential smoothing, and grey theory are some data mining techniques. Logistic regression, support vector machine, decision tree, neural network, Bayesian network, and other machine learning techniques are also available. Data mining is a broad term that refers to the collection of previously unknown, usable, and practical information from large datasets and its application to decision making or knowledge gain. Data mining is used to predict customer purchasing behaviour using machine learning algorithms. The prediction procedure is depicted in Figure 2.

The model divides the data mining process into six stages, as shown in Figure 3. The step sequence is arbitrary and heavily influenced by the previous phase's results. The diagram's arrows represent the most powerful relationships. The outer circle represents the circular nature of data mining tasks: data mining project lessons and solutions frequently lead to new business questions and spark a new process

Figure 2. Customer purchase behaviour prediction process

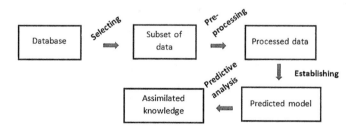

Figure 3. Major steps in learning task

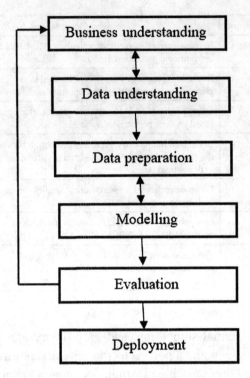

(Chapman et al., 2000). The six steps are described in more detail below. Table 2 delineates the six stages in greater detail.

- Business understanding: This phase examines the project's goals from a business standpoint. An issue definition for data mining is derived from a collection of insights.
- Data understanding: Data is collected and analyzed during the data comprehension phase to gain early insights and become comfortable with the data.
- Data preparation: At the end of this stage, a final dataset of variables is generated from raw data and used as input into the modelling software.
- Modelling: During this stage, modelling techniques are employed—model parameter selection and fine-tuning. The same data mining problem can be modelled in a variety of ways.
- Evaluation: After the models have been implemented, they must be reviewed and compared. It's vital to evaluate whether the objectives set during the business understanding phase were reached.

Table 2. Steps involved in each stage of learning

Stage	Steps Involved
Business understanding	· Identifying the objectives of the business · Assessing the Situation · Finding the goals of Data Mining · Preparing the project plan
Data understanding	· Sample Data collection · Data description and statistics · Exploratory Data Analysis · Data quality check
Data preparation	· Description of the data · Data selection · Data cleaning · Data construction · Data Integration · Data formatting
Modelling	· Choose the modelling technique · Test Design generation · Training the model · Assess Model
Evaluation	· Evaluate Results · Review Process
Deployment	· Deployment of plan · Monitoring the plan · Final Report generation · Project review

- Deployment: The model must be deployed to gain its benefits. The model must be connected into live systems and fed with live data to produce useful predictions.

From the analysis of various research works on C.P.P., the conventional structure of each ML model is shown in Figure 4.

The purchase of various things, goods, and services is one of the most typical financial decisions that we make practically daily. In some circumstances, the purchase choice is solely focused on price. Still, the purchasing decision is more complex in many cases, with many additional elements influencing the decision-making process before the ultimate commitment is made. Retailers are well aware of this and strive to take advantage of it to obtain a competitive advantage in a crowded market. To improve the possibility of a purchase, companies frequently add additional features to the offer to increase the perceived value of the investment to the consumer and balance the scalability and profit in establishing the selling price of a product. The flow of this work is shown in Figure 5 (Baderiya et al. (2018)).

Figure 4. Conventional flow of C.P.P. by researchers

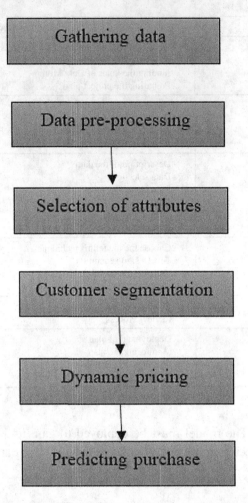

RELATED WORKS

Several studies have been conducted to investigate purchase prediction. Recently, studies established frameworks to investigate purchase prediction in a market environment using prior session data and physical mobility. Experiment results indicate that including user behaviour/session variables in ML models improves their accuracy in predicting purchase intent. Zeng et al. (2019) proposed a purchase prediction model to analyze user behaviour during a Chinese holiday. A user is more likely to spend more time on a product that piques their interest. Wu et al. (2015) created a purchase behaviour prediction model for virtual environments instead of session features. According to the study's findings, using click-based characteristics

Figure 5. Architecture used for CPP

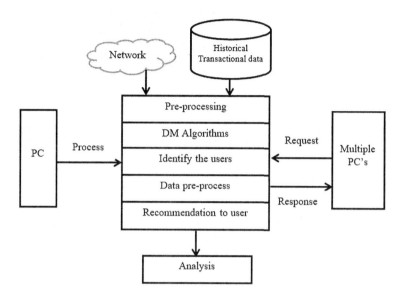

can improve purchase prediction as much as using session-based features. Lo et al. proposed purchase prediction models for registered Pinterest users (2016). When prediction models were run on extracted features, the authors discovered that purchase intentions increased over time. The studies' findings revealed that prediction models developed using the entire timeline up to the purchase were more accurate.

D.T., N.N., R.N.N., and logistic regression are some of the most advanced ML models used for purchase prediction. Mokryn et al. (2019) investigated and compared the performance of various machine learning models in predicting user purchases. Li et al. (2016) proposed three machine learning models (Bagging, D.T., and Random Forest) combined using linear regression. Their proposed strategy improved purchase prediction accuracy by 8%. Mokryn et al. (2019) used temporal features to investigate the effect of Bagging on purchase prediction performance (time, product trendiness, etc.). Suh et al. (2004) discovered that integrating D.T., N.N., and Logistic Regression ML models improved performance. ML models performed well when trained on anonymous sessions with extracted session attributes despite their anonymity.

CHALLENGES

Despite these advancements, it is still impossible to foresee a customer's purchasing intention. For the most part, earlier studies on the prediction of purchase intent

Table 3. Recent works about purchase prediction in literature

Reference	Key Findings
Zeng et al. (2019)	First, a prediction model was constructed, and then a recommender system model was built to determine which product could be purchased.
Wu et al. (2015)	A neural network model was used to analyze click patterns to make purchase predictions.
Li et al. (2016)	An L.R. model was developed to forecast purchasing behaviour on a Chinese e-commerce website.
Baumann et al. (2018)	Data from the user's navigation was used in the graph modelling process to create a model for predicting purchases.
Lo et al. (2016)	Models of user behaviour were used to explore how registered users' purchase intentions are formed after each visit to the website.
Mokryn et al. (2019)	When temporal variables are taken into account, compare purchase prediction models.
Park and Park (2016)	A Bayesian probabilistic model was used to examine purchase conversion factors.
Martinez et al. (2020)	The authors Modeled a mechanism to anticipate future purchasing habits based on historical data.
Kim et al.(2020)	Camera sensors in an unmanned product cabinet were used to detect objects in real-time and analyze purchasing activity on merchandise.

employed data collected from customers of e-commerce platforms (Tsagkias et al. (2021)). The models tested ranged from feature-based models such as boosted decision trees to sequence-based neural models such as R.N.N.s. However, de-identified data from an e-commerce website shows that anonymous visitors account for more than half traffic. It is difficult to detect purchase intent for anonymous users because many existing algorithms rely on user history. Features that predict purchase intent. An unknown and identified setup is used to identify purchasing intent signals. We test the features based on our observations on a production-ready model. We use five more classifiers to test the generalizability of the feature sets.

Two examples of session-based data we collect are page dwell time and the number of days since the last transaction. Session-based functionality can be used for both identifiable and anonymous sessions provided the user has logged in or is recognized by cookies (when the customer is not known). Feature availability is limited to the times and dates stated. For some reason, purchase intent prediction for anonymous sessions has received little attention in earlier proposals (Seippel et al., (2018)). Researchers studied over 95 million anonymous user sessions from a European e-commerce platform to fill this gap.

The following research questions are addressed:

RQ1: What separates buy and non-purchase sessions?

Customers are more likely to buy in the evening and on a weekday, and they are more likely to own multiple devices.

RQ2: What key session-based characteristics distinguish purchase sessions from non-purchase sessions?

What should key historical characteristics be considered while developing predictors for identified sessions?

What changes in the relevance of features as the session progresses?

We conclude that historical data related to earlier purchasing behaviour is extremely significant for recognizing purchases in the defined scenario based on the tests presented in Section 5. However, dynamic elements such as page dwell time and page sequencing are most significant in the anonymous setting. Furthermore, as the session progresses, the importance of dynamic features grows, while the volume of static features declines.

RQ3: How effective are models for predicting buy intent for anonymous vs identifiable sessions?

In addition, how helpful are the proposed features in terms of increasing anonymous session performance?

The authors analyzed that tree-based and neural classifiers outperform in the unknown environment and that adding new features to models improves F1 by about 17%. In contrast, all models perform well in the identified scenario, and adding unique characteristics does not provide a meaningful advantage.

METHODOLOGY

The authors used a data-miner to gather product information from Amazon, Flipkart, Jabong, Myntra, and other e-commerce sites. Web scraping is a sophisticated approach to collecting data from multiple websites at once.

The web pages are difficult to navigate. Web scraping seeks to discover unstructured data storage locations. When we execute the web scraping app, we will send a query to the URL you provided. Upon request, the server transfers the data and displays the HTML tab. The application then examines the HTML file and removes unnecessary stuff. Using supervised machine learning as a decision tree algorithm to predict consumer intensity. Two studies discuss the application

Figure 6. Predictive model workflow for client purchases

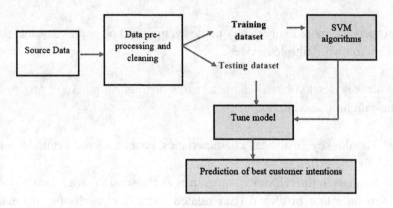

of machine learning algorithms in healthcare. This is due to a bag estimation error demonstrated to be objective and straightforward to calculate in many studies. An example of this is shown in Figure 6.

Scrapping Data

To obtain Price, Name, Rating, and so on, we must scrape Flipkart with a data miner extension. Scanning the website for information to scrape is the next step. Examine the product's price, name, and rating page, which are saved in the I.D. identifier. You may want to keep the data in CSV format after distilling it. Figure 7 shows how web scraping can convert unstructured data to structured data.

Figure 7. Web scraping of data from webpages

Data Validation and Pre-processing

The extracted dataset is imported into the library's packages. The libraries analyze the dataset and help with delicacy removal, missing value correction, and data shaping to perform operations and produce accurate results. The extracted data must be corrected before the algorithms can be applied. This is a critical step known as data cleaning or pre-processing. It is a systematic process for converting an outlier or data set to a clean data set that can be analyzed. This step speeds up the process because the extracted raw data is unsuitable for analysis. Figure 8 shows the methodology used for the effective CPP model.

Figure 8. Methodology used for effective CPP model.

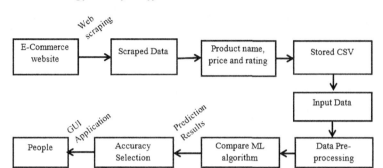

Visualization of Data and Training Dataset

To train a model a specific attribute, statistics need specialization in quantitative knowledge estimation. Data visualization is a powerful tool for conditional comprehension. This can help with trends, bad data, and many other things when evaluating and functioning on a dataset. This is done after the data has been cleansed and prepared for analysis. Results are generated and presented in a statistical table or graph by the user. The results are easier to comprehend when visualized. This strategy is called Data Visualization. An overall summary of the data set is also obtained.

They infer the customer's intent based on the selected items and ratings. Retailers, as end consumers, must produce simple-to-understand results. We use a web application to display the results and categorize them as positive, negative, or neutral. We used Linear Support Vector Machine to rate customer products and compared the results to those from other Machine Learning models. Figure 9 compares SVM-Linear to other machine learning methods regarding user buy intent.

CONCLUSION

With the growth of e-commerce, the consumer now has a say in purchasing a product. The internet is a goldmine of researchable data. Using machine learning algorithms, data is acquired from the internet. Once the data has been pre-processed, it is cleaned

Figure 9. SVM-Linear Method compared with other ML models

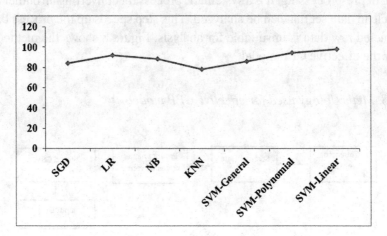

and analyzed before algorithms are run on it. The outcomes are graphically used to predict client intent. Because retailers are the ultimate users, the results must be presented in plain English. The authors employed a user interface, a webpage, to give the results and categorize them as positive, bad, or neutral. The suggested approach is fully based on website data and algorithmic training data. This is increasingly likely to work in the future as e-commerce, and customer-focused businesses grow. As technology, cloud computing, and e-commerce evolve, so will customer-generated outcomes. This process can be automated further to view the results on a desktop programme. The work can also be used in an Artificial Intelligence setting. Customers' input or marks may be important in future technologies such as sales force and supply chain management.

REFERENCES

Agrawal, A., Gans, J., & Goldfarb, A. (2018). *Prediction machines: the simple economics of artificial intelligence*. Harvard Business Press.

Baderiya, M. S. H., & Chawan, P. M. (2018). Customer buying Prediction Using Machine-Learning Techniques. *Survey (London, England)*.

Ballestar, M. T., Grau-Carles, P., & Sainz, J. (2019). Predicting customer quality in e-commerce social networks: A machine learning approach. *Review of Managerial Science, 13*(3), 589–603. doi:10.100711846-018-0316-x

Batra, R., & Keller, K. L. (2016). Integrating marketing communications: New findings, new lessons, and new ideas. *Journal of Marketing, 80*(6), 122–145. doi:10.1509/jm.15.0419

Baumann, A., Haupt, J., Gebert, F., & Lessmann, S. (2018). Changing perspectives: Using graph metrics to predict purchase probabilities. *Expert Systems with Applications, 94*, 137–148. doi:10.1016/j.eswa.2017.10.046

Chakraborty, I., Kim, M., & Sudhir, K. (2019). Attribute sentiment scoring with online text reviews: Accounting for language structure and attribute self-selection.

Chou, P., Chuang, H. H. C., Chou, Y. C., & Liang, T. P. (2022). Predictive analytics for customer repurchase: Interdisciplinary integration of buy till you die modeling and machine learning. *European Journal of Operational Research, 296*(2), 635–651. doi:10.1016/j.ejor.2021.04.021

Cui, D., & Curry, D. (2005). Prediction in marketing using the support vector machine. *Marketing Science, 24*(4), 595–615. doi:10.1287/mksc.1050.0123

Hartmann, J., Huppertz, J., Schamp, C., & Heitmann, M. (2019). Comparing automated text classification methods. *International Journal of Research in Marketing, 36*(1), 20–38. doi:10.1016/j.ijresmar.2018.09.009

Huang, D., & Luo, L. (2016). Consumer preference elicitation of complex products using fuzzy support vector machine active learning. *Marketing Science, 35*(3), 445–464. doi:10.1287/mksc.2015.0946

Jacobs, B. J., Donkers, B., & Fok, D. (2016). Model-based purchase predictions for large assortments. *Marketing Science, 35*(3), 389–404. doi:10.1287/mksc.2016.0985

Kim, D. H., Lee, S., Jeon, J., & Song, B. C. (2020). Real-time purchase behavior recognition system based on deep learningbased object detection and tracking for an unmanned product cabinet. *Expert Systems with Applications, 143*, 11306. doi:10.1016/j.eswa.2019.113063

Kim, S., & Lee, H. (2022). Customer Churn Prediction in Influencer Commerce: An Application of Decision Trees. *Procedia Computer Science, 199*, 1332–1339. doi:10.1016/j.procs.2022.01.169

Lee, J., Jung, O., Lee, Y., Kim, O., & Park, C. (2021). A Comparison and Interpretation of Machine Learning Algorithm for the Prediction of Online Purchase Conversion. *Journal of Theoretical and Applied Electronic Commerce Research, 16*(5), 1472–1491. doi:10.3390/jtaer16050083

Li, Q., Gu, M., Zhou, K., & Sun, X. (2016). Multi-classes feature engineering with sliding window for purchase prediction in mobile commerce. In *Proceedings - 15th IEEE international conference on data mining workshop, ICDMW*, (pp. 1048–1054)

Liu, X., Lee, D., & Srinivasan, K. (2019). Large-scale cross-category analysis of consumer review content on sales conversion leveraging deep learning. *JMR, Journal of Marketing Research*, *56*(6), 918–943. doi:10.1177/0022243719866690

Lo, C., Frankowski, D., & Leskovec, J. (2016). Understanding behaviors that lead to purchasing: a case study of pinterest. In *Proceedings of the ACM SIGKDD international conference on knowledge discovery and data mining*, (pp. 531–540) 10.1145/2939672.2939729

Ma, L., & Sun, B. (2020). Machine learning and AI in marketing–Connecting computing power to human insights. *International Journal of Research in Marketing*, *37*(3), 481–504. doi:10.1016/j.ijresmar.2020.04.005

Mart'ınez, A., Schmuck, C., Pereverzyev, S. Jr, Pirker, C., & Haltmeier, M. (2020). A machine learning framework for customer purchase prediction in the non-contractual setting. *European Journal of Operational Research*, *281*(3), 588–596. doi:10.1016/j.ejor.2018.04.034

Miguéis, V. L., Camanho, A. S., & Borges, J. (2017). Predicting direct marketing response in banking: Comparison of class imbalance methods. *Service Business*, *11*(4), 831–849. doi:10.100711628-016-0332-3

Mokryn, O., Bogina, V., Kuflik, T. (2019). Will this session end with a purchase? Inferring current purchase intent of anonymous visitors. *Electronic Commerce Research and Applications, 34*, 100 836

Park, C. H., & Park, Y. H. (2016). Investigating purchase conversion by uncovering online visit patterns. *Marketing Science*, *35*(6), 894–914. doi:10.1287/mksc.2016.0990

Rai, A. (2020). Explainable AI: From black box to glass box. *Journal of the Academy of Marketing Science*, *48*(1), 137–141. doi:10.100711747-019-00710-5

Seippel, H. S. (2018). *Customer purchase prediction through machine learning* [Master's thesis]. University of Twente.

Suh, E., Lim, S., Hwang, H., & Kim, S. (2004). A prediction model for the purchase probability of anonymous customers to support real time web marketing: A case study. *Expert Systems with Applications*, *27*(2), 245–255. doi:10.1016/j.eswa.2004.01.008

Tsagkias, M., King, T. H., Kallumadi, S., Murdock, V., & de Rijke, M. (2021, February). Challenges and research opportunities in ecommerce search and recommendations. In *ACM SIGIR Forum, 54*(1), pp. 1-23. ACM.

Wu, H., & Li, B. (2022, January). Customer Purchase Prediction Based on Improved Gradient Boosting Decision Tree Algorithm. In *2nd International Conference on Consumer Electronics and Computer Engineering (ICCECE)*, (pp. 795-798). IEEE. 10.1109/ICCECE54139.2022.9712779

Wu, Z., Tan, B. H., Duan, R., Liu, Y., & Mong Goh, R. S. (2015). Neural modeling of buying behaviour for E-commerce from clicking patterns. In *Proceedings of the international ACM recommender systems challenge 2015*, (p. 12). 10.1145/2813448.2813521

Zeng, M., Cao, H., Chen, M., & Li, Y. (2019). User behaviour modeling, recommendations, and purchase prediction during shopping festivals. *Electronic Markets*, *29*(2), 263–274. doi:10.100712525-018-0311-8

Zhang, M., & Luo, L. (2018). Can user-posted photos serve as a leading indicator of restaurant survival? Evidence from Yelp. *Evidence from Yelp.*

Chapter 7
Failed IPO Stories:
Stories of Initial Public Offering

Swarnasree Vutharkar
Woxsen University, India

C. A. Narasimha Swamy
Woxsen University, India

Krishna Hitesh
Woxsen University, India

ABSTRACT

Initial public offerings (IPOs) have long been a popular term on Wall Street and among investors. By selling shares of the Dutch East India Company to the general public, the Dutch are credited with launching the contemporary IPO. Since then, firms have utilised IPOs as a means of raising funds from the general public by issuing shares of stock to the general public. IPOs have experienced uptrends and downtrends in issuance over the years. Due to innovation and several other economic reasons, individual industries also undergo uptrends and downtrends in issuance. At the height of the dotcom boom, companies scrambled to list themselves on the stock market as technology IPOs surged. There are essentially two steps in the IPO process. The pre-marketing stage of the offering is the first, and the actual initial public offering is the second. A company that wants to go public will either request private bids from underwriters or make a public announcement to pique interest.

PAYTM

India's top financial services provider, Paytm, provides customers, physical businesses,

DOI: 10.4018/978-1-6684-4246-3.ch007

and internet platforms with full-stack financial solutions. The company wants to integrate half a billion Indians into the global economy through payments, commerce, financial services, banking, and investments. Vijay Shekhar Sharma launched One97 Communications Limited, which has the trademark Paytm and has its headquarters in Noida, Uttar Pradesh. Softbank, Ant Financial, AGH Holdings, SAIF Partners, Berkshire Hathaway, T Rowe Price, and Discovery Capital are among of its investors.

The country's largest digital bank, Paytm Payments Bank, is owned by Vijay Shekhar Sharma, founder, and CEO of Paytm, and One97 Communications Limited. It has over 58 million account holders. To fulfil its goal of integrating under- and un-served Indians into the formal banking system, it has developed creative technological solutions that have made banking convenient for people all over the nation.

Its wholly owned subsidiary, "Paytm Money," has the distinction of becoming India's largest investment platform within its first year and is currently one of the largest contributors of new Systematic Investment Plans (SIPs) to the Mutual Funds industry. It has already received approvals to launch Stock Broking, Demat Services, and National Pension System (NPS) services, and it aims to continue to enlarge the financial services and wealth management opportunities available to the public.

Millions of consumers all throughout India now turn to Paytm First Games, a member of the same group of companies and a joint venture between One97 Communications Ltd and AG Tech Holdings, for their gaming and at-home entertainment needs. The platform offers a vast selection of games for beginners as well as professional esports to accommodate all different types of gamers.

A brokerage licence has been obtained by Paytm Insurance, a wholly owned subsidiary of One97 Communications Ltd (OCL). It provides insurance products in four categories, including two-wheeler, four-wheeler, health, and life, to millions of Indian consumers. The business wants to make insurance simpler and give customers a simple, intuitive online experience.

There are two different Paytm revenue /model structures. Paytm receives commissions from customer transactions made using its platform. The accounts from which they derive their money are escrow accounts. It provides customers with little intrigue, as is evident from the absence of its hidden capital. Paytm has accrued income totalling 3.314.8 crore INR since 2018.

In 2017–18, Paytm verified 2.5 billion transactions. Paytm said that it increased its gross transaction value (GTV) from $25 billion to $50 billion from 2018 to 2019. GTV is a measurement of the intensity of its transactions.

Paytm has launched a lot more. On the portal, users may purchase tickets for events, movies, theme parks, and flights. Later, Paytm QR was introduced along with gift cards. Citibank and Paytm even collaborated to introduce credit cards. The Paytm IPO failed for a variety of reasons. Its unreasonably inflated listing was the main reason behind Paytm's stock market decline. Analysts and industry professionals have long brought attention to the unicorn's exaggerated value, which ended up being a reason for disaster.

The IPOs was priced at Rs. 2,150 per share which was substantially more than the company's true valuation, the shares where subscribed more than 1.8 times in the IPO. Paytm's parent company, One97 Communication, was trading at 49.7 times its FY21 sales. At that time, the business wasn't even showing a profit. The absence of a licence to operate in the loan industry is one of the main causes of fear.

Any fintech company's lending sections generate the most profitable revenue. To earn the respect of analysts, a financial services provider needs to have a lending business. But Paytm lacks the license to operate in this area of the fintech business. This might be another reason for the questionable future of Paytm and failed of IPO.

PhonePe, which accounts for 42% of all UPI transactions in the nation, poses the biggest threat to the business. Other well-known brands like BHIM and Google Pay come after it. Together, PhonePe and Google Pay account for more than 82 percent of the UPI market in India, which has significant implications for Paytm's future in this market (Mahajan, 2022; Pandey, 2021).

E – COMMERCE

Car Trade

A multi-channel car platform with presence and coverage across all vehicle types and value-added services is Car Trade Tech Limited. CarWale, Car Trade, Shriram Auto mall, BikeWale, Car Trade Exchange, Adroit Auto, and AutoBiz are just a few of the company's platform names. Through these platforms, the company makes it possible for buyers and sellers of new and used cars, as well as auto dealers, OEMs, and other companies, to do business quickly and easily. The goal of Car Trade is to establish a digital automotive ecosystem that links auto buyers, OEMs, dealers, banks, insurance providers, and other interested parties. The company provides a range of options for marketing, purchasing, financing, and selling new and used cars, two-wheelers, as well as pre-owned commercial vehicles, agricultural equipment, and construction equipment.

Car Trade Tech Ltd., India's top online auto marketplace, acts as a marketplace for those interested in buying and selling both new and old cars. The Car Trade IPO's total issue size is expected to be Rs 2,998.51 crore, according to the DRHP submitted to SEBI. The car trade IPO was subscribed more than 20.29 times.

The Car Trade IPO consists of a pure offer by the company's current shareholders and promoters to sell 18,532,216 equity shares. The market lot size for the Car Trade Tech IPO is 9 shares. Retail investors may submit applications for as few as 1 lot

(9 shares, or 14,265) and as many as 13 lots (117 shares, or 185,445). The offer consists of a purchase proposal. 18,532,216 shares totalling 2,998 crores are up for sale in the offer, and the selling shareholder will receive all the profits. To reap the advantages of listing equity shares on stock exchanges is the issue's main goal.

When compared to their main rivals over the period from April 2020 to March 2021, the platforms of Car Trade Tech, CarWale, and BikeWale ranked first in terms of relative online search popularity, and Shriram Auto mall is one of the top platforms for used car auctions based on the volume of vehicles listed for auction for the fiscal year 2020. The business provides a range of services along the whole value chain of an automobile transaction, including discovery and research tools, pricing and financing information, and connections between customers and dealers and OEMs for both used and new car transactions. Through their financial platforms, Car Trade Tech also offers financing alternatives that are dynamic, tailored, and available in real time to vehicle buyers. Combining online and offline auctions with complementary services increases consumer traffic, fosters competition among their network of reputable dealers, and ensures that users are getting the best price.

The strength of the Car Trade Tech brands and their link with dependability, quality, and trust are important company attributes that boost consumer confidence and affect purchasing decisions. Consumer traffic has consistently increased across all of the company's platforms thanks to its known brands as well as the high calibre and dependability of its user interface and user experience. For the three months ended June 30, 2021, the financial years 2021 and 2020, respectively, the company's monthly average of unique visitors was 27.11 million, 25.66 million, and 20.51 million. For the same time periods, their online and offline auction platforms had 212,552, 814,316, and 809,428 listings, respectively. This brand-based expansion has enormous network effects that produce a constructive feedback cycle. We have been able to create additional products including price tools, financing options, and trade-in solutions because to our strong, recognised brands.

A significant competitive advantage is decision-making that is driven by analytics. Data science and proprietary algorithms are used by Car Trade Tech to analyse vehicle sales that take place through their auctions as well as those offered for sale by dealers on CarWale, CarTrade, and BikeWale. These factors include vehicle-specific information on automotive transactions, vehicle registration records, consumer buying patterns and behaviour, demographic data, and macroeconomic data. The company's statisticians and data scientists have created sophisticated, proprietary algorithms to use this data to provide pricing tools, product reviews, market insights, and reports in an engaging, simple-to-understand manner to customers, dealers, financial institutions, and OEMs through their web and mobile user interfaces.

Some of the risk elements include Trends, such as youngsters choosing ride-sharing services, that may cause a reduction in demand for vehicles, may negatively affect demand for cars supplied through the platforms. The firm can suffer as a result of this. Any extended pandemic phase could cause revenues to drop and have a significant effect on the company. Their business and reputation may suffer if their technology platforms are disrupted or fail, which has major legal, financial, and public relations concerns (Ellikkal et al., 2022; Salo, 2020).

Zomato

As of March 31, 2021, Zomato Ltd. was one of the top food services platforms in India in terms of the amount of food sold. 32.1 million average MAU used its platform in India during Fiscal 2021. Zomato was available in 525 Indian cities and had 389,932 active restaurant listings as of March 31, 2021. According to App Annie's estimates, its mobile application has received the most downloads for food and beverages in India over the course of the last three fiscal years, from fiscal 2019 to fiscal 2021, on the iOS App Store and Google Play combined.

Customers, restaurant partners, and delivery partners are all connected through Zomato's technological platform, which meets their various needs. Customers can order food delivery, reserve a table, read and post reviews from other customers, browse and submit photos, and pay for their meals at restaurants using this platform. On the other side, the business offers its restaurant partners sector-specific marketing tools that let them draw in clients to expand their clientele while simultaneously offering a dependable and effective last-mile delivery service. Hyperpure, a one-stop procurement service run by Zomato, provides premium products to its restaurant partners. As a result, the organisation offers flexible and transparent income opportunities to its delivery partners.

Although the company had a presence in 23 countries outside of India as of March 31, 2021, it has made a strategic decision to limit its attention to the Indian market going forward. It believes that a more focused Zomato will increase value for all of its stakeholders given the huge market opportunity in India. The COVID-19 pandemic caused a setback in its activities in the fiscal year 2021. As a result, the financials and key performance metrics of the company for Fiscal 2021 account for the pandemic's effects on its operations.

Zomato is launching its first stock offering totalling Rs. 9375.00 cr. to partially finance its goals for funding organic and inorganic growth initiatives (Rs. It has established a price range of Rs. 72 to Rs. 76 for each share with a Re.1 face value (FV). The subscription of IPO was more than 38.25 times. A minimum application is required for 195 shares, followed by applications for multiples of that number. The offering comprises of a new equity issuance for Rs. 9000.00 crore and a selling offer for Rs. 375.00 crore. Zomato will issue a total of 1233552730 shares at the highest price range of the offering, including a new equity offering of 1184210625 shares. Shares will be listed on BSE and NSE after allotment. The issue makes up 15.72% of the company's post-issue paid-up capital.

For its qualified employees, Zomato has reserved 6500000 shares of its ownership. It has allotted 75% of the remaining amount for QIBs, 15% for HNIs, and 10% for ordinary investors. The company raised further equity between July 2010 and March 2021 in the price range of Rs. 641.00 and Rs. 155690.27 (for FV of Re. 1) after issuing initial equity at par. Additionally, bonus shares were issued at a ratio of 6699 shares for each share held as of April 2021. The selling stakeholders paid an average of Rs. 1.16 per share for the shares they purchased.

The current issued and paid-up capital of Zomato is Rs. 666.10 cr. will be raised to Rs. 784.52 crore. A market cap of Rs. 59623.37 cr. is what the company is aiming for based on the IPO's upper band price.

In terms of financial performance, Zomato has reported a total turnover/net loss (Loss) of Rs. 1397.72 cr. / Rs. - (1010.51) cr. (FY19), 2742.74 crore rupees / Rs. - (2385.60) cr. (FY20) and 2118.42 crore rupees. / Rs. - (816.43) cr. (FY21). It has suffered significant losses for several years. After additional efforts and the declining top line, FY21 reported a reduced loss.

Zomato has (on a consolidated basis) reported negative EPS of Rs. - (2.99) and a negative RoNW of - for the previous three fiscal years (49.09). The issue's price is 5.04 P/BV based on its NAV of Rs. 15.09 and 2.91 P/BV based on its NAV of Rs. 26.10 after the issuance (at the upper price band). It has a positive NAV despite suffering significant operational losses. Thanks to the significant premiums raised on the stock placements, it has posted a positive book value (Pandey, 2021; Yadav et al., 2022).

INSURANCE

LIC

Since 1956, Life Insurance Corporation of India (LIC) has been the only PSU life insurance provider in India. Until recently, LIC operated under a unique LIC act. But now that the IRDA system is in place, it has joined to clear the way for its first float. It is the most dependable Brand and has a stronghold in the home market. It adheres to the meaning of its catchphrases, "Jindagi Ke Saath Bhi, Jindagi Ke Baad Bhi," "LIC that knows India better," and "Har Pal Aapke Saath."

For the nine months ended December 31, 2021, LIC held a 71.8% market share in terms of the number of individual policies issued, an 88.8% market share in terms of the number of group policies issued, and a 61.6% market share in terms of premiums (or GWP) and new business premium (or NBP), respectively. Over 65 years ago, LIC began providing life insurance in India.

For Fiscal 2021, LIC had a market share of 64.1% in terms of GWP, 66.2% in terms of NBP, 74.6% in terms of individual policy issuance, and 81.1% in terms of group policy issuance in the Indian life insurance sector. When compared to the market leaders in the top seven markets worldwide, it had the biggest disparity in market share by life insurance GWP relative to the second-largest life insurer in India (in 2020 for the other players and in Fiscal 2021 for LIC). This, according to CRISIL, is due to LIC's vast agent network, solid track record, enormous trust in the name "LIC," and 65-year history. In terms of total assets, LIC is ranked 10th globally (comparing its assets as of March 31, 2021, with other life insurers' assets as of December 31, 2020) and fifth globally in terms of life insurance GWP (comparing its life insurance premium for Fiscal 2021 to its global peers' life insurance premium for Fiscal 2020).

As of December 31, 2021, LIC was the largest asset manager in India, with AUM (comprising policyholders' investments, shareholders' investments, and assets held to cover linked liabilities) of Rs. 40.1 trillion on a standalone basis, more than 3.2 times the combined AUM of all private life insurers in India, roughly 15.6 times the AUM of the second-largest player in the Indian life insurance industry, and more than 1.1 times the entire India.

As of December 31, 2021, the CRISIL Report estimates that LIC's investments in listed stock represented about 4% of the NSE's total market capitalization. On September 1, 1956, 245 private life insurance companies in India were combined, and LIC was established with a Rs. 50.00 million beginning capital. It was the sole life insurer in India from the time of its incorporation till 2000. Based on its size, market relevance, and domestic and international interconnectedness, IRDAI designated LIC as a Domestic Systemically Important Insurer ("D-SII") in September 2020. According to Brand Finance's "Insurance 100 2021 study," its brand, LIC, was ranked as the third strongest and tenth-most valuable worldwide insurance brand. The effectiveness of a brand's performance on intangible metrics in comparison to its competitors is known as its strength, which is assessed by taking into account the brand's marketing investment, shareholder equity, and the effects of those factors on business success.

32 individual goods—16 participating products and 16 non-participating products—as well as 7 individual riders make up LIC's portfolio of individual products in India. The company's group offerings include group term insurance, group savings insurance, group pension insurance, and group annuity products. There are 11 group products in the LIC portfolio in India.

By December 31, 2021, LIC has 1,559 satellite offices and 2,048 branch offices throughout India, serving 91% of the nation's districts. Individual agents, partners in bancassurance, members of its sales staff for group products, and other channel partners make up its multi-channel distribution platform for group products (other corporate agents and brokers).

In addition to its operations in India, the firm also has branches in Fiji, Mauritius, and the United Kingdom, as well as subsidiaries in Bangladesh, Nepal, Singapore, and Sri Lanka in the life insurance sector. Bahrain also has operations in Qatar, Kuwait, Oman, and the United Arab Emirates. On a consolidated basis, its premium from outside India made up 0.93%, 0.99%, 0.73%, and 0.69% of the total premium for Fiscal 2019, Fiscal 2020, Fiscal 2021, and the nine months ended December 31, respectively. Although it faces competition from private firms, it is still India's top life insurer overall and would remain so given its function.

LIC is a corporation that offers both insurance and investment goods. With a guaranteed return, their products combine investment and insurance. Over 13.5 lakh LIC agents bring in most of the new business. LIC programmes provide both life insurance and "fixed returns." This makes it simple for brokers to sell and gives insurers peace of mind. The public has a high level of trust in LIC for both life insurance and investments made with them. In India, the word "insurance" is equated with LIC. A 39-lakh crore asset is managed by LIC. That sum exceeds the aggregate total of the mutual fund industry. They use these funds to buy bonds and stocks. They own more government bonds than the RBI and 4% of all Indian listed stocks. Leading Indian insurance carrier and fifth-largest insurer globally according to GWP. a variety of life insurance plans to accommodate different insurance demands of people.

As they continue to lose market share to private insurance providers, particularly in metropolitan areas, LIC has weak new policy growth. Products that combine insurance and investing have a poor margin. Due to the unique nature of the LIC business model, valuation is extremely challenging. LIC demands payment up advance with the promise of later paying out benefits to policyholders. They cannot classify the premiums they collect as revenue because they are a mix of insurance and investments. The purpose of the IPO is to sell 221,374,920 shares by selling stockholders and to use the net proceeds to reap the rewards of listing the equity shares on the stock exchange.

A LIC policyholder may submit 2 IPO applications for LIC IPO shares under the categories of Policyholder + Retail and Policyholder + HNI (NII). Reserved quotas for the LIC IPO have investment caps of Rs 2 lakh for workers, policyholders, and retail investors. By placing a bid in the "policyholders + retail" quota (Rs 2 + 2 lakh), policyholders can increase limits. By placing a bid in the "employee + policyholders + retail" quota (Rs 2+2+2 lakh), employees can increase limitations. The benefits of reserved quota in the LIC IPO include a discount of Rs 60 per share on the final offer price as well as a reduction of Rs 45 per share in the retail and employees' quotas. The LIC IPO was subscribed more than 2.95 times.

Following the filing of the DRHP in February 2022, LIC further increased the buzz surrounding its IPO plans. Investors from all sectors were occupied with determining its valuations in light of its enormous size of business and market share in the face of competition. Its pricing, which mirrors embedded value and the trend of corporate growth, now that it has filed a RHP and made its offering details public, seems reasonable. The issue has become more appealing because to its investor-friendly approach and a discount to its pillars, namely policyholders and retail investors. With these actions in the midst of unsettling events like the Russia-Ukraine war, spiralling inflation, and poor global markets, the Indian government has once again demonstrated its investor-friendly gestures. For medium- to long-term benefits, investors might think about participating in this major insurer's first mini-offer (Dimovski et al., 2007; Selvam, 2022).

ASSET MANAGEMENT COMPANY

Aditya Birla Sun Life AMC

Over the past seven decades, the multi-national conglomerate known as the Aditya Birla group has expanded to become one of India's largest and most prestigious multinational companies. This group's ABSLAMC is the one becoming public

According to the CRISIL Report, Aditya Birla Sun Life AMC Ltd. (ABSLAMC) has been listed as the largest non-bank affiliated AMC in India by QAAUM since March 31, 2018 and has been among the top four AMCs in India by QAAUM since September 30, 2011. As of June 30, 2021, ABSLAMC handled a total AUM of Rs. 2,936.42 billion across its suite of mutual funds, portfolio management services, offshore offerings, and real estate offers (excluding domestic FoFs). According to the business, it has attained this position of leadership by putting an emphasis on steady investment performance, a wide distribution network, brand, an accomplished management group, and first-rate customer service.

It has built a geographically varied Pan-India distribution presence since its start in 1994, with 284 locations spanning 27 states and six union territories. As of June 30, 2021, the company's distribution network included over 66,000 KYD-compliant MFDs, over 240 national distributors, and over 100 banks/financial intermediaries. It is large, multi-channelled, and has a strong physical as well as digital presence. As of June 30, 2021, it managed 118 schemes, including two liquid schemes, five ETFs, and six domestics FoFs. These included 37 equity schemes (including, among others, diversified, tax-saving, hybrid, and sector schemes), 68 debt schemes (including, among others, ultra-short-duration, short-duration, and fixed-maturity schemes), and two liquid schemes.

Aditya Birla Sun Life Frontline Equity Fund and Aditya Birla Sun Life Corporate Bond Fund are two of ABSLAMC's flagship programmes that have developed under its administration into top funds in India. As of June 30, 2021, March 31, 2020, and 2019, respectively, the total QAAUM (excluding domestic FoFs) was Rs. 2,754.54 billion, Rs. 2,692.78 billion, Rs. 2,475.22 billion, and Rs. 2,464.80 billion. As of June 30, 2021, it also offered offshore, real estate, and portfolio management services, managing a total AUM of Rs. 115.15 billion as part of those services.

Through its Pan-India network and customer solutions, ABSLAMC serves a broad range of clients, including both individuals and institutions. This puts it in a good position to draw clients with a variety of needs and risk profiles from the Indian mutual fund market and to build a strong retail clientele. According to the CRISIL Report, its MAAUM from institutional investors was Rs. 1,503.04 billion as of June 30, 2021, ranking fourth among peers. Like this, as of June 30, 2021, ABSLAMC's MAAUM from individual investors was Rs. 1,333.53 billion. The company's exceptional financial success is a result of its market leadership, product mix, cost structure, and scale.

Over time, it has kept a market-leading position in B-30 penetration, which has helped to increase the number of individual investors and boost profitability. Similar growth has been seen in its systematic transactions, with the number of outstanding SIPs rising from 0.86 million as of March 31, 2016, to 2.80 million as of June 30, 2021.

ABSLAMC is launching its first initial public offering (IPO) by way of an offer for sale (OFS) of 38880000 equity shares worth Rs. 5 each, with a price range of Rs. 695 to Rs. 712. This is done in an effort to examine the benefits of listing and give some of its stakeholders an exit. The company is considering raising Rs. 2768.26 cr at the highest price band. The subscription of shares was more than 5.25 times than the actual shares issued. Applications must be submitted for a minimum of 20 shares and in multiples of that number afterwards. Shares will be listed on BSE and NSE after allotment. 13.50% of the company's post-issue paid-up capital is made up by the issuance.

For the shareholders of ABCL (Aditya Birla Capital Ltd.), ABSLAMC has set aside 440000 shares, and from the remainder, it has distributed 50% to QIBs, 15% to HNIs, and 35% to ordinary investors. After issuing its initial equity at par, the business raised further equity in May 1999 at a price of Rs. 9.405 per share (based on a Rs. 5 paid-up value) and issued bonus shares in April 2021 at a ratio of 7 for 1. The promoters' and selling stakeholders' respective average purchase costs per share are Rs. 2.30 and Rs. 2.77. Since this is a pure OFS, ABSLAMC's post-issue paid-up equity capital remains at Rs. 144.00 cr. The company is aiming for a market cap of Rs. 20505.60 cr. at the upper cap of the offer price.

The Book Running Lead Managers (BRLMs) for this issue are Kotak Mahindra Capital Co. Citigroup Global Markets India Pvt. Ltd. BoFA Securities India Ltd. and Ltd. As opposed to KFin Technologies Pvt. Axis Capital Ltd., HDFC Bank Ltd., ICICI Securities Ltd., JM Financial Ltd., IIFL Securities Ltd., Motilal Oswal Investment Advisors Ltd., SBI Capital Markets Ltd., and Yes Securities (India) Ltd. are few examples of the companies that participate in the market. Ltd. is the issue's registrar.

ABSLAMC has reported a total income/net profit of Rs. 1407.25 cr. on the financial performance front. / Rs. 446.80 cr. (FY19), 1234.77 crore rupees / Rs. 494.40 cr. & Rs. 1205.84 billion (FY20). / Rs. 526.28 cr. (FY21). It reported a net profit of Rs. 154.94 cr. for the first quarter of FY 22 that ended on June 30, 2021. on a revenue of Rs. 336.25 billion. in contrast to Rs. 97.35 crore. / Rs. 260.75 cr. and for the corresponding prior period, respectively. As a result, despite dropping top lines, it has been reporting growth in bottom lines. The occasional decline in fees and commission costs is blamed for this spike in income.

For the previous three fiscal years, it had average EPS of Rs. 17.44 and average RoNW of 34.05%. On the basis of the issue's NAV of Rs. 62.57 as of June 30, 2021, the P/BV for the issue is 11.38. The asking price is fully priced if annualised FY22 earnings are applied to the post-issue paid-up equity capital, which results in a P/E of 33.09.

Investors from all sectors anticipated this offer with great anticipation. The issue is completely priced, despite the fact that it has been reporting growth for bottom lines. With expanding stock market investments and an increase in the number of Demat accounts, this company is positioned for promising futures. Investors with a long-term outlook may store money in this offering (Baral et al., 2016; Singh et al., 2017).

CONCLUSION

Tech companies are well known for their tendency to fall sharply in value because of their huge growth possibilities, but these suffer greatly during bear markets. The decline gets worse when it appears that the valuation is excessive. The most recent hit to the stock was the exit of the private equity fund. The share price of Zomato was further lowered as a result. Analysts contend that the insurance industry is quite vulnerable to changes in the market, which could have an effect on its inherent value. The stock has been in a downturn as a result. Concerns about inflation and investors' apprehensive attitudes toward economic growth hurt LIC in the short run.

Brokerage firms awarded the initial IPO a favourable rating, but many experts now think the stock is best for long-term investors or those who are more willing to take on risk. They are under more selling pressure as a result of the stock.

REFERENCES

Baral, P. K., Das, D., & Kumar, K. (2016). Mutual Funds Industry in India: A Growth Trend Analysis. *International Journal of Multidisciplinary Research and Development*, *3*(1), 1–13.

Dimovski, W., Brooks, R., & van Eekelen, A. (2007). The costs of raising equity capital for closed-end fund IPOs. *Applied Financial Economics Letters*, *3*(5), 295–299. doi:10.1080/17446540701222391

Ellikkal, A., Rajamohan, S., & Prakash, M. O. (2022). IPOs in Indian Stock Market: Analyzing Pricing and Performance of IPO Listed in 2021. *Journal of Management*, *10*(2), 1–8.

Mahajan, S. (2022). Paytm IPO: Case of Failure and the Behemoth. *JBIMS*.

Pandey, D. (2021). Coronavirus Impact on Indian IPO Market. *IUP Journal of Accounting Research \& Audit Practices, 20*(4), 603–609.

Salo, T. (2020). *Incorporating CSR Activities into the Company's Financial Strategy: A Case Study* [Thesis]. Metropolia University of Applied Sciences.

Selvam, M. (2022). Lic IPO. *SMART Journal of Business Management Studies*, *18*(2), 6–7.

Singh, D., Denesh, R., Balakrishnan, J., Vijayan, N., & Ghosh, D. (2017). Department of Management Studies. *International Journal of Mental Health and Addiction, 16*, 15.

Yadav, N., & Goyal, S. (2022). *Regaining partner trust in the food delivery business: case of Zomato*. Emerald Emerging Markets Case Studies.

Chapter 8
Fin–Cology or Tech–Nance?
Emergence of FinTech

Swarnasree Vutharkar
Woxsen University, India

Rajesh Kumar K. V.
iD https://orcid.org/0000-0002-7989-1824
Woxsen University, India

ABSTRACT

The words "financial" and "technology" are combined to form the phrase "fintech." Despite being a wide expression with numerous interpretations, it typically refers to the growth of a sector when new technology use-cases are developed and put into place to expedite more traditional-looking financial activities. When it first arose in the 21st century, the term "fintech" was used to describe the technology employed in the back-end systems of reputable financial organisations. Since then, nevertheless, there has been a shift toward more client-centered services, and thus, a more client-centric definition. Currently, the term "fintech" is used to describe a wide range of professions and businesses, including investment management, retail banking, education, and non-profit fundraising, to name a few. In this chapter you will be reading the relation between python and finance; SQL and finance; Tableau and finance; Power Bi and finance; and Block Chain and finance.

INTRODUCTION

In this chapter we will be learning about the emergence of Fintech in this world. Is technology used in finance industry? Does finance and technology go hand in

DOI: 10.4018/978-1-6684-4246-3.ch008

hand? What changes technology had bought into finance industry? Has technology changed finance or finance changed technology?

Did you ever get such doubts? Let's find the solution for all your finance and technology related questions in this chapter.

Any innovation that includes financial transactions, whether for personal or professional usage, falls under the umbrella of financial technology. Since the invention of the credit card in the 1950s and the ATM in the 1960s, fintech has been upending our world.

In reality, financial technology is all around us. Many of us utilise fintech instead of cash while making purchases. It is widely used to conduct different financial transactions in methods that are much more practical than in the past.

Our society will continue to change as a result of fintech. So, let's get acquainted with this category of financially disruptive developments (An et al., 2021; Hilpisch, 2014, 2018; Lin, 2016; Raef Lawson et al., 2018; Reddy et al., 2019; Shahrokhi, 2008; Zetzsche et al., 2020).

PYTHON AND FINANCE

Python is one of the best general-purpose, high-level programming languages available today. With its straightforward grammar and close resemblance to the English language as a whole, this language aims to be user-friendly for beginners.

In addition, when it comes to employing Python for finance, its general application is a blend of English and mathematics. Thus, Python's syntax is not all that far from the standard format for expressing mathematical and financial methods.

The three primary components of financial analytics—data collection, sophisticated mathematical calculations, and result visualization—can be made simpler with Python. Finding the ideal module for your data analysis is simple thanks to the large number of Python packages available.

The most popular computer language for undertaking quantitative and qualitative analysis in finance is Python. This language is used for construct payments and internet banking systems, analyse the status of stock market, lower financial risks, calculate the rate of return on stocks, and much more.

Regular data analysts find it expensive, time-consuming, and difficult to grasp and base statistical computations on massive amounts of data. Analysts can streamline these processes and create illuminating visualisations of the outcomes by utilising Python. Financial and data analytics is the idea of gathering, processing, and analysing data using technology, programmes with complex algorithms, and mathematical calculations. The obtained data can be used to make judgments, forecast future trends,

Figure 1. Ideal image of Python Programming Language

and find other useful information. When developing risk management strategies or forecasting prospective changes in financial markets, such projections are important.

Python is a famous choice for finance because it has a good foundational of building neural networks and artificial intelligence. These machine learning models are capable of making predictions based on the collected data. When it comes to stock market investing, Python in finance can assist you get to a calculated and lower-risk decision. You must download the financial information from particular interest-bearing time periods in order to perform such an analysis. To interface with the financial data from Google Finance, Quandl, Enigma, or other databases, you must utilise the Pandas online data reader extension.

Data visualisation is one of the important components of financial ventures. Therefore, importing these features from the Matplotlib package is convenient. To present data in a way that is user-friendly, you can use a variety of charts and plots. Additionally, you can filter data based on expected return rates or average price markings.

Given these options and its simple syntax, it is not surprising that Python has taken over as the standard language for financial projects. It is changing the way analysts do framework-supported data-driven financial assessments. Python is a great option for performing quantitative analysis in relation to the examination of large financial data sets. You may easily manage sizable databases and visualise the findings using libraries like Pandas, Scikit-learn, PyBrain, or other comparable modules.

As a result, creating charts of the fluctuating prices and other financial market trends is simple. To create a context for additional forecasts and insights, you can use sophisticated mathematical calculations.

Lots of Fintech firms chose Python because of its efficiency in financial chores, which sort of naturally matches Fintech solutions that are related with data and mathematics. Python's reputation as the most user-friendly programming language for finance professionals may also be a contributing factor.

Businesses may now accept payments online thanks to Stripe, a Fintech start-up. The business created APIs for integrating into websites and mobile applications using Python. Stripe streamlines the transaction process for internet businesses. Invoicing, subscription management, and fraud protection are some of its offerings. With thousands of businesses using it, Stripe was valued at $9 billion (Hilpisch, 2014, 2018)

SQL AND FINANCE

Microsoft Excel is one of the most widely used programmes in the finance industry, and spreadsheets are now the main way to store and analyse financial data. The spreadsheet programme Excel may be used to gain a lot of insights regarding financial data that is gathered and saved by using features like Pivot Tables and statistical calculations.

However, there are numerous data science tools that perform data storage, cleaning, and analysis chores even better than Microsoft Excel, which may be used for data analytics and some database tasks. Financial Analysts can create more sophisticated database systems that are built on a structure that is quite similar to a spreadsheet thanks to their knowledge of the SQL programming language. Spreadsheets and other data analytics tools will enable many financial analysts to apply their theoretical knowledge to comprehend the workings of a SQL database management system.

In SQL, there are entities that make up the tables' objects of interest and are described by attributes (columns). When we declare and use those relationships in a certain way, entities that are related to one another might create what is known as a relational model. Each and every attribute has a domain; examples are INT, DECIMAL, VARCHAR, CHAR, and DATETIME.

Working with big data requires knowledge of databases, especially now that data collection is a necessity across a range of disciplines and sectors. Big data collection is built on databases, and as consumers interact with a platform or a company gathers data about itself, all of this information is needed to keep in a scalable repository.

For financial institutions, it's also crucial to make sure that the data which is being gathered can be stored in a safe location. Fortunately, there are only a few number of SQL tools that are specifically designed to collect financial data, such as user transactions and industry trends, while also ensuring the security of the information and data being stored. Tables are used to convey big data. A main key, also known as a candidate key, is used in tables to uniquely identify each row (sometimes referred

Figure 2. Image of Microsoft SQL Server

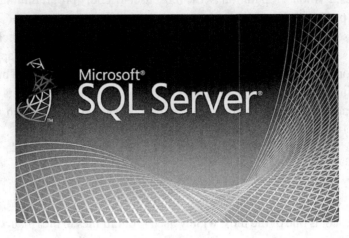

to as entity integrity) and is combined with various non-key properties. A column with the ID prefix is all that a primary key is.

Foreign keys, which are simply columns that are the primary key of another table, can be used to merge two tables. There are two primary methods for building a table: building the columns (with column types, and specifying the primary key).

SQL is one of the various computer languages that Financial Analysts can use, and it's particularly helpful for employing tools for business intelligence, predictive analytics, and financial modelling. Any of Noble Desktop's SQL courses can be combined with supplementary training in business and finance for students and professionals who are interested in learning more about utilising SQL for financial analysis. In order to build a portfolio of data science and financial analysis projects, the FinTech Bootcamp combines teaching in SQL databases with Python.

The Financial Modelling Bootcamp teaches participants how to develop financial models and value businesses. Although the focus of this bootcamp is on using Excel for financial analysis, many of the techniques covered can also be applied to using SQL databases. The data analytics technologies from Noble Desktop Students and professionals who want to combine their knowledge of SQL with the ability to display data and convey business conclusions might consider bootcamp as a great choice. The SQL programming language and relational database management systems provide both students and professionals with a more in-depth grasp of how to interface with databases for financial research, making them crucial data science tools. There are numerous additional SQL codes that are applicable to the financial sector.

SQL is incredibly important in the realm of finance. Morgan Stanley, one of the largest companies, manages its databases using SQL. The most often examined abilities in the Morgan Stanley Data Analyst interview process are in probability,

Figure 3. Image of Tableau software

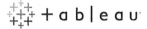

algorithms, and SQL. This contrasts with conventional SQL and Analytics questions from interviews for data analysts (Rajan et al., 1990; Walstra et al., 2015).

TABLEAU AND FINANCE

Tableau can satisfy the various needs and demands of the organisations by doing a thorough analysis of its data. The needs of an organisation may depend on those of the client and how a product, programme, or application is used.

Business intelligence and analytics software called Tableau provides views of interactive data visualisation. Tableau was created by Tableau, a company which develops software with headquarters in Seattle, Washington, in the United States. Pat Hanrahan, Chris Stolte, and Christian Chabot started it. It was established in 2003.

The major objective of business intelligence applications is the topic of this article. Users can design interactive dashboards according to their specific tailored preferences. This utility can be customised to accept connections from many data sources. This programme makes it simple to analyse real-time data. In the areas of business intelligence and data analytics, it has consistently held a high spot.

It is simple to examine data from many sources, and reports that are immediately understandable can be produced. The data will be extracted, loaded, and transformed in order to be studied in various ways. The data can be processed and evaluated using a variety of techniques, procedures, and steps.

There is another type of process where Tableau is used to analyse data by condensing or summarising the content or primary, crucial aspects of the data sets are to non-redundant information. Tableau's visual dashboards offer a variety of representations, including pictorial, tabular, graphical, pie chart, and bar graph displays.

Tableau can be used with a wide range of database features, such as those found in RDBMS, No SQL Databases, Object-Oriented Databases, etc. Relational Database Management Systems store structured data, whereas No SQL and Object-Oriented Databases store semi-structured and unstructured data, such as JSON, text files, and other file types.

The management of various forms of data is simpler, and it is also simpler to customise that data to meet the needs. Tableau's technique only requires a form of drag and drop or tool feature that is simpler to use and it also has a lower learning curve. It does not require any kind of programming, coding, or designing.

The visual analysis may take the form of a graph or another type of representation that is simpler to comprehend or that is clear at first glance. This is how the method of data visualisation influences the visual analysis.

The method of obtaining data and analysing it from many sorts of data sources is flexible thanks to the connections made to numerous data sources and the pulling or crawling of that data into Tableau. The analysis of the data can then be done from there.

The Tableau tool offers a wide range of uses in data analytics and data visualisation, offering more advantages like processing data and decreasing data redundancy in the fastest execution time dynamically. Tableau is among the greatest business intelligence and data visualisation technologies available for quickly and effectively delivering extremely complicated business solutions without the headache of managing the data transformation functionalities. The demand for some software applications or tools to handle and manage their large-scale customer content data securely is driven by the daily rise in the customer's business needs or customer-business handling requirements.

Tableau has been a great tool for many businesses in the most recent scenario of the digital world with great innovations and technological breakthroughs for highly complex data visualisation in data reporting, which has increased the customer base and daily requirements or activities related to customer data handling.

Sales Force Company uses Tableau in this manner. Sales Force Company's finance team uses data and visual analytics on a daily basis to better understand the financial situation of our EMEA operations and provide the executive team with the necessary information.

Accounts Receivable is included in the financial dashboards. Discover current insights by location or account. Treasury, Simple to grasp operating balance and cash flow. Cost management, look at the dashboard to see how much money Tableau is able to save each month. Live Demo on Profitability, utilizing variance analysis, create your own profitability dashboard. Use of offices, map the occupancy rate of your international offices to reduce expenditures. Purchasing, by visualising your PO spend, you can get the best value from your vendors. The insurance and finance firm Allstates utilises Tableau for running the firm (Batt et al., 2020; Murphy, 2013; Reddy et al., 2019)

Figure 4. Image of Power Bi Software

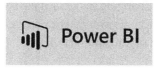

POWER BI AND FINANCE

Bring Your Data to Life, is the Power BI tagline. Power BI is a collection of several data analytics-based services and platforms with a primary focus on presenting and enhancing the interactivity of business data for enterprises.

A cloud-based service company called Power BI provides data warehouse and data visualisation services. Data organisation, custom visualisation, data discovery, data warehousing, reporting, and data preparation are just a few of the services offered.

Power BI is a powerful tool for organising business data. Various types of constraints are frequently placed on the quantity, kind, and complexity of data as well as their reporting and classification across a variety of data management mediums. Regardless of the size of the firm or the sophistication of its data, this application offers outstanding financial data management services with no restrictions on reporting financial data.

Power BI has exceptional data projection systems. Financial predictions are a crucial component of a business' operations, and they serve as the basis for many important decisions. It is therefore a crucial component of all organisations' data management operations.

What-if parameters, a function in the programme that generates interactive data predictions that are excellent for comparison, is available. Using this anyone should be able to create Projections statements using all the types of assumptions.

Power BI has a built-in time intelligence. Additionally, it offers the capability of organising data according to various data dimensions and attributes. Using such features, it is quite easy to spot data trends or patterns over a number of years or across the market competition. They are especially valuable in arriving at critical business operations conclusions and in helping to make critical financial decisions on profitability, budgeting, operating costs, etc.

Power View, a crucial part of Power BI, makes it possible to create interactive graphs, charts, and data maps. It helps in creating charts and graphs from the financial facts to draw conclusions and make financial decisions.

Power BI, a platform for collaboration that makes it easy for users to exchange and access information while yet maintaining high security and safety standards. This makes it possible for project financial management teams or a company's finance department to collaborate. They can effectively operate together by exchanging important data conclusions, exchanging financial datasets, publishing financial reports and dashboards, and cooperating. Power Bi is a piece of software used by Berkshire Hathaway Inc. to manage the organisation (Pukala et al., 2020; Zheng et al., 2019)

CRYPTO AND FINANCE

Almost every industry has been significantly impacted by the radical, new ideas that blockchain introduced, including finance, supply chain management, and healthcare. The public first became aware of blockchain start-ups about two to three years ago. Nearly all contemporary businesses are currently exploring for prospects in blockchain technology. Blockchain essentially functions as a distributed ledger and is a decentralised ledger system. In 2009, it was able to attract widespread interest.

Therefore, conventional wisdom claimed that blockchain technology will primarily be used in finance. A fascinating aspect of blockchain is that it has the potential to have a significant impact on the financial sector. As the applications of blockchain develop across numerous industries, it is necessary to look at the role of blockchain in banking sector in the next times.

Any new technology is typically challenging to comprehend. The fact that it is rare to discover a technology with a name that accurately conveys what it performs is most essential. In such instance, the blockchain serves as the ideal illustration since it signifies precisely what its name implies. Blocks of information can be created and stored using blockchain technology.

To construct a "digital ledger," each new block that is created for a transaction is added to the chain. Blockchain ledgers have made significant improvements over traditional digital ledgers, expanding the potential for its use in finance.

Using blockchain technology, a digital ledger can be distributed among numerous nodes. As a result, processing and storing transaction data do not require the involvement of a single third party. As a result, the use of blockchain in the financial sector can reduce the risk of transaction data being compromised due to the absence of a centralised repository with a unified security mechanism. Blockchain technology also eliminates the intermediaries' monopoly over financial transactions. With this we can say, accessibility and cost efficiency will increase because of using Blockchain in finance.

Security with blockchain technology is unquestionably unique among the many factors that support the need for blockchain integration in banking. Blockchain employs encryption to ensure the security of the transaction ledger. As a result, only those in possession of a certain key code could access the information. High

Figure 5. Cryptocurrency

levels of security are also ensured because blockchain transactions are decentralised and peer-to-peer.

Worldwide, financial services continue to operate using a centralised, traditional, and multi-layered model. The majority of financial data is stored in centralised databases and must go via numerous middlemen. The centralised mechanisms also don't provide transparency. Additionally, database security and intermediates are the only factors that affect data security.

On the other hand, even the most secure databases are susceptible to data breach and hacking. Lack of transparency frequently creates complex security risks because no one is aware of any irregularities until a data breach or other system error is discovered. At the end not everyone would support the idea of open financial records, both clients and financial service providers would benefit from some degree of transparency.

Blockchain applications in banking and finance assist to simultaneously ensure transparency and security. Immutability is the key characteristic of blockchain that guarantees security and transparency. Blockchain can guarantee the confidentiality, accuracy, and validity of data since it eliminates the possibility of data manipulation. Blockchain use in the finance industry also makes the most of privacy advantages.

There are two security keys, a private key and a public key, are used in blockchain applications. All network users have access to the public key, whereas only the participants in a given transaction can access the private key. As a result, the transaction can be seen by all network users, and only participants can see the transaction's specifics. Blockchain can therefore preserve financial system transparency while protecting the private financial data of participants in transactions.

Due to centralization, the financial sector must allocate a considerable sum of money among numerous businesses. Providers of financial services must make significant investments in accounting, database upkeep, value transfer systems, central database procurement, database security, labour costs, and intermediary commissions. Additionally, because all of these investments are recurring, financial service providers must routinely provide funds to cover them. Because of all the extra expenses, a financial service system may be rather pricey.

Is blockchain the future of finance? has a perfect answer thanks to its cost advantage. Because it can result in significant cost savings for financial service companies. A recent study found that by 2022, distributed ledger technology could help financial service companies cut expenses by $15 to $20 billion yearly. Blockchain technology can increase security, guarantee cost savings, and promote transparency. By implementing smart contracts, blockchain applications in banking can lower the expenses associated with recordkeeping, middlemen, and value transfers.

It is obvious that blockchain technology is a vital solution to many problems facing the banking sector. New ideas like DeFi and CBDCs have the potential to become well-known in 2022 as businesses and start-ups continue to develop fresh perspectives on "how blockchain is used in finance."

Additionally, blockchain technology would continue to be a model for financial service providers in terms of security, transparency, speed transactions and risk management. The use of blockchain in banking, however, still faces a number of difficulties. Better results may result from businesses' capacity to predict emerging trends in blockchain-related financial applications and changing blockchain features.

El Salvador, country of Central America, is a place where Crypto is actually considered as currency. The people over there can buy products using crypto currency. Crypto is accepted as legal currency in that country. This shows the world is moving fast and accepting new technology (Joo et al., 2019; Murphy, 2013; Scott, 2016, 2016; Zheng et al., 2019).

CONCLUSION

Fintech now refers to a range of financial activities that are typically performed without the help of a person, such as money transfers, checking your account balance on your smartphone, applying for credit without visiting a bank branch, raising money for a startup business, or managing your investments. Customers are increasingly aware of fintech as a part of their daily lives, with one-third of consumers using at least two or more fintech services.

REFERENCES

An, J., & Rau, R. (2021). Finance, technology and disruption. *European Journal of Finance*, *27*(4–5), 334–345. doi:10.1080/1351847X.2019.1703024

Batt, S., Grealis, T., Harmon, O., & Tomolonis, P. (2020). Learning Tableau: A data visualization tool. *The Journal of Economic Education*, *51*(3–4), 317–328. doi:10.1080/00220485.2020.1804503

Hilpisch, Y. (2014). *Python for Finance: Analyze big financial data*. O'Reilly Media, Inc.

Hilpisch, Y. (2018). *Python for finance: mastering data-driven finance*. O'Reilly Media.

Joo, M. H., Nishikawa, Y., & Dandapani, K. (2019). Cryptocurrency, a successful application of blockchain technology. *Managerial Finance*.

Lawson, R., C. M. A., C. S. C. A., Smith, D., C. A. E., C. M. A., & C. P. A. (2018). Developing data fluency. *Strategic Finance*, *100*(3), 68–69.

Lin, T. C. W. (2016). Compliance, technology, and modern finance. *Brook. J. Corp. Fin. \&. Com. L.*, *11*, 159.

Murphy, S. A. (2013). Data visualization and rapid analytics: Applying tableau desktop to support library decision-making. *Journal of Web Librarianship*, *7*(4), 465–476. doi:10.1080/19322909.2013.825148

Pukala, R., Hlibko, S., Vnukova, N., & Korvat, O. (2020). Power BI in ICT for Monitoring of Insurance Activity Based on Indicators of Insurance Portfolios. *IEEE International Conference on Problems of Infocommunications. Science and Technology (PIC S\&T)*, 393–401. 10.1109/PICST51311.2020.9467993

Rajan, A. (1990). *Information technology in the finance sector: an international perspective*.

Reddy, C. S., Sangam, R. S., & Srinivasa Rao, B. (2019). A survey on business intelligence tools for marketing, financial, and transportation services. In *Smart intelligent computing and applications,* (pp. 495–504). Springer. doi:10.1007/978-981-13-1927-3_53

Scott, B. (2016). *How can cryptocurrency and blockchain technology play a role in building social and solidarity finance?* Shahrokhi, M. (2008). E-finance: Status, innovations, resources and future challenges. *Managerial Finance*.

Walstra, R., Drougas, A., & Harrington, S. (2015). Integrating Excel, SQL, and SPSS within an Introductory Finance Intrinsic Value Assignment. *Journal of Finance and Accountancy, 20,* 1.

Zetzsche, D. A., Arner, D. W., & Buckley, R. P. (2020). Decentralized finance. *Journal of Financial Regulation, 6*(2), 172–203. doi:10.1093/jfr/fjaa010

Zheng, X., Zhu, M., Li, Q., Chen, C., & Tan, Y. (2019). FinBrain: when finance meets AI 2.0. *Frontiers of Information Technology \& Electronic Engineering, 20*(7), 914–924.

Chapter 9
Forecasting the Space Utilization Trend in Corporate Offices

Apurva Patil
Liverpool John Moores University, UK

Rajesh Kumar K. V.
iD https://orcid.org/0000-0002-7989-1824
Woxsen University, India

ABSTRACT

The research is mainly focused on forecasting office space utilization trends in the organization using information such as office space count, space occupancy count, holidays, leaves. Space occupancy data is collected using PIR sensors. Descriptive analytics is done using creative visualizations, and model building is done using univariate and multivariate time series methods. Descriptive analytics explains that there is a positive autocorrelation in the data with no outliers and randomness. There exists a pattern of space occupancy for different office locations at different times of the day. Univariate time series models are suitable for forecasting space occupancy for single office locations, whereas multivariate time series model VAR is suitable when considering multiple office locations of a client or multiple office locations of different clients at the same time. Empirical research has exhibited that out of tested models, SARIMAX has shown better performance on multiple test datasets.

DOI: 10.4018/978-1-6684-4246-3.ch009

INTRODUCTION

In today's era, companies are focusing more on the utilization of their real estate by wisely managing financials and operations. They are also leveraging space utilization metrics. Organizations require different types of assets to function profitably. Employee workspace defines the required privacy to the employee, and security of their belongings. Failure of the organization to provide enough area, architectural accessibility, social space to the employees will create a negative impact on the work environment.

Space is the biggest asset of the organization. Space Utilization will change with conditions of demand and trend. Space management is an ongoing process for an employee workspace; though its capacity remains the same, with efficient space management its occupancy can be varied (Reagan Nickl (SpacelQ), 2019). For any office, examination of how much workspace is utilized will give the ideal ratio of occupancy. For proper utilization of office workspace, we need to take into consideration total number of desk spaces, employee count, occupancy pattern and architectural view using which office workspace can be utilized properly. If employee count increases, it would be easier to rearrange office space arrangement to accumulate more number employees while managing basic requirements of employee space and safety. It is common for companies to invest in real estate as they grow, but the questions that come up are how efficiently office space can be utilized and what if any unpredicted critical situation comes and these owned or leased office spaces will become a financial burden for these companies.

Companies realized space as their major liability at the time of financial crisis happened in the US in the year 2008, where the financial, investment firms, banks, etc were broken and the only way for the IT industry left was to save them money by reducing the amount they are paying for the lease. So the main focus at that time was only limited to the IT/ITES industry (Material, 2016).

Prior to the financial crisis in the year 2008, organizations used to consider their huge office spaces as their asset, but later on office spaces became liability to the organization. Considering the current situation of the COVID-19 pandemic, many companies are focusing on reducing cost concerning office space that is under-utilized or not utilized. It would also help them to reduce real estate cost and increase profitability. This would allow organizations to focus on managing the safety of the employees who are returning to the office by using facility management. Companies also need to ensure space management with optimal investment in real estate and its utilization.

Space utilization trends for an organization can be arrived at on the basis of past data of office space occupancy. Space utilization trends will help organization to adopt Activity Based Working (ABW) approach in continuously evolving business and working structure. These trends will help designers and facility managers to understand & match the space requirement. As per the article 'Advanced Workplace' (Karen Plum, Director of Research & Development, n.d.) the concept of space utilization trend has started rolling in the market around 2000 where the employee count was inversely proportional to the lease amount that firms were paying for space.

The focus of this research paper is on building a forecasting model to forecast office space utilization. This forecast will be based on the parameters provided such as client and their office locations, total space available with the status of the space occupancy captured by the sensors. Along with the data, space has become the important and biggest asset for the organization. Space optimization can be done at the architectural phase of the office space construction or if space is on lease or owned and cannot be modified, based on the historical trend of space utilization and current market scenario of space utilization can be analyzed by predicting the space occupancy count for future days. Additionally, the current COVID-19 pandemic situation has made all the organizations think about the investment made in office space.

Though, all the employers and employees have now become very much comfortable with the new normal of the work from home culture. Still due to some reasons employees can choose to work from office, so they can view the space utilization forecast of a particular day and decide whether to work from office for that day or not. Organizations can easily keep a check on employee safety and security by maintaining social distancing and can utilize infrastructure if the employee count increases or decreases in the future. This will help organizations to optimize space requirements based on the forecast and wisely use office space by maintaining employee safety and security.

The main aim of this research is to create a forecasting model which will predict the space utilization by week, by day, and by hours, considering the parameters such as available space for desks, number of employees, number of teams along with the total number of members, etc.

The research objectives are formulated based on the aim of this study which are as follows:

- To study the current processes and methods used in organization for space utilization.
- To build the forecasting model to predict the usage of space in the organization (considering holidays and leaves).
- To build UI that can be used for real-time resource management and track and analyze usage patterns to make space and resource utilization on a real-time basis.

LITERATURE REVIEW

Space Utilization in the corporate offices has now become the main concern from the current COVID-19 pandemic. Before that 2008 financial crisis has thrown a light on this issue, due to which organizations were more focused on investing more time and money from the architectural phase to reduce investment in office assets intelligently and plan better office space design to accommodate more employees in the future (Lik Lau et al., 2017).

The advancement in the Internet-of-Things (IoT) and Big Data allows users to collect various information remotely and send it to the cloud for further processing (Bhongaraju S.D, Kumar K.V.R, Anjaiah P., Shaik J,H, 2021). Various sensors are used to gather data related to office space utilization. Heat sensors use thermal imaging or temperature grid to get space occupancy. Other sensors like Pyroelectric Infrared Sensors (PIR) sensors used to detect room occupancy, Sound detection sensors can be used to detect the activity around the space. Space occupancy detection using the camera through Computer Vision is possible, but it is computationally & financially expensive (Lik Lau et al., 2017).

In this paper the data is given by Workplace Fabric Ltd., they are using the PIR to detect the presence of the employees and provides an occupancy optimization solution. PIR sensor nodes are installed under the desk to sense the presence and location of the employee and collect their space utilization data. PIR sensors are accurate in measuring occupants' presence at the desk, room, or collaborative spaces level (Zhou et al., n.d.).

History of Space Utilization Management

As we go by the basic definition of space utilization which is given as building's occupancy vs capacity. Space utilization rate is the number of square feet per worker, it varies as per industry. Earlier the space utilization process was manual, known as "Bed Checking" (City, 2014). Though the process was inexpensive, it was time-consuming, labour-intensive to measure the utilization and feed the data in computer regularly.

Various types of techniques are used to perform the task of sensing space occupancy. Few of them are such as heat sensors using thermal imaging or temperature grid, Pyroelectric (PIR) Sensor, sound detection method, density-based method, computer vision approach using the camera which is very computationally expensive and cost of implementation is high (Lik Lau et al., 2017, Zhou et al., n.d.).

Space occupancy focus started from design in the architectural phase depending upon the parameters such as room size, weather, disruptions, number of employees, number of meeting rooms, etc. using different models such as 'User Simulation Space

Utilization (USSU)'. This model has been built to predict and display occupancy schedules in an office building (Tabak, 2009). To overcome the loopholes in the USSU model 'Discrete-Choice Modelling (DCM)' has been built where the probability of space occupancy is determined based on the available integration information about space preferences and space attributes (Cha et al., 2018). Here, the relation between space and activity is not defined clearly, due to a lack of activity definition. To overcome the limitation of DCM and increase the focus on predicting the occupancy of the building where 'Occupancy Simulator' is designed using Markov-chain model which is an agent-based web application and used to simulate the presence of occupants and movement in the buildings considering details on spatial and temporal diversity (Cha et al., 2018). Data they have gathered was the number of office rooms, employee time steps, holidays, and similarly for meeting rooms the data collected from google calendar was the duration of a meeting room, number of people in the meeting room. Based on all these data occupancy schedules were generated.

Predictive Modelling Using Various Techniques

Different methods have been used and developed by researchers to study the forecasting capability of the data which is majorly based on time (KUMAR K.V.R, ELIAS S,n.d). Few of the researchers have used the ANOVA method where random variables using the overall mean, deviation from the mean due to time-of-day, and random error term with daily variability for forecasting. Similarly using, the day of the week, the effect of a particular month with weekly and monthly patterns have been used in ANOVA forecasting (Hellerstein et al., 2001).

Time series models have been used extensively for forecasting over years . Depending on the frequency of time series, either ARIMA or SARIMA models are used. Considering the inconsistency in the performance of the ARIMA/SARIMA model researchers have tried to improve its performance by using multivariate time series (Yao & Jiang, 2019).

A few of the researchers have also used reinforcement allocation and control theory for adaptive allocation of resources by using the ARIMA model which represents the time series model in a more flexible way (Zia Ullah et al., 2017). Time series forecasting assumes a combination of patterns with some random error and for analysis and the main goal of prediction is to understand the long-term trend, seasonality, change caused by seasonal factors. Additionally, the time series (Bhogaraju S.D, Korupalli V.R.K, 2020) model also captures resources as per dynamically changing requirements and expected load. The main advantage is that they capture transient behavior while incorporating nonlinearity in the system model and its accuracy appears in each application.

141

Holt-Winter (HW) exponential smoothing can be used when there is both trend and seasonality in the data. Adaptive HW technique, time-series parameters are constantly updated for recently observed data. Even the time series changed its behavior using the adaptive (HW) technique the model parameters should adapt to this change (Kalekar, 2004). Using auto ARIMA() function ARIMA model can be selected for the further model building based on the lowest Akaike Information Criteria (AIC) and Bayesian Information Criteria (BIC) values. This model fits the data and predicts the next utilization values. Based on the stationarity and white noise variance of the model order and penalty factor are introduced with a combination of AIC and BIC to avoid prediction errors due to overfitting (Zia Ullah et al., 2017).

When it comes to multivariate prediction time series model gets computationally complex, through both empirical and theoretical techniques employ an empirical method for forecasting and standard statistical methodology. In this case, substitute can be non-parametric regression and neural network, as their inherent multi-input nature they are suitable for space-time and multi-variant model (Ghosh et al., 2009). Data with too much noise and dimension complexity, ANN fall back with limitations such as inconsistent and unpredictable performance. Back Propagation Neural network model also fails when there is high noise and complexity in the data while selecting controlling parameters such as input variables, hidden layer size, learning rate, momentum rate. Support Vector Machine (SVM) uses risk function with empirical error and regularized terms derived from structural minimization principle can also be used for time-series prediction (Kim, 2003). The traditional method of predicting accuracy is based on comparing it with the threshold value, but SVM can help in predicting more accurately and reduce prediction error (Wang et al., 2017). As it reduces the upper bound of the generalization error, hence overfitting rarely occurs in SVM (Kim, 2003). The genetic algorithm's approach to feature dividing and determining connected weights of ANN can be used for prediction. This will also reduce the dimensionality of feature space and increase prediction performance (Kim & Han, 2010).

Parametric techniques for time-series models are also there such as linear and non-linear regression, historical average algorithms, autoregressive linear processes (Kumar K.V.R, Zachariah A.A., Elias S., n.d). Out of these Auto-Regressive Linear processes and SARIMA models perform better than other time series techniques. Researchers have developed STM and MST. Structural Time Series Model is similar to the Holt-Winters exponential smoothing model with more complexity. MST is developed using SUTSE and it does not use a cause-effect relationship between variables. Univariate Structural Time Series Model is based on unobserved components with the direct interpretation of temporal visibility of the time-series dataset. Whereas MTS is classified as panel data and interactive data, where panel data influence each other and elements never interact with each other, but they show dynamic interaction amongst each other (Ghosh et al., 2009).

As compared to ARIMA class of models, STM handles missing values very easily. While building a model using STM explanatory variables, outliers, structural breaks, etc can be easily considered and migrated from univariate to the multivariate regime (Ghosh et al., 2009). The Moving Average (MA) method is the simplest forecasting method, which uses historic time-series data to calculate the arithmetic mean and the main advantage is that it removes inconsistent changes or seasonal factors. Additionally, the SARIMA model worked more effectively when time-series components are changing rapidly and proved its usefulness in forecasting short-term volatility, as the model consists of auto-regression, differencing, and moving average with the seasonal and non-seasonal part. Based on research, the univariate and multivariate SARIMA model has constant deviation and the autocorrelation function lies within the confidence interval, which is indicative of residuals that are independent and attain criteria of white-noise (Hye Jin Kam, Jin Ok Sung, 2010).

RESEARCH METHODOLOGY

The dataset used for this research is provided by 'Workplace Fabric Ltd'. They are collecting this data using the PIR sensors. Space occupancy status is recorded based on the set time and multiple policies that have been defined for different spaces such as desks, collaboration spaces, meeting room, etc. For this research, we will be considering only desk spaces. The space occupancy count has been represented as column 'stat_value' is a dependent variable, whereas information including ID, Account ID, Location ID, UTC Time are independent variables. The observation in this step was that time-related columns 'UTC_TIME' and 'Local_US_TIME' columns have datatype as 'object', hence as these are the main columns for time series forecasting their datatypes are changed to 'datetime'.

Data Pre-Processing and Analysis

The received dataset is loaded into the Jupyter notebook for pre-processing. The initial step of the pre-processing is understanding the dataset along with the data types of all the columns for the data present in the column for data uniformity and standardization. Null value check is done on the dataset for data cleansing and the dataset has no null values and value zero represents that no employees are present there like for example during the night-time or on holidays. 'UTC_TIME' is set as an index of the table for space occupancy prediction i.e. column 'state_value'. 'UTC_TIME' column split into 'Year, Month, Day, Hour, Time' and using the new

Table 1. Dataset description

Variables	Definition of Variables
Id	Auto incrementing sequence number
Account_id	Client id which is a unique number
Location_id	Floor id for the location of client's office
Stats_type	Space occupancy status 'Space_Occupied' and 'Space_Free'
Observed_at	Current observation time as per location
Stat_value	Count of Space Occupied and Free
UTC_time	Observation Time as per UTC (UK Std time)
Local_US_time	Observation Time as per US standard time

columns exploratory data analysis is performed. Space occupancy analysis based on the day is high on weekdays and almost zero on weekends similar to the normal case. Similarly, based on time shows that space occupancy in the morning time is high and gradually starts decreasing till midnight, and the occupancy count is zero till the next day morning. This will vary depending upon the client, location, and their employee shifts as per their different projects.

Additionally, based on the exploratory data analysis for different clients and their respective different locations, we can say that the data has strong pattern and cyclic behaviour. A few variations in their pattern can be seen depending upon the office location, working pattern, and the employee office timings, and along with this various interesting and informative visualizations are generated. Additionally, there is no perceptible trend has been observed in the data over the period.

Data Stationarity

The stationarity of the time series will define whether the trend or seasonality has any effect on the time series at any time of series. Time series with cyclical behaviour is stationary, as the cycles are not of a fixed length so the peaks and throughs of the cycles will be at any point in time. Based on the univariate analysis of the space occupancy count of the data, the series is horizontal with some cyclic behaviour. These cycles are aperiodic and as the employee and desk space count varies in the long term the timings of these cycles become unpredictable. Hence, we can conclude that the series is stationary.

The stationarity of the time series was examined using Augmented Dickey-Fuller (ADF) test.

Null Hypothesis (H_0): Time series is not stationary

Alternate Hypothesis (H$_1$): Time series is stationary

If the value of p > 0.05 then we cannot reject the null hypothesis and if the value of p <= 0.05 null hypothesis can be rejected. In this case, the p-value is low and less than 0.05. Hence, we rejected the null hypothesis and concluded that the time series is stationary.

Proposed Method

In this research paper, we will be focusing only on time series forecasting, as space utilization is highly dependent upon date and time. Hence, for future predictions using time series analysis will be more useful in terms of accuracy, a sudden change in data, increase or decrease in effecting parameters, lower complexity as compared to more sophisticated and complex techniques.

Univariate Time Series Model

Dataset variable 'stat_value', considering that these column observations are recorded sequentially over equal time increments of 15 mins and ignoring other variables building model based on this will be referred to as the univariate time series analysis. In this research based on the goal of the study, the first step is to identify the appropriate model based on the dependent variables. For a more realistic model, first the focus will be on the univariate model, and then based on its success multivariate model is built. First, we concentrate on a class of models created by the linear combination of past observations of the same variable and past forecast errors, the auto regressive moving average models (ARMA):

AR model forecasts future observations as the linear regression of past observations. The model has a lag order or autoregressive component denoted as 'p'. This value is determined by plotting PACF. Here, the significantly high values of partial autocorrelation are at 1, 2, 3, 17, 39, 44, 46 points. For AR model order is determined based on the AIC which fixes the number of lags from the past observations to use in correlation analysis to determine the state space vector dimension. Here, there is no seasonality in the dataset hence, as the data is stationary the order of the AR model is low. Hence, the value of lag order is 2 which is an immediate value where partial autocorrelation is significantly high [ARIMA(2,0,0)] and the model equation is:

$$\widehat{y_t} = \beta_0 + \beta_1 y_{t-1} + \beta_2 y_{t-2}$$

Figure 1. Partial Autocorrelation (PACF): Space Occupancy

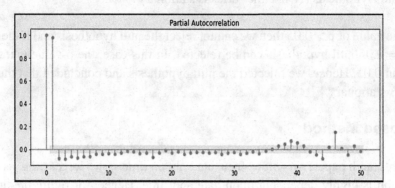

Where $\widehat{y}_t$ is future value to be forecasted i.e. dependent variable, y_{t-1} past value, independent variable. β_1 coefficient of lag of time series.

MA model predicts future observations using past forecast errors in a regression-like model. The model has the parameter 'q' which defines the window size over which linear combinations of errors are calculated. Value of 'q' is determined by plotting ACF, where autocorrelation measures relationships within one variable measured at regular intervals over time on only one subject.

Figure 2. Autocorrelation (ACF): Space Occupancy

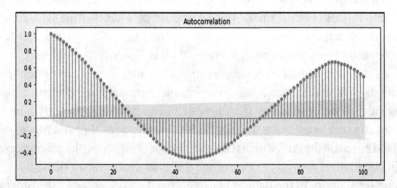

Beyond 25 autocorrelation dies, hence the suitable value for 'q' in this case is 3 [ARIMA(0,0,3)]. Moving Average equation is:

$$\hat{y}_t = \mu + \phi_1 \varepsilon_{t-1} + \phi_2 \varepsilon_{t-2} + \phi_3 \varepsilon_{t-3}$$

Where $\hat{y}_t$ is future value to be forecasted i.e. dependent variable, ε_{t-1} represents the past error of lags, ϕ_1 is coefficient of error lag of time series, μ is mean of Y.

The Fitting MA model is more complicated as compared to the AR model, as error terms are considered in AR. ACF and PACF may suggest MA would be better, but sometimes both MA and AR terms require to be used in the model. The main drawback of this method was that it removes the seasonal factor which led to a reduction in accuracy (Hye Jin Kam, Jin Ok Sung, 2010). An approach where both MA and AR are combined is termed as Box and Jenkins Approach, also called as ARMA model. Box-Jenkins model assumes the time series as stationary and also, data used in the research paper is stationary. This model is flexible as it includes both AR and MA and also this model can be extended to include seasonal auto regression and seasonal moving average terms (Huang, 2015). For this research, we have considered characteristics of AR('p') and MA('q') and built ARMA(p,q) model. For the ARMA model based on AR and MA model value pf 'p' is 2 and 'q' is 3 [ARIMA(2,0,3)]. ARMA equation will be:

$$\hat{y}_t = \beta_0 + \beta_1 S_{t-1} + \beta_2 S_{t-2} + \phi_1 \varepsilon_{t-1} + \phi_2 \varepsilon_{t-2} + \phi_3 \varepsilon_{t-3}$$

ARIMA model is a linear regression of one or more past observations along with past forecast errors. It considers three parameters 'p', 'd', and 'q', where 'd' is a degree of differencing to make series stationery. In comparison with ARMA new parameter 'I' called integrated has been introduced which removes the trend and then integrates with the original series. Though the ARIMA model was implemented just to check the performance and accuracy, this model is not suitable as data is stationery and the value of the differencing parameter by default is zero.

SARIMA model is exactly similar to ARIMA with an extra feature of seasonality. Hence, we have considered the SARIMAX model instead of SARIMA which considers non-seasonal and seasonal parameters along with this it also considers exogenous variable which models future observations as the linear regression of an external variable which is given as SARIMAX $(p,q,d)(P,Q,D)_m$. For SARIMAX model, suitable value for non-seasonal component and seasonal is 1; periodicity of the seasons is 12 as we have yearly data [SARIMAX(1,1,1) (1,1,1,12)]. SARIMAX equation will be:

$$\hat{y}_t = \mu + y_{t-12} + \phi_1 \left(y_{t-1} - y_{t-13} \right) - \theta_1 \varepsilon_{t-1} -_1 \varepsilon_{t-12} + \theta_{11} \varepsilon_{t-13}$$

Multivariate Time Series Model

Once the univariate analysis is completed, the multivariate time series forecasting model was developed using Vector Autoregression (VAR) which provides a flexible means to model and forecast. Multivariate time-series analysis estimates the vector of parameters and vector of dependency coefficient simultaneously. Here, the variables are one independent variable and multiple dependent variables and appropriate analysis is the time-series equivalent of an analysis of covariance (Salkind, 2012). For the analysis, we have first determined the appropriate lag between the covariate and dependent variables and if there is a dependency between the covariates, then transformation will require before performing analysis. Variables in the dataset there is no dependency in the covariates, hence no transformation is required.

Univariate time series analysis model can be used to predict space occupancy for one client with one office location and multivariate analysis will consider client id with their office location id and will forecast space occupancy for all clients and their all-office spaces. This model can be used to forecast space occupancy for the client who has multiple offices and they will have a space occupancy forecast of all locations together. VAR model has n-equation with an n-variable linear model that relates each variable to the past values of other n-1 variables (Jones et al., 2009). VAR is a collection of multivariable linear regression models. It can be stated as, it is an extension of the univariate autoregression where the vector of time-series variables, Y_{t+1} is represented as a linear function of $Y_t,\ldots\ldots\ldots,Y_{t-p+1}$ with deterministic terms (Stock, 2001).

VAR maxlag length has been decided based on the number of observations. The value of maxlag started with 10 and then increased up to 16. The most suitable value for maxlag was 15, as AIC value, in this case, is low as compared to the other values and for maxlag 16 AIC was low as compared to maxlag 15, and values of t-stat & probability were null for alternate location id. The stationary VAR model for p-lags and ($n \times 1$) vector of time-series variables can be represented as:

$$Y_t = c + \Pi_1 Y_{t-1} + \Pi_2 Y_{t-2} + \ldots + \Pi_p Y_{t-P} + $$

Where t=1……, T, Π_i are ($n \times n$) coefficient matrices and $_t$ is an unobservable zero-mean white noise vector process with a time-invariant covariance matrix. In this case, the VAR model was applied first and it was successful, hence as of now, other multivariate techniques have not been applied.

Model Validation and Forecasting

Based on various studies on time series forecasting univariate models with simple linear equation often performs better than more complicated multivariate models. The forecast over a period of the next few months produces a root mean square error for both univariate and multivariate time series models. AIC is calculated for every model and the order of the model with minimum AIC was identified. This determines the number of lags into the past to be used in canonical correlation analysis. The sample canonical contribution of the past with variables increasing the number of steps into the future are considered. AIC type criteria with penalty weight contribute to the canonical correlation of the variable, and variables with a large contribution are added to the state-space vector. Once the parameters and standard errors are estimated, t-ratio significance levels and AIC models have been evaluated. Along with AIC, more suitable time series model to space utilization forecast has been selected using evaluation parameter technique RMSE. The main point to consider RMSE as an evaluation technique is that it emphasizes the most significant errors as compared to the other evaluation techniques such as Mean Absolute Error (MAE), Mean Absolute Percentage Error (MAPE).

MSE is a distance of a data point from the line. To measure MSE vertical distance from point to Y axis is taken and values is squared. RMSE is the average distance of a data point from fitted line, measured along vertical line. It is a square root of mean square error. Lower the value of MSE and RMSE closer is the fit to the data.

$$MSE = \frac{1}{N} \sum_{i=1}^{N} \left(y_t - \widehat{y_t} \right)^2$$

$$RMSE = \sqrt{\frac{1}{N} \sum_{i=1}^{N} \left(y_t - \widehat{y_t} \right)^2}$$

Where y_t is the actual observation for time period t, $\widehat{y_t}$ is the forecast for the same time period and N is the length of the dataset.

Based on the RMSE value of all the models that we applied, two of them have been finalized to proceed for forecasting in the future and they are ARMA and SARIMAX. But out of these two models, SARIMAX is preferred for univariate time series analysis, as along with autoregression and moving average it considers the seasonal changes in the data, so that will help to predict correctly for holidays and leaves taken by the employees. Similarly for VAR the multivariate time series analysis.

Table 2. Time Series Techniques with RMSE Score

Model	AIC	MSE	RMSE
AR	22157	178.4	13.36
MA	28219	1487.16	38.56
ARMA	22047	170.91	13.07
ARIMA	22139	7160.47	84.61
SARIMA	22163	180.01	13.42
VAR	-40.68	352.25	13.28

Features regarding forecasting results are:

- There is a consistent downward pattern in the forecasting performance of the univariate model when the autoregression order increases.
- The data is stationary with no trend, hence MA and ARIMA models are not suitable for the dataset before the pandemic situation. As in the current pandemic dataset, there has been trend and seasonality, hence the list of current better performing models will change because a sudden decrease in the space occupancy in the current pandemic situation has made the dataset non-stationary.
- There is not much difference in the AIC value of all the univariate and multivariate models, but a significant decrease in RMSE value can be seen in the suitable models ARMA, SARIMAX, VAR. Models with a slight decrease in AIC have shown a significant decrease in the RMSE values as well.

From the experiments on various datasets of one client and its different locations, we found that there is a consistent performance between training and test datasets. Currently, the forecasting model has been built for one client and its different locations individually. The predictive results for this based on days and hours are quite impressive. Multivariate time series model has been built for simultaneous forecasting of multiple clients and their office locations. The predicted data can be cumulatively added to view the forecast of weeks, months and years. At present such cumulative forecast has not been shown, it will be added once the model is finalized.

For further study, the effect of Covid-19 will be taken into consideration by using the pre-and post-office reopening data. This will help organizations to be ready with all safety measures for their employees who are willing to work from the office in any such pandemic or unforeseen situations.

ANALYSIS

Data Description

Dataset has a total of 7 variables or columns. Column representation is as stated: Account ID is a unique id assigned to client, Location ID represents unique floor id of different office locations of a client, Stat Type states whether the observed record is of free space or occupied space, Stats Value states the count of Stat Type, Observed At is the time at which the space occupancy has been observed at the local time of client's office location, UTC Time is Observed At time is converted to the time in UTC.

For this research, the UTC Time column has been considered for value observation and forecasting to maintain uniformity when the model is deployed in production. Later, this column in the model can be replaced with the local time, or while displaying the converted time as per the region can be shown.

Data Preparation

For uniformity and standardization, the data type of all the columns was checked and rectified wherever applicable. Columns such as ID, Account ID, Location ID have unique values and their datatype is 'int64'. The ID column is an auto-incrementing sequential number, does not have any significance in this forecasting, and hence can be eliminated. Account ID and Location ID are very important for prediction as a model will be trained based on these columns along with the time parameter for future forecasting.

Column Stat Type is a categorical variable where data type is Object and for each client's location based on total available spaces the values have been recorded as 'Space Occupied' and 'Free Space'. Total count of space can be calculated for each location id and only one row is considered for prediction which is 'Space Occupied'. For more understanding new column 'Total Space Count' can be added to represent space occupancy forecast based on total available space on each floor.

The datatype of the UTC Time column has been changed to DateTime from Object so that this column is then set as an index to build time series, forecasting model. Once the column is set as index exploratory data analysis can be done using UTC Time column as X variable and space occupancy count, status, etc. as Y variable, to study the variation, trend, and pattern in the data.

EDA Analysis and Data Visualization

Model building has been simplified by removing the redundant columns which are not providing any relevant information for forecasting. This will help to consider only relevant columns and reduce the time required to train the model. ID, Local US Time, and Observed At columns are eliminated from the model building step.

Based on the value of the Stat Type column new table is created with the remaining other columns with the value of the 'Space Occupied' category. This table is further used for univariate and multivariate time series forecast model building. In terms of Univariate Time Series forecasting along with ID and other time-related columns Account ID and Location ID columns are eliminated as the forecast will be only for a single client for its single location. In the case of Multivariate Time Series forecasting, the Account ID column can be eliminated if there many locations of a single client to be considered or this can also be used to forecast occupancy for different clients and their different locations.

As per the analysis, there are no missing values in the dataset. The dataset shows count of occupied and free spaces, when for example at night time or on weekends the free space count is equal to the number of spaces available and the occupancy count is zero. Hence in this case there and no missing or null values in the dataset and as per the status of the desk occupancy, the count is shown.

But there are cases where null values have been recorded when the sensors could not communicate with the router to send the recorded data. In this case, data correction is done from the backend, to maintain data uniformity and consistency and avoid updating data with false values.

EDA helps to analyse and investigates the dataset and summarizes its main characteristics, by employing visualization methods. It helps to determine the best ways to manipulate the dataset by discovering the patterns, anomalies, finding interesting relationships among variables, test hypothesis, and assumptions. Here we have done Univariate and Bivariate analysis of the dataset.

Simple Univariate analysis states that space occupancy data has a specific pattern, where based on the day type (weekday or weekend) and time occupancy count varies.

The histogram shows bins on X-axis and counts on Y-axis by dividing the variables into bins, count data points in each bin. Here, bins represent the total space of all locations and the total count of spaces occupied at that time. Based on the output of different values of binwidth the best value of bins is 10. Smaller bandwidth made the plot cluttered and larger bandwidth may add modulation in the data. From the histogram, we can see that the space occupancy count of 140 to 160 is quite high, and also considering the night-time and weekends the space occupancy count is zero, hence its frequency is very much high as compared to others.

Figure 3. Space Occupancy Based on Time

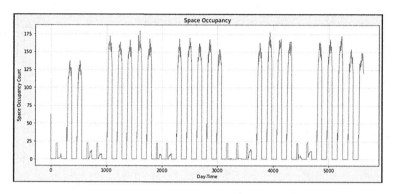

The density plot gives a smooth, continuous version of the histogram where we can get the single smooth density estimation by plotting to add the continuous curves of all space occupancy count added together. The kernel used here is Gaussian hence which has produced a bell curve at each data point (Reddy E.M.K, Gurrala A., Hasitha V.B., Kumar K.V.R, 2022). The main point to be considered is that in the density plot total area under the curve integrates to one (Koehrsen, n.d.). This probability density is the probability per unit on X-axis and Y-axis represents the probability density function for kernel density estimation. With the density plot, we have compared a few of the locations of a single client, where we can see that, location ids have almost same Space Occupancy Count distributions.

Lag plot a special type of scatter plot which is plotted against the K_{th} lag time period before the time i. The lag plot has been plotted for first-order. Here, data shows a positive linear trend, which suggests that positive autocorrelation is present in the data and there is are no outliers in the dataset. Data has been tightly clustered

Figure 4. Space Occupancy Spread Using Histogram

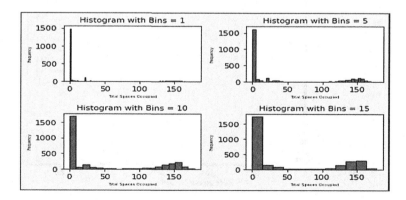

Figure 5. Space Occupancy Spread Using Density Plot

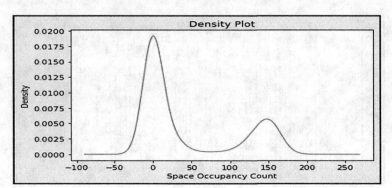

along the diagonal and we can say that data has strong positive autocorrelation i.e., there is a very strong association between observation and succeeding observation. The value of Y_i will have a strong guess for the value of Y_{i+1}.

The ACF plot provides the graphical representation of the autocorrelation structure of time series variables to determine the past forecast errors which are used to decide the extent to which past values are reliable to predict future values (Jones et al., 2009). Autocorrelation plots have been used to check the randomness present in the data. Data has autocorrelations with data of varying time lags and hence the dataset is non-random. The ACF plot indicates that based on the day and time-space occupancy is characterized by wave type patterns.

Univariate analysis has provided an understanding of the spread and randomness of the data. Along with this, the density of the data is smooth with an equal distribution

Figure 6. Space Occupancy of Different Locations Using Density Plot

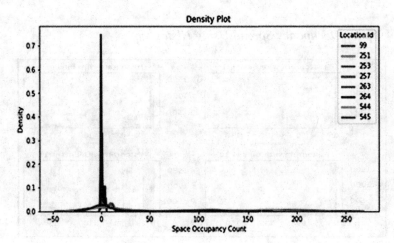

Figure 7. Space Occupancy Spread Using Lag Plot

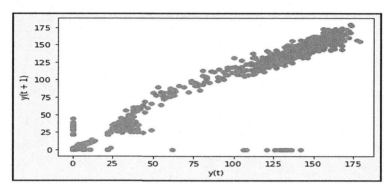

count for different locations. There is a pattern in the space occupancy data, where on 1st Jan there is a holiday, on 2nd Jan after 11:00 am we can see that the space occupancy count has started increasing and count reduces to zero at night time and similarly for other days. In this way all the holidays, weekends have been taken care of in the model building.

Figure 8. Space Occupancy based on Time

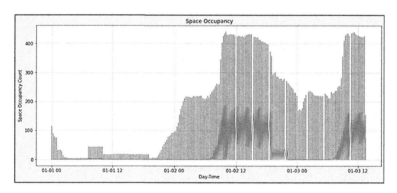

For different location ids based on the day of the week, we can track the space occupancy. This bivariate analysis helps to understand the relation between office locations and the day of the week. Day 1 is the weekend; hence space occupancy count is zero. For Day 2 and 3 based on the office location and employee count, there are some spikes for particular locations.

Similarly, for office locations based on time of the day, there is a pattern in the space occupancy count like at around 11:00 am there is a sudden increase in office space, during lunchtime between 2:00 pm to 3:00 pm there is a drop-in space

Figure 9. Space Occupancy Based on Day for different Office Locations

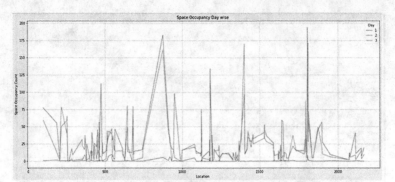

occupancy count and after 10:00 pm space occupancy count starts decreasing till midnight, from midnight till next morning. Based on the shift timings in certain office locations, the spaces have been occupied by few employees.

Figure 10. Space Occupancy Based on Time for different Office Locations

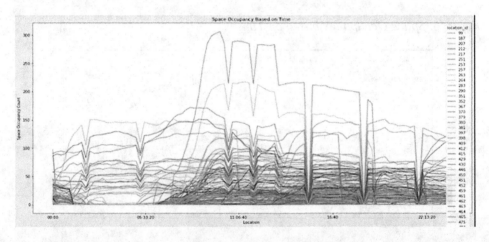

Based on bivariate analysis there is a relation between office location & office timings and these parameters will affect the forecast. For future forecast, parameters that will affect the forecast are holidays, weekends, weekdays, number of employees present each day, and office location. For holidays we do not need separate data to build a model to forecast space occupancy and similarly, employee leaves will be taken care of in the same dataset.

Once the exploratory data analysis is done, the dataset is then split into training and test set with a ratio of 70:30. We have a large amount of data for model training and the rest of the test dataset can be further used for both validation and test. For validation and test purpose different sets of client data has been used to check the model accuracy, correctness, and robustness.

Based on the performance the model that were finalized are ARMA and SARIMAX out of tested Univariate Time Series Models and VAR model from Multivariate Time Series Model. Out of these models Univariate Models will be used to forecast space occupancy of a single office location of a client and Multivariate Model for multiple office locations of a client or multiple office locations of different clients at the same time.

RESULTS AND DISCUSSIONS

Interpretation of Visualizations

Visual representation of the office space occupancy count showed that depending upon the office location and type of work meaning working shifts and employee type, there is a certain pattern present in the space occupancy. That pattern can be seen based on year, month, week of the month, day of the month, and the same pattern can be seen for holidays, if there are any leaves taken by the employees, the pattern change has been observed for such days. Space occupancy pattern is almost similar for different clients and various office locations data.

The main focus was on Univariate analysis, to understand the relationship between data and whether it is completely random or not. This helped to decide which time series forecasting model will be suitable for this data. Histogram of space occupancy has given the range of space occupancy based on its occupancy period in different office locations. As the data varies the histogram view has changed but the pattern of the histogram is the same which is kind of asymmetric and bimodal. Boxplot view was not helpful to gain any analysis of the data. The quantitative range of the bins has shown the distribution of space occupancy values falling in the range of the bin. The density plot has smoothed out all the noise present in the data by using kernel smoothing, but there was no noise present in the data. The density plot has no bins like histograms and easy to understand. Here, the density plot is bimodal with smooth distribution and as per the occupancy density, the value on X-axis has been adjusted automatically. Based on the Lag plot, we can see that data is tightly clustered along the diagonal hence we can conclude that data has strong positive autocorrelation and data is non-random. As we have seen that there is a correlation between data points, ACF has shown sinusoidal pattern and Histogram, Density

Figure 11. Auto Regression Forecast Accuracy

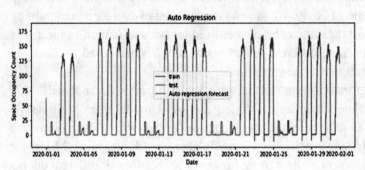

MSE value: 178.40
RMSE value: 13.36

Plot and Lag Plot pattern is same for space occupancy data of different clients and their office locations with some variations.

Model Diagnosis

Based on the literature that we have identified for office space utilization researchers have proposed different ways to utilize the office space wisely and along with that, the parameters that researchers have identified can be considered to granularize research on office space utilization trends. Based on data analysis, parameters on which space occupancy count is dependent, and a forecasting model has been built using time series analysis. Models suggested in the previous work can be replicated as their prediction parameters were different as per use cases and future data forecast was not applicable in most of the cases.

Based on the stationarity test result, we have found out that the dataset is stationary, hence the time series model applied directly without any transformation. As per the data analysis first, the univariate time series analysis is done to study lag order i.e. 'p' value, past forecast errors 'q' value, differencing 'd' but the data is stationary, hence its value is zero and models which work on these parameters are not suitable as the value of AIC and RMSE is very high. Validation of these models on the test dataset represents that prediction accuracy is very low as RMSE value is very high and there is a huge difference between the actual value and predicted value based on the visualization of actual & forecasting values.

Considering the AIC, RMSE values ARMA and SARIMAX are suitable and hence, the accuracy provided by them is sufficiently high as compared to other univariate models. The model's comparative study has been done by using various sets of different client data and results were quite impressive that the SARIMAX model was performing with almost consistent accuracy whereas the ARMA model

Figure 12. Moving Average Forecast Accuracy

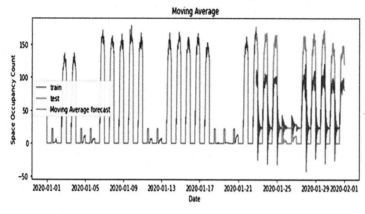

MSE value: 1487.16
RMSE value: 38.560

Figure 13. Auto Regressive Moving Average Forecast Accuracy

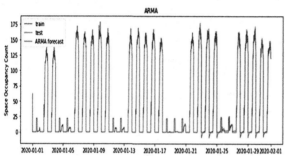

MSE value: 170.91
RMSE value: 13.07

Figure 14. Auto Regressive Integrated Moving Average Forecast Accuracy

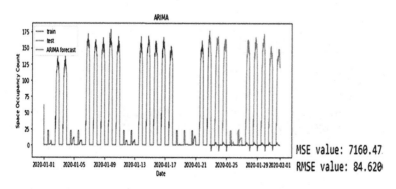

MSE value: 7160.47
RMSE value: 84.620

159

Figure 15. Seasonal Auto Regressive Integrated Moving Average Forecast Accuracy

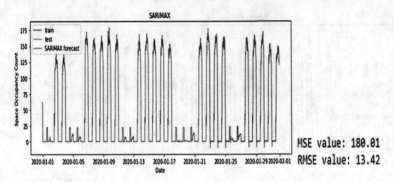

was not that consistent. While trying the model on different sets of data, model parameters p,d,q were changed accordingly.

Univariate models were first used for testing purposes to check the compatibility of the forecasting methods used on the data. Based on the results received models are compatible with the dataset and future space occupancy count can be forecasted using them. But these models were built only considering a single client and its single office location, hence the rest of the other variables were not considered while building the model. As per the production environment setup this model will be used for clients having a single office location.

But to predict all client's data simultaneously considering multiple office locations, a multivariate time series model has been developed using VAR. The multivariate model considers all variables to forecast, in future if any additional variable is added that can be easily taken into consideration in the model. This model has been run on different datasets and lag order varies as the data changes. Hence set of lag orders defined to avoid its manual selection and save time & resources. As it has

Figure 16. Vector Autoregression Forecast Accuracy

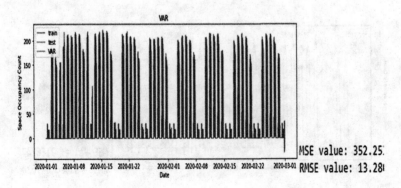

been run on different sets of data with various combinations of clients and their different office locations RMSE value and accuracy of the model varies but it has been consistent between a moderate range.

However, we have not proposed Holt-Winter exponential smoothing technique in this study, but based on results provided on the test dataset multivariate VAR model accuracy was high as compared to the smoothing technique. There is no trend and seasonality in the data smoothing technique that can be avoided as of now. We did not consider multivariate forecasting using neural network models like LSTM and RNN. As of today, no work has been done in space optimization using neural networks. For now, multivariate VAR model performance is satisfactory considering RMSE value and accuracy, neural network model requires more time and resources as compared to VAR. As the data will increase the complexity of the model will also increase.

Discussion

However, based on this study of pre-COVID data, there is a consistent predictable pattern in the space occupancy count for any office locations of any country and also the occupancy pattern is predictable considering the holidays and leaves taken by employees. This suggests that in normal conditions office space optimization data will help to improve the processes and it will reduce space mismanagement issues and improve proper utilization of the office architecture. In addition to this, in the future, if the employee count increases or decreases then office space can be properly utilized without any major changes requiring in the existing architecture.

Out of the two Univariate models, SARIMAX performance was better, it is a more versatile model as compared to ARMA. With seasonal and non-seasonal parameters, it also considers the time step for a seasonal period and accordingly forecasts considering the period data that we are providing. As the model parameters need to change with the variation in the data those values have been recorded and will be accordingly added into the model as per the data with few modifications. A similar thing will be done for the multivariate VAR model as well.

With this, both univariate and bivariate models will be in the examination for few days with the latest data or more dummy test data to study their performance. Along with this model will be trained on the post-COVID dataset separately and later both datasets would be combined to see the effect on current models. With merging before and after dataset, data would show some trend, seasonality and the stationarity of the data would get affected, and accordingly, the models which are not proposed in this research would be considered.

Limitations

Time series forecast can be uncertain as we do not know the future events that will happen which will affect the forecast. This uncertainty comprises of the error term ε_{t+h} with random measurement error with series being forecast and unforeseeable data revisions. Additionally, the forecast uncertainty might occur due to model approximation error and estimated model parameters.

For more accurate and certain forecasts, forecast interval can be defined based on historical parameters & residuals or by simulation for more complicated nonlinear models. If the model fails to incorporate forecast estimation uncertainty, then forecast error distributions can be constructed using simulated out-of-sample prediction methodology. Where model will be estimated using data through the same date, say t then a forecast for a-step ahead will be $t + h$. The model then estimates using data through date $t + 1$ and forecasts for $t + h + 1$. The impact lag order uncertainty of the ARMA model can be analysed by using Monte Carlo experiments, by generalizing the replicates of the AR(p) model.

Variables show sudden changes because of different reasons such as change in employee policies, change in work timings then, model instability increases. These changes are structural and gradual; hence it becomes critical to monitor model performance. To detect such changes different statistical techniques can be applied which detects instability in estimated coefficients or through forecast errors. Practically, to determine instability expert judgement will be required to draw more information and incorporate the changes in the existing models.

FUTURE RECOMMENDATIONS

In Future, the dataset would include the pre-COVID data, where normal offices were open and COVID data where lockdown has imposed and offices were completely closed for different time periods globally and post-COVID data where in some cases offices were opened with some percentages of their total capacity. For this current and past situation data would be considered together, and based on the analysis both univariate and multivariate models would be built. This development could provide invaluable advances in determining space occupancy in any unavoidable circumstances. There are chances that analysis from the past might not be useful for this new dataset.

Later, the new dataset can be merged with the old dataset to study the impact on models, this would help to create a more robust model considering all the real-life possibilities and their impacts. Models built have highlighted the importance of having a smooth and well-grounded forecast which can be used as a benchmark for new forecasts. This forecasting model would then be used in real-time and considering the pandemic situation and in future also it will be better & easy to maintain a safe distance in the office premises starting from office desks.

Employees would be able to track the forecast with an enhancement of real-time dashboard view given to them and accordingly they can decide whether to work from home or office on that day. Also, with these new additions can be done along with the space utilization forecast such as time would be suggested when space will be available based on employee entry time, meeting room occupancy rate with its booking frequency, space occupancy in the collaboration area, alarm if a count of employees in the meeting room increases beyond the threshold and similarly on collaboration area.

CONCLUSION

In summary, the research paper is focused on developing the forecasting model of office space utilization, using both univariate and multivariate time series approaches. The univariate time series forecasting models ARMA and SARIMAX are best fit to forecast space occupancy for single office location and multivariate time series forecasting model VAR is best fit to forecast space occupancy for multiple clients and their multiple office locations or single client and its multiple office locations.

However, as the test dataset varied the model performance has varied. Hence, more the models are trained, more of office space's demand and supply equation is getting smoother. Based on the other research works the parameters that they have suggested for office space utilization can be taken into consideration in the future, depending upon the social and professional situations then.

The development of a forecasting model help organizations in planning space allocation for the employees who are willing to work from the office every day and those who want to work from office for a few days in a month. As the employee count increases accordingly desk spaces can be managed and becomes easier to maintain safe distance between each desk. As per the methods proposed in this research paper, the focus was more on developing a robust, analytical forecasting model that provides decision support for important, real-time, and critical forecasting and monitoring.

REFERENCES

Bhogaraju, S. D., & Korupalli, V. R. K. (2020, January). Design of smart roads-a vision on indian smart infrastructure development. In *2020 International Conference on COMmunication Systems & NETworkS (COMSNETS)* (pp. 773-778). IEEE. 10.1109/COMSNETS48256.2020.9027404

Bhogaraju, S. D., Kumar, K. V. R., Anjaiah, P., & Shaik, J. H. (2021). Advanced Predictive Analytics for Control of Industrial Automation Process. In Innovations in the Industrial Internet of Things (IIoT) and Smart Factory (pp. 33-49). IGI Global. doi:10.4018/978-1-7998-3375-8.ch003

Cha, S. H., Steemers, K., & Kim, T. W. (2018). Modeling space preferences for accurate occupancy prediction during the design phase. Automation in Construction, 93, 135–147. doi:10.1016/j.autcon.2018.05.001

Chen, Y., Hong, T. & Luo, X. (2018). An agent-based stochastic Occupancy Simulator. *Building Simulation*, *11*(1), 37–49.

Ghosh, B., Basu, B. & O'Mahony, M. (2009). Multivariate short-term traffic flow forecasting using time-series analysis. *IEEE Transactions on Intelligent Transportation Systems*, *10*(2), 246–254.

Hellerstein, J.L., Zhang, F. & Shahabuddin, P. (2001). Statistical approach to predictive detection. *Computer Networks*, *35*(1), 77–95.

Huang, L. (2015). Auto regressive moving average (ARMA) modeling method for gyro random noise using a robust kalman filter. *Sensors, 15*(10), 25277–25286.

Jones, S.S., Evans, R.S., Allen, T.L., Thomas, A., Haug, P.J., Welch, S.J. & Snow, G.L. (2009). A multivariate time series approach to modeling and forecasting demand in the emergency department. *Journal of Biomedical Informatics*, *42*(1), 123–139.

Kalekar, P. (2004). Time series forecasting using Holt-Winters exponential smoothing. *Kanwal Rekhi School of Information Technology*, 1–13. Available from: https://www.it.iitb.ac.in/~praj/acads/seminar/04329008_Expon entialSmoothing.pdf

Kam, H. J., & Sung, J. O. (2010). *Prediction of Daily ED Patient Numbers*. Available from: www.e-hir.org

Kim, K.J. (2003). Financial time series forecasting using support vector machines. *Neurocomputing*, *55*(1–2), 307–319.

Kim, K.-J., & Han, I. (2010). *Genetic algorithms approach to feature discretization in artificial neural networks for the prediction of stock price index.* Available from: www.elsevier.com/locate/eswa

Koehrsen, W. (n.d.). *Histograms and Density Plots in Python. Towards Data Science.* Available from: https://towardsdatascience.com/histograms-and-density-plots-in-python-f6bda88f5ac0

Kumar, K.V.R., & Elias, S. (n.d.). Use Case To Simulation: Muscular Fatigue Modeling And Analysis Using Openism. *Turkish Journal of Physiotherapy and Rehabilitation, 32,* 2.

Kumar, K.V.R., Zachariah, A.A., & Elias, S. (n.d.). *Quantitative Analysis of Athlete Performance in Artistic Skating using IMU, and Machine Learning Algorithms.* Academic Press.

Li, S., Joe, J., Hu, J., & Karava, P. (2015). System identification and model-predictive control of office buildings with integrated photovoltaic-thermal collectors, radiant floor heating and active thermal storage. Solar Energy, 113, 139–157. doi:10.1016/j.solener.2014.11.024

Lik Lau, B.P., Wijerathne, N., Kiat Ng, B.K., & Yuen, C. (2017). *Sensor fusion for public space utilization monitoring in a smart city.* Academic Press.

Ma, R., Boubrahimi, S. F., Hamdi, S. M., & Angryk, R. A. (2017). Solar flare prediction using multivariate time series decision trees. In: *Proceedings - 2017 IEEE International Conference on Big Data, Big Data 2017.* Institute of Electrical and Electronics Engineers Inc. 10.1109/BigData.2017.8258216

Material, M. (2016). *The Evolution of Office Space Utilization in the U.S.* Academic Press.

Plum, K. (n.d.). *What is a Workplace Utilisation Study?* Available from: https://www.advanced-workplace.com/what-is-a-workplace-utilisation-study/

Reagan Nickl (SpacelQ). (2019). *Sapce Utilization Metrics.* Available from: https://spaceiq.com/blog/space-utilization-metrics/

Reddy, E. M. K., Gurrala, A., Hasitha, V. B., & Kumar, K. V. R. (2022). Introduction to Naive Bayes and a Review on Its Subtypes with Applications. In *Bayesian Reasoning and Gaussian Processes for Machine Learning Applications* (pp. 1–14). Chapman and Hall/CRC. doi:10.1201/9781003164265-1

Ryu, S. H., & Moon, H. J. (2016). Development of an occupancy prediction model using indoor environmental data based on machine learning techniques. Building and Environment, 107, 1–9. doi:10.1016/j.buildenv.2016.06.039

Salkind, N. (2012). Time-Series Study. In *Encyclopedia of Research Design*. SAGE Publications, Inc.

Stock, J. H. (2001). Time Series: Economic Forecasting. In *International Encyclopedia of the Social & Behavioral Sciences* (pp. 15721–15724). Elsevier. doi:10.1016/B0-08-043076-7/00526-X

Tabak, V. (2009). *User Simulation of Space Utilisation: System for Office Building Usage Simulation*. Academic Press.

Tabak, V. & de Vries, B. (2010). Methods for the prediction of intermediate activities by office occupants. *Building and Environment*, *45*(6), 1366–1372.

Wang, Z., Zhang, M., Wang, D., Song, C., Liu, M., Li, J., Lou, L., & Liu, Z. (2017). Failure prediction using machine learning and time series in optical network. *Optics Express*, *25*(16), 18553. doi:10.1364/OE.25.018553 PMID:29041054

Yao, J., & Jiang, K. (2019). A fast intra prediction algorithm with simplified prediction modes based on utilization rates. In *Proceedings - 18th IEEE/ACIS International Conference on Computer and Information Science, ICIS 2019*. Institute of Electrical and Electronics Engineers Inc. 10.1109/ICIS46139.2019.8940153

Zhou, Y., Tagliaro, C. & Hua, Y. (n.d.). *From Hour to Minute: Non-technical Challenges for Measuring Office Space Utilization with Smart Technologies*. Academic Press.

Zia Ullah, Q., Hassan, S., & Khan, G. M. (2017). Adaptive Resource Utilization Prediction System for Infrastructure as a Service Cloud. *Computational Intelligence and Neuroscience*. doi:10.1155/2017/4873459 PMID:28811819

Chapter 10
How Customer Relationship Management Influences Business and How It Impacts Customer Satisfaction and Loyalty:
How Has Technology Impacted CRM?

Anuska Sanyal
Woxsen University, India

P Ritwik
Woxsen University, India

ABSTRACT

In this chapter, the foundation of customer relationship management has been explored along with its history and how it has evolved in the past few years. Metrics to measure CRM are important to check its effectiveness. It also determines the impact of CRM on customer satisfaction and loyalty. The way CRM has helped business over the years has also been discussed. In business-to-business and business-to-consumer, CRM has made a large impact. With CRM technology, both business and relationship areas have been improved.

DOI: 10.4018/978-1-6684-4246-3.ch010

INTRODUCTION

CRM has attracted the expansion of business from over the years now. Companies rely on efficient CRM technology, tools, and strategies for effective long-term relationship with customers and improve their profits. Marketing and sales department of a business are widely accepting the process of customer relationship management. It is expected that companies not only sell products for profit but also meet customers' needs and demands in order to provide them a good experience which later cater to building customer loyalty (Sulaiman & Said Musnadi, 2018). The companies are meant to build trust and communication with their customers through CRM, thus establishing a relationship with them. The mission of CRM is giving customers the best experience and values. It is a method to attract and retain customers by improving customer satisfaction and maintain relationship.

Customer relationship management is used to create competitive advantage by optimising communication, deliverables, and existing customer relationships. Earlier a small business used to start with trust, personal attention to customers, meeting their demands, customisable orders, manual orders and customers tracking and all other things to meet customer requirement. All of these processes were time-consuming and used to create a complicated workflow. But when a business starts to scale, they had to adopt measures such as mass production, mass distribution to meet growing demand. This is when CRM comes in use. It allows any user to handle and edit any data at any point of time instead of handling them manually.

The use of CRM is not only limited to keeping track of customers and orders but also provides information and data about the customers, their buying pattern, preferred choices. Inferences based on these data help the companies to understand the consumers well and provide insights on communication and other marketing and sales strategies thereby creating values and satisfaction for the customers. It helps in streamlining sales process and customer service (Agrawal, 2004). Thus, CRM influences customer satisfaction which in turn help increasing company's revenue and bring in loyal customers.

CRM has the power to connect the departments of an organisation like marketing, sales, customer service and maintain all their data and activities under one system. Every user has easy access to all the data. This CRM software is a success due to the integration of SaaS and cloud computing. Because of these two technologies, today CRM is able to help grow and scale business irrespective of the size of the company.

Building customer relationships is equally important for both B2B and B2C markets. There are two perspectives to customer relationship: the breadth and depth of the relationship. Width describes the different stages of a relationship and how it developed. An organisational strategy must be developed to maintain the relationship and move it to the desired stag (Campbell et al. 2009, p.109). A CRM helps facilitate the relationship between an organisation and its customers. Loyal customers are more profitable and valuable than customers who are not loyal.

Evolution of CRM

A misconception regarding CRM prevails that it is something new whereas it originated at the middle of the twentieth century. It started with handwritten notes and Rolodexes but with the boom in the digital technology CRM software evolved into something more complex with databases.

Before the invention of computer, pen and paper were used to document business data. In 1950 Rolodex was introduced that helped keep track of customers. In 1980s sales representatives introduced database marketing which was upgraded to Contact Management Software in late 1980s which is presently regarded as the basic CRM system and mark the foundation of CRM. Early 1990s saw software development with Sales Force Automation (SFA) expected to refine sales process and boost productivity. In 1995 'Customer Relationship Management' term was introduced and CRM software were installed in individual computers. Late 1990s CRM went online with first mobile CRM by Siebel. In 1999, CRM began moving to cloud with the introduction of Software as a Service (SaaS) CRM by a company named Salesforce. From 2000s we have seen Cloud based CRM trends and with increasing presence of social media business shifted their customer relationship focus from transaction to interaction. Refer to the following timeline flowchart for evolution of CRM over time (Salesforce, 2021).

The market for CRM seems to be growing though existing vendors struggles to keep up with the latest development and transformation. Increased social and mobile data has created the latest shift in CRM. But the cloud based, and SaaS CRM have been the focus for building business. CRM software focus on marketing, sales, and customer service for providing solution. Salesforce, Infusionsoft and AgileCRM are making continuous changes in their platforms according to the latest trends and development. (Evolution of CRM, AgileCRM)

The advent of computers and technologies have helped in growing de-intermediation process in many industries which helped CRM evolve and develop in recent times. Industries such as airlines, insurance, household appliances, software and banking, are undergoing a process of de-intermediation which has made relationship marketing more demanding and thus has proven to change the marketing pattern. (Salesforce, 2021)

Figure 1. Evolution of CRM over time

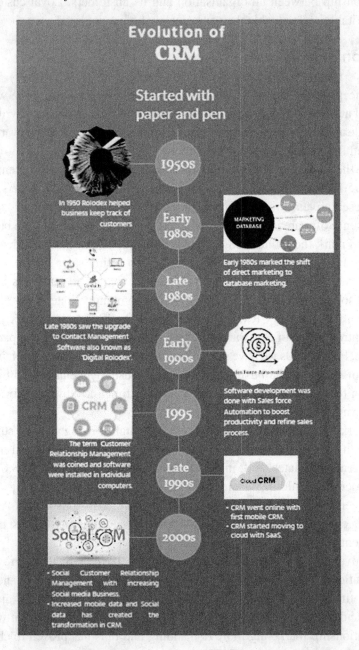

LITERATURE REVIEW

Customer Relationship Management works as an integration of sales, marketing, and customer service with the goal of maximizing revenue through customer satisfaction (Kalakota and Robinson, 2010). It is a concept of building relationship between the management and customers (Sutedjo, 2011). To flexibly respond to the growing demand and achieve customer loyalty, businesses must strive to build long-lasting relationships with customers. Companies that ignore this trend, have the risk of losing market share and future growth opportunities (Peppers and Rogers (2011)). So, customer relationship management technique of customer service which hopes to build and maintain long-lasting relationships (Ardiyhanto, 2011). Initially CRM was often cited to as IT-based customer solutions (Payne and Frow, 2005). However, it is an integrative business strategy that includes more than just information technology (Crosby, 2002).

Customer satisfaction is an important factor of business. CRM tools allow businesses to customise and enhance the customer experience, reliability of their products, and assist businesses in managing customer relationship more successfully, hence it can affect customer satisfaction (Reinartz et al., 2004; Mithas et al., 2005). Increased customer satisfaction, increased plant profitability, reduced labour costs and engineering processing times, improved product quality, & improved organisational processes are all cited as benefits of CRM implementation. Since CRM's benefits are varied and impact many different areas, it is difficult to quantify their effectiveness. As a result, multiple effectiveness indicators will be needed depending on the industry and the nature of the business (B2B or B2C), and other organisational traits. (Chen, I.J. & Popvich, K., 2003) Nevertheless, as CRM adoption is a strategic matter that has an impact on the organization's competitiveness, it is essential to be able to quantify its advantages (Teng et al., 2007; Mithas et al., 2005; Sin et al., 2005).

CRM PERFORMANCE METRICS

CRM performance need to be regularly assessed in order to determine whether strategies are successful and long-term viable. Enhancing relationship marketing strategic objective and features or taking corrective measures in terms of relationship governance both are aided by performance evaluation. Without relevant performance metrics to evaluate customer relationship management activities, it seems to be difficult to make decisions about CRM modification or termination process. Creating performance measurements is never an easy task because most businesses choose to analyse CRM using existing marketing KPIs. However, a lot of currently used marketing metrics, such market share and overall sales volume, might not be applicable in the context of CRM.

To assess CRM performance, it is recommended to use a **balanced scorecard** with multiple metrics, depending on the purpose of each of the initiatives (Kaplan

& Norton, 1992). The set of objectives of a project should be reflected by CRM performance evaluation metrics. However, there are certain global metrics that can measure impact of CRM on a business.

One of the global measures used in monitoring CRM performance in business is the measure of **relationship satisfaction**. Measuring relationship satisfaction determines how satisfied relational partners are with their current cooperative and collaborative partnerships, similar to how customer satisfaction does, which businesses generally use nowadays. Customer satisfaction measures, which are only used to evaluate satisfaction on one side of the dyad. On the contrary, Relationship satisfaction measures can be used on either side of the dyad. Both customers' and company's relationship satisfaction should be assessed because both of them must perform in order to attain a cooperative partnership (Biong, Parvatiyar, & Wathne, 1996). By evaluating relationship satisfaction, one may predict the propensity whether each side would be more likely to keep the relationship continuing or terminate it. Customer loyalty can likewise be used to measure such propensity. When measurement scales for relationship satisfaction or loyalty are created based on the antecedents, they can offer detailed information on the factors that determine these variables, helps in strategizing the managerial actions that are most likely to increase relationship satisfaction and/or loyalty.

How Customer Relationship Management Benefits Businesses

Since we have seen how CRM is responsible for driving customer satisfaction and loyalty, customer reviews are also considered essential for large as well as small firms for building strategies and boosting sales. A CRM approach is not only for customer service but also help in effective business to enhance the current strategy and increase revenue. So, lets dive into how CRM benefits businesses.

Builds Connection With Customers and Loyalty

Customers loyalty is a sign that a company values them and forges connections. Additionally, it may be the secret to developing even more leads and expanding its customer base. Adopting a customer relationship management strategy has several important benefits, one of which is that it improves communication between a company and both potential and current customers.

Using CRM software to create a precise, thorough strategy for how a company will engage with its customers is an excellent method to do this. Collecting data on a company's target market can be another approach to use a CRM system to increase customer loyalty. Businesses need to understand exactly how their target market prefers to be communicated to, what they hope to learn from the services and goods they buy, and which brands they connect the most with. CRM systems should be used to gather data from customer information and support the growth of a firm by identifying trends that are pertinent for audiences and ways to raise customer satisfaction. (Mukesh K. Singhmar)

Information Storage

The ability to store information about a company in one location is one of the major benefits of CRM systems. Keeping all data in one location makes it possible for all employees, to access information at any moment. Since interactions with leads and customers can be monitored and shared among groups, CRM provide opportunities for upselling or account expansion in sales. Second, because information can be traced back to specific time, information storage space contributes in minimising problems and errors and saves time. (Mukesh K. Singhmar)

It's Inexpensive

CRM solutions help businesses spend less money on ineffective strategies by providing current data at the flick of a switch.

It is easier to learn what the customer expects from a business and what products, advertising and marketing techniques, and communication channels perform best since CRM helps in knowing more about a brand's consumers.

CRM systems give businesses the ability to analyse customer buying patterns, sales data, and the effectiveness of their goods and services, allowing for more effective future marketing initiatives. Companies can increase their revenue margins by cutting costs on items or services that are ineffective. (Mukesh K. Singhmar)

It Supports the Organization

Utilizing a CRM system also helps to internally organise an organisation. With streamlining the sales process, CRM also allows departments within an organisation to better organise their workloads. All information is monitored by CRM systems, which makes daily operations considerably more organised. Meetings can be booked through a CRM system, tasks can be prioritised, and timetables help teams keep track of deadlines or goals. Customers will undoubtedly be thrilled by the well-organized and efficient sales procedure, and internal effectiveness within a company will undoubtedly shine outwardly. (Mukesh K. Singhmar)

Better-Targeted Marketing Campaigns

Marketing campaigns can be considerably more effectively targeted at customers using a CRM system, depending on where they are in the sales cycle. Depending on whether they are leads, new customers, or loyal customers/ brand enthusiasts' organisations can tailor their strategies to them. Future marketing and sales procedures become considerably more structured and specific to each target market with better-targeted and more personalised strategies based on past sales record. (Mukesh K. Singhmar)

B2B Vs B2C With Respect to CRM

The volume of transactions, in B2B compared to B2C markets, is substantially larger (Kumar and Reinartz 2012, s. 261). There are several resources which claims that there are less subjects in the B2B market, which is why the value of each purchase amount and transaction size are significantly larger. The biggest difference between B2B and B2C is in B2B there are a large degree of independence between buyers and sellers (Gummesson, 2008, s.174). There are evidence-based researches which show B2B business generate more benefit than B2C using CRM technology (Saini et al, 2010, s.366). In B2C customers are not so loyal therefore they tend to switch often (Saini, Grewal and Johnson, 2010). There is more loyalty in B2B due to the need of more trust between business partners. Also, in B2B customer relationship is more valuable than service or goods (Davis et al. 2012, s.200).

Though we have seen the importance of customer satisfaction, customer loyalty which helps in customer retention, few managers admit it publicly that they do not want any relationship with their customers. In fact, there the enough evidence present that shows most of the time customer also don't look for a relationship with the goods or service they buy. People usually lack motivation, interest, time, and energy to develop a relationship with their products. This is because relationships are special and they require mutual respect, dedication and cooperation. B2B connections are also created with the idea that both sides support each the other's business success.

A seller-customer relationship takes on a paradoxical turn in B2C markets. The paradox is the challenge of attempting to build a "relationship" with a customer while also seeking to generate revenue by offering them goods and services. A distinct kind of "connection" may only be possible in specific circumstances, according to the social character of relationships and reality of business. According to recent research, consumers can comprehend this dilemma. (Grahame Dowling, 2002)

There is experiential evidence, which shows building a relationship with a brand or the retailer selling it is important. There may be a considerable "brand component" that influences consumer choice, behaviour and commitment in marketplaces in spite of psychological and social factors that predominates (such as luxury items, cosmetics, and lifestyle brands). Some customers might love the brand influenced by a personality and desire for a relationship with it.

Even if customers are not looking for a relationship with the goods or service yet they might enjoy and value a relationship with the salesperson who sells the goods or service to them. Several such programmes have been introduced in a variety of retail formats. Multiple retail CRM methods have proven effective in industries where product bundling is essential for assisting the customer in constructing their desires (such as apparel, home goods, cosmetics). Supporting customers in starting a conversation with the business is another possible value-adding channel for CRM tools. Such a line of contact has been established using numerous consumer call centres, loyalty programmes, and websites. Real conversation, however, requires two-way communication. It demands current, precise, and thorough customer data. (Grahame Dowling, 2002)

The objective in both B2B and B2C sales cycle is to lead potential customers via a sequence of communications and (specific) content that starts with building brand awareness and leads, ultimately, to a sale. This sale may result in repeat business and brand loyalty if it is followed up with thorough customer service.

In B2B business is significantly more complicated and multidimensional than a single consumer. Companies may find it challenging to determine what they need and where because there are likely to be several constraints and obligations at each touchpoint. The CRM system steps in to help with this.

A B2B customer relationship management helps marketing and sales team track individual leads in detail, and identify exactly how and when to progress to the next level of the sales funnel, and automate a variety of tasks.

CRM Integration With Technology

The type of technology companies use is believed to influence business performance and relationship building.

The introduction of this technology can be viewed as a strategic marketing decision. Companies using contact management software are unlikely to dramatically improve their business and relationship performance. According to IT adoption literature, a comprehensive structure of user acceptance, functionality and integration is the foundation of technology adoption. Habitual use of technology as part of job duties and to achieve results is known as recruitment. IT researchers found CRM technology integration to be key factor in technology success in an organization. (Woodburn, 2002)

There is a difference between a standalone customer contact application for individual dealers and a central enterprise-wide customer database accessible to all users. The integration aspects show how well your technology links with the rest of your business, ensuing a seamless customer experience.

Customer knowledge management and good process for customer data collection, information analysis and knowledge retrieval are what business and customer want in their sales and marketing tools.

Customer perceived value of the application appears to be industry related. Companies in the financial services industry agree that the knowledge management capabilities provided by CRM are important and valuable in fostering customers relationships. Most companies agree that technology can be used to improve customer loyalty.

Many users and customers have presented the concept of customer knowledge management and how CRM technology can be used to "Package" customer knowledge.

Larger organizations are more likely to have more complex business processes, large customers portfolios, larger customer relationship database, and more difficult customer management. Larger organizations are more likely to realize the intelligence they can bring to their operations and customer understanding efforts because of the size and complexity of their customers and databases. They are likely to get more out of the software implementation.

Face-to-face contact between organization and their customers is common in B2B and service sectors. In some industries, the need of an effective CRM is gradually increasing. According to service market literature, customers perceive a higher risk with respect to services due to their intangibility and variability. As such, service companies are more likely to build relationships than non-service companies. Service companies should also be more likely to use CRM technology than non-service companies.

The software provides the ability to identify strategically important customers, segment customers, and track and model customer behavior. The importance of personalization and customization in service delivery is more important for service companies than for non-service companies.

Longevity of CRM technology with an organization -The length of time CRM software has been in operation within an organization can impact it usage and potential benefits from the software. Employees initial resistance subsides and they are more likely to exploit the full potential of the system.

Learning curve theory suggests that as employees become more comfortable with technology, they will use it more often to maximize its potential. Employees will naturally likely to use customer relationship management technology if they know how to use it properly.

CONCLUSION

This book chapter significantly discussed what Customer relationship management is and how companies rely on CRM software for growing their business. Later it focussed on how CRM has evolved over the years with the advent of technology. Also factors of CRM that benefit business. Next, CRM effect on B2B and B2C markets has been discussed. Performance metrics to evaluate CRM in customer satisfaction and customer loyalty has also been discussed. Lastly the integration of CRM with technology is discussed briefly.

REFERENCES

Agrawal, M. L. (2004). Customer Relationship Management (CRM) & Corporate Renaissance. *Journal of Service Research*, *3*(2), 149–167.

Biong, H., Parvatiyar, A., & Wathne, K. (1996). Are Customer Satisfaction Measures Appropriate to Measure Relationship Satisfaction? In A. Parvatiyar & J. N. Sheth (Eds.), *Contemporary Knowledge of Relationship Marketing* (pp. 258–275). Emory University Centre for Relationship Marketing.

Campbell, D., Wells, J., & Valacich, J. S. (2009). Diagnosing and Managing Online Business-to-Consumer (B2C) Relationships: Toward an eCommerce B2C Relationship Stage Theory. *AIS Transactions on Human-Computer Interaction*, *1*(4), 108–132. doi:10.17705/1thci.00008

Chen, I. J., & Popvich, K. (2003). Understanding customer relationship management (CRM): People, process and technology. *Business Process Management Journal*, *9*(5), 672–688. doi:10.1108/14637150310496758

Crosby, L. A. (2002). Exploding some myths about customer relationship management. *Journal of Service Theory and Practice*, *12*(5), 271–277. doi:10.1108/09604520210442056

Davis, D. F., Golicic, S. L., & Marquardt, A. (2012). *Business-to-business Marketing Management: Strategies, Cases, and Solutions*. Emerald Group Publishing. doi:10.1108/S1069-0964(2012)18

Day, G. S. (2000). Managing Market Relationships. *Journal of the Academy of Marketing Science*, *28*(1), 24–30. doi:10.1177/0092070300281003

Dowling, G. (2002). *Customer Relationship Management: In B2C Markets Often Less Is More*. doi:10.2307/41166134

Evolution of CRM. (n.d.). *AgileCRM*. Retrieved from https://www.agilecrm.com/crm/evolution-of-crm#:~:text=In%20the%20last%20decade%20or,to%20interactive%20client%20relationship%20management

Gummesson, E. (2008). Quality, service-dominant logic and many-to-many marketing. *The TQM Journal, 20*(2), 143–153. doi:10.1108/17542730810857372

Johnson, Clark, & Barczak. (2012). Customer relationship management processes: How faithful are business-to-business firms to customer profitability? *Industrial Marketing Management*. Advance online publication. doi:10.1016/j.indmarman.2012.04.001

Kaplan, R. S., & Norton, D. (1992, January-February). The Balanced Scorecard – Measures that Drive Performance. *Harvard Business Review, 70*, 71–79. https://hbr.org/1992/01/the-balanced-scorecard-measures-that-drive-performance-2 PMID:10119714

Kumar, V., & Reinartz, W. (2012). *Customer Relationship Management: Concept, Strategy, and Tools*. Springer. doi:10.1007/978-3-642-20110-3

Mithas, S., Krishnan, M. S., & Fornell, C. (2005). Why do customer relationship management applications affect customer satisfaction? *Journal of Marketing, 69*(4), 201–209. doi:10.1509/jmkg.2005.69.4.201

Payne, A., & Frow, P. (2005). A strategic framework for customer relationship management. *Journal of Marketing, 69*(4), 167–176. doi:10.1509/jmkg.2005.69.4.167

Peppers, D., & Rogers, M. (2011). *Managing Customer Relationships: A Strategic Framework*. John Miley & Sons. doi:10.1002/9781119239833.fmatter

Saini, A., Grewal, R., & Johnson, J. L. (2010). Putting market-facing technology to work: Organizational drivers of CRM performance. *Marketing Letters, 21*(4), 365–383. doi:10.100711002-009-9096-z

Salesforce. (2021a). *The B2B Sales Funnel and the Role of CRM Systems*. Retrieved from https://www.salesforce.com/uk/learning-centre/crm/b2b-crm

Salesforce. (2021b). *The complete history of CRM*. Retrieved from https://www.salesforce.com/in/hub/crm/the-complete-crm-history

Sin, L. Y. M., Tse, A. C. B., & Yim, F. H. K. (2005). CRM: Conceptualization and scale development. *European Journal of Marketing, 39*(11/12), 1264–1290. doi:10.1108/03090560510623253

Singhmar, M. K. (n.d.). *Why Customer Relationship Management is Important for Your Business*. Retrieved from https://seeresponse.com/blog/why-customer-relationship-management-is-important-for-your-business/

Sulaiman & Said Musnadi. (2018). Customer Relationship Management, Customer Satisfaction and Its Impact on Customer Loyalty. *ICMR 2018*, 692-698. DOI: doi:10.5220/0008892606920698

Teng, K. L., Ong, S. G., & Ching, P. W. (2007). The Use of Customer Relationship Management (CRM) by Manufacturing Firms in Different Industries: A Malaysian Survey. *International Journal of Management*, 24, 386.

Woodburn, D. (2002). Customer relationship management: Hard lessons learned in B2B pose tough questions for B2C. *Journal of Direct, Data and Digital Marketing Practice*, 4(1), 19–32. doi:10.1057/palgrave.im.4340160

ADDITIONAL READING

Agrawal, G. K., & Berg, D. (2009). The Development of Services in Customer Relationship Management (CRM) Environment from 'Technology' Perspective. *Journal of Service Science and Management*, 02(04), 432–438. doi:10.4236/jssm.2009.24052

Ata, U. Z., & Toker, A. (2012). The effect of customer relationship management adoption in business-to-business markets. *Journal of Business and Industrial Marketing*, 27(6), 497–507. doi:10.1108/08858621211251497

Baker, M. J., Buttery, E. A., & Richter-Buttery, E. M. (1998, Autumn). Relationship Marketing in Three Dimensions. *Journal of Interactive Marketing*, 12(4), 47–62. doi:10.1002/(SICI)1520-6653(199823)12:4<47::AID-DIR5>3.0.CO;2-B

Berry, L. L. (1995, Fall). Relationship Marketing of Services—Growing Interest, Emerging Perspectives. *Journal of the Academy of Marketing Science*, 23(4), 236–245. doi:10.1177/009207039502300402

Coltman, T., Devinney, T. M., & Midgley, D. F. (2011). Customer relationship management and firm performance. *Journal of Information Technology*, 26(3), 205–219. doi:10.1057/jit.2010.39

Crosby, L. A., & Stephens, N. (1987, November). Effects of Relationship Marketing and Satisfaction, Retention, and Prices in the Life Insurance Industry. *JMR, Journal of Marketing Research*, *24*(4), 404–411. doi:10.1177/002224378702400408

Das, K. (2009). Relationship marketing research (1994-2006): An academic literature review and classification. *Marketing Intelligence & Planning*, *27*(3), 326–363. doi:10.1108/02634500910955236

Dwyer, F. R., Schurr, P. H., & Oh, S. (1987, April). Developing Buyer-Seller Relationships. *Journal of Marketing*, *51*(2), 11–27. doi:10.1177/002224298705100202

Kale, S. H. (2004). CRM Failure and the Seven Deadly Sins. *Marketing Management, 13*(5), 42–46. Retrieved from https://www.researchgate.net/publication/232608105_CRM_Failure_and_the_Seven_Deadly_Sins

Mousavy, S. K. (2012). Customer Relationship Management (CRM) and Study of Its Effect on Competitive Advantage. *Life Science Journal-Acta Zhengzhou University Overseas Edition*, *9*(4), 4167–4173.

Parvatiyar, A., & Sheth, J. N. (2001). Customer Relationship Management: Emerging Practice, Process, and Discipline. *Journal of Economic and Social Research*, *3*(2), 1–34. https://www.researchgate.net/publication/312458264_Customer_relationship_management_Emerging_practice_process_and_discipline

Reinartz, W., Krafft, M., & Hoyer, W. D. (2004). The customer relationship management process: Its measurement and impact on performance. *JMR, Journal of Marketing Research*, *41*(4), 293–305. doi:10.1509/jmkr.41.3.293.35991

Richard, J. E., Thirkell, P., & Huff, S. L. (2007). The strategic value of CRM: A technology adoption perspective. *Journal of Strategic Marketing*, *15*(5), 421–439. doi:10.1080/09652540701726793

Richard, J. E., Thirkell, P. C., & Huff, S. L. (2007). An examination of customer relationship management (CRM) Technology adoption and its impact on business-to business customer relationships. *Total Quality Management & Business Excellence*, *18*(8), 927–945. doi:10.1080/14783360701350961

Sheth, J. (2000). *The Domain And Conceptual Foundations Of Relationship Marketing*. Retrieved from https://www.jagsheth.com/relationship-marketing/the-domain-and-conceptual-foundations-of-relationship-marketing

Ulaga, W., & Eggert, A. (2006). Relationship value and relationship quality: Broadening the nomological network of business-to-business relationships. *European Journal of Marketing*, *40*(3/4), 311–327. doi:10.1108/03090560610648075

Chapter 11
Indian Economic Growth Concerning the Impact on FDI (Foreign Direct Investment):
Impact of FDI on Indian Economic Growth in the Pharmaceutical Sector

Pingili Sravya
Woxsen University, India

Rajesh Kumar K. V.
iD https://orcid.org/0000-0002-7989-1824
Woxsen University, India

ABSTRACT

The present empirical study has explained the part of foreign direct investment (FDI) in India's economic growth in the pharmaceutical sector. The study has detailed information about the relationship, impact, and forthcoming action of the FDI on the Indian economy. This study applies the e-views software concerning statistical tools used are VECM, ordinary least squares, and VAR. It has considered the secondary data with the year starting from 2011 to 2021. The study has evaluated the results as a good association between the FDI and the pharmaceutical sector. This study suggests that it affected the positive long-term connection of FDI in the pharmaceutical industry and the short-term affinity between FDI and GDP. The study also concluded that the outcomes of foreign direct investment would have positive future movements in GDP.

DOI: 10.4018/978-1-6684-4246-3.ch011

INTRODUCTION

Foreign Direct Investment (FDI) is described as "cross-border expenditures to acquire or extend corporate ownership of productive assets." FDI is paramount to a nation's economic growth. Foreign investors' money helps India enhance infrastructure, raise production, and deliver career opportunities. Furthermore, FDI performs as a conduit for formulating sophisticated technology and mobilizing foreign currency resources. The country's foreign trade aid allows the RBI (Reserve Bank of India) to intervene in the foreign exchange market and limit adverse movements to stabilize exchange rates. Consequently, it creates a more favorable economic climate for the growth of the Indian economy.

India is regarded as a worldwide center for low-cost generic pharmaceuticals, which is critical in ensuring the right to health in impoverished nations. Foreign direct investment (FDI) is required to introduce newer and safer technologies to India. However, India's current FDI laws need to be reviewed. The Indian government should also ensure that excessive foreign investment does not harm local businesses and enterprises (particularly those engaged in generic medication), the market, and the price of pharmaceuticals in India. The present NDA government's start-up policies, Pharma Vision 2020, and their effective execution are critical. If the recommendations mentioned earlier are effectively executed, FDI in the pharmaceutical industry will fulfill its objective. The pharmaceutical business in India is significant in implementing the people's welfare state. Economic development in the sector, the availability of generic products, and robust competition are critical for India. After weighing the benefits and drawbacks of FDI in the Indian pharmaceutical industry, it has been determined that India needs sufficient FDI and its spillovers for the industry's development. The government has been engaged in developing policies to guarantee the industry's overall growth. Since 2001, 100 percent of FDI in the pharmaceutical industry has been permitted. This has benefited the pharmaceutical industry. MNCs bought as many as six major Indian companies between 2006 and 2010. This has not resulted in price increases or a scarcity of generic products. With skilled and inexpensive labor, India is a big prospective market for MNCs. However, worries about FDI in the pharmaceutical industry persist. Though the data do not indicate them, they may emerge over time (Bhogaraju et al., 2021; Seeja et al., 2021).

Some government supervision over FDI in the pharmaceutical industry was required. The Central Government has announced that FDI would be permitted via the FIPB clearance route for up to six months in instances of Brownfield investments in the pharmaceutical industry. During this time, the government would put the necessary enabling framework for supervision by the Indian Competition Commission. After six months, the Competition Commission of India (CCI) would oversee the process in line with the country's competition rules. The existing (FIPB) and planned (CCI)

Figure 1. Graphical representation of the sector

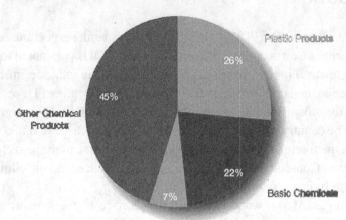

permission procedures seem to be a swiftness breaker for prospective unfamiliar investors since they may be required to demonstrate that they do not intend to collude or engage in predatory pricing or any other anti-competitive activity. If the government makes the needed changes and CCI's authority is expanded to cover all significant pharma acquisitions by MNCs, it will guarantee transparent competition in the pharma sector. The government may implement alternative public policies such as the public purchase of generic products and price control of critical medicines concerning the public interest. CCI, on the other hand, is a relatively new entity. Its knowledge is restricted to the industry's competitiveness. The Government of India has made a highly hopeful choice to enable CCI to be the watchdog of overall mergers and 43 acquisitions in the pharmaceutical sector. Still, it must guarantee essential changes to the Competition Act 2002 are made, and the commission's jurisdiction is expanded.

LITERATURE REVIEW

According to the results of an investigation into the function of artificial intelligence (AI) in the digital transformation of the pharmaceutical value chain, increased competitiveness in the pharmaceutical industry draws international investment. Increased healthcare expenditure, such as healthcare insurance policies and life insurance policies, leads to growth in the pharmaceutical sector, attracting investment. As a result, the Indian pharmaceutical industry remains an attractive location for international pharmaceutical firms and investors. The research is about an analytical analysis of foreign direct investment in India's pharmaceutical industry. However, India's current FDI laws need to be reviewed. The Indian government should also ensure that excessive foreign investment does not harm local businesses and enterprises (particularly those engaged in generic medication), the market, and the price of pharmaceuticals in India. In this respect, the present NDA government's startup policies, Pharma Vision 2020, and their effective execution are critical. In response to India's drive towards conformity with the World Trade Organization's intellectual property agreements, TRIPS, Multinational Corporates (MNCs) have boosted the amount and quality of FDI (FDI) in pharmaceutical Research & development (R&D) and production. On the other hand, MNCs have adopted a more cautious approach to breaking and marketing pharmaceutical products in India, waiting to monitor the interpretation of new regulations by Indian courts and patent agencies and adopt the exclusive data law (Dhar & Joseph, 2019; Jain & Rautela, 2018; Yadav, 2017).

However, policy should be designed to reduce, if not eliminate, any objections or disadvantages to FDI inflows into a nation. This is also necessary as 100% foreign direct investment in this sector is permitted. This "poses a direct threat to our overall health and IPR framework regarding access to medicines, affordability, advantages, and our congestion." Foreign Direct Investment (FDI) is a significant source of capital for many countries and foreign finance. The Research is being conducted over ten years, beginning in 2000-01 and ending in 2009-2010. The study's research shows that FDI does not affect the growth of pharmaceutical businesses as assessed by foreign currency earnings, sales, exports, profit, and assets. The author found that FDI in pharmaceutical companies did not affect the aggregate growth of selected financial parameters (Jain & Rautela, 2018; Joseph & Ranganathan, 2016; Safiuddin & Samad, 2015). A research on the issue and prospects of FDI inflows into the Indian pharmaceutical industry, Because FDI brings financial and managerial resources, access to vast markets, technical support, and strategic assets such as brand name, host companies gain local and international comparative advantages. It has been observed that there has been considerable potential for the concentration of FDI in the industry, especially in terms of export and profitability.

According to a study on Foreign Direct Investments in the Indian Pharmaceutical Industry, even though India has significantly liberalized its foreign investment policy, foreign direct investment inflows have remained significantly below objectives until recently. Market leaders in the pharmaceutical sector should increase their R&D spending. Academic cooperation would benefit the pharmaceutical industry in terms of drug development (Akhtar, 2014; Dhande & Magar, 2015; Mehta, 2012; Mudassir & Safiuddin, 2015).

According to "A Study of Foreign Direct Investment in the Indian Pharmaceutical Industry," the foreign direct investment method is the quickest, safest, and most effective way of bringing in the most current technology in India. India is a generics center that will draw significant FDI inflows in the following years. According to "Research on Foreign Direct Investment in the Indian Pharmaceutical Industry," foreign direct investment is the fastest, safest, and most efficient means of bringing in cutting-edge technology in India. India is a generics hub that will receive substantial FDI inflows in the following years. Greetings, Mr. Ronny Thomas. Research will attempt to illustrate India's chances in the liberalization of its economy since 1991. Furthermore, it will show how India has developed both socially and economically due to FDI promotion by comparing the country's record to that of other developing countries. Finally, it will demonstrate how foreign direct investment has aided India's infrastructure development projects and the difficulties the nation still confronts in delivering a quality of life equal to the developed world (Akhtar, 2014; Bergman, 2006; Dhande & Magar, 2015; Maathai, 2005; Mehta, 2012; Mudassir & Safiuddin, 2015).

The author researched FDI and its spillover effects in the Indian pharmaceutical sector. This study of FDI and its spillover effects on India's pharmaceutical industry. MNCs' horizontal productivity spillover effects on local Indian pharmaceutical companies are investigated, and possible transmission routes via which spillover effects may arise. The pharmaceutical sector is highly technical and capital demanding, and India is one of the few developing nations with a competitive advantage. A Study of Foreign Investment Trends in India's Healthcare Sector This suggests that hospitals and clinics in India have relied on private equity investors interested in making a quick buck and have no long-term plans for growth. This raises significant implications for the general population in a nation like India, where state investment in healthcare is minimal, and out-of-pocket healthcare expenditure is driving millions of people into poverty. The primary goal of this study is to investigate the long-run connection between Foreign Direct Investment (FDI) and Gross Output (GO), Export (EX), and Labour Productivity (LPR) in the Indian economy at the sectoral level using yearly data from 1990-91 to 2000-01 The Panel co-integration (PCONT) test is used in the Research, and the findings show that the flow of FDI into sectors has helped to increase production, labor productivity, and export in specific sectors, but a better role for FDI at the sectoral level is still anticipated. The findings also show no substantial cointegrating connection between variables such as FDI, GO, EX, and LPR in the economy's key sectors. We can conclude that the introduction of FDI at the sector level has not positively impacted the Indian economy (Bergman, 2006; Kathuria & Das, 2005; Maathai, 2005; Mehta, 2012; Pawar & Argade, n.d.). The author saw FDI as a conduit for MNCs to transmit their superior technical abilities and know-how to local businesses. Using firm-level data between 1996 and 2001, the study used the Probit and Tobit models to investigate the drivers of R&D. The Research found a substitution connection between technology imports and R&D. While the FDI's impact on Indian economic growth is higher, in his comparative

FDI study and economic development in the Indian and Bangladeshi economies, it is unacceptable. The multiple regression approach was used to estimate the influence of the FDI on the export performance of the Indian economy. Research has shown that FDI has no statistically meaningful impact on the Indian economy's export promotion (Akhtar, 2014; Bergman, 2006; Dhande & Magar, 2015; Dhar & Joseph, 2019; Kathuria & Das, 2005; Maathai, 2005; Mehta, 2012; Mudassir & Safiuddin, 2015).

HYPOTHESES OF THE STUDY

1. **Null Hypothesis:** There is no relationship between FDI investment in the Indian Economy and Pharmaceutical Sector Index.
2. **Alternative Hypothesis:** There exists an association between FDI acquisition in the Indian Economizing and Pharmaceutical Sector Index.
3. **Null Hypothesis:** FDI flows have no impact on the Indian Economy and Pharmaceutical Sector Index.
4. **Alternative Hypothesis:** FDI flows impact the Indian Economy and Pharmaceutical Sector Index.

RESEARCH METHODOLOGY

The study contains believed secondary data. The analysis predominantly concentrates on the association, consequence, and forthcoming tendency of the FDI with the Indian Economizing. *VECM:* The vector error Correction Model has been applied to know the long and short-run relationship of FDI with the Indian Economy. The present study has identified the relationship between the FDI with pharmaceutical sector and GDP.

Granger Causality Test: The granger causality is used to identify the cause-and-effect relationship between the two or more time series. It is given by (Granger, 1969), It only suggests that logic does not precede cause. Granger Causality is a method that helps determine whether one-time series is helpful to estimate another time series.

Ordinary Least Square: The Ordinary Least square method has been applied to examine the multiple independent variables on one dependent variable. The study has applied to know the effect of FDI flows on Indian Economy.

Stationary of the Data: The present study has considered the time series data of the FDI, GDP, and pharmaceutical sector data. Thus, both are observed to be

Table 1. Division Root examination with Augmented Dickey-Fuller

Variables	Grade	1st Distinction	2nd Distinction
FDI	0.001*	-	-
Pharmaceutical sector	0.002*	-	-
GDP	0.003*	-	-

Source: Secondary data

time-series data and applied to the Augmented Dickey-Fuller test. Below is the result depicting the result of stationary of selected variables.

SCOPE OF THE STUDY

The exploration primarily focused on the connection between FDI acquisitions with the Indian Scrimping, and contemplation has regarded secondary data. The study has been considered to be the secondary data for 2011-2020, i.e., ten years. The introspection endeavored to examine the linkage and result of FDI assets on the Indian Economy and has also tried to indicate India's future tendency on FDI flows.

DATA ANALYSIS

Objective 1: To determine the relationship of FDI investments with the Indian Economy and Pharmaceutical Sector Index

The analysis remarked on the division root examination outcome under the Augmented Dickey-Fuller test for FDI cruises on the Indian Economizing. This introspection consequence revealed that FDI stands at Rank as the P-value is significant at the 5% level. The Pharmaceutical sector and GDP stand substantial in the Grade test as the p values stood effective at 5%, i.e., 0.002 and 0.003. Consequently, three of the variables are contended to be stagnant. Therefore, these variables are suitable for research intents.

H0: There exists no association between the FDI investments and the Indian Economy.
H1: There exists an association between the FDI investments and the Indian Economy.

The above examination reveals step 1 of the vector misconception correction standard. Here, the outcomes indicate that the Lag order section is at lag one and declares there is a subsequent step steered with the implementation of lag 1 in vector

Table 2. VAR lag order selection criteria of FDI with the Pharmaceutical sector

VAR Lag Order Selection Criteria						
Endogenous variables: FDI PHARMA Exogenous variables: C Sample: 1 17 Included observations: 10						
Lag	LogL	LR	FPE	AIC	SC	HQ
0	-384.8250	NA*	3.43e+18*	48.35313*	48.44970*	48.35808*
1	-383.0714	2.849633	4.58e+18	48.63393	48.92365	48.64876

* indicates lag order selected by the criterion
LR: sequential modified LR test statistic (each test at 5% level)
FPE: Finalpredictionerror
AIC: Akaikeinformationcriterion
SC: Schwarz information criterion
HQ: HannanQuinn information criterion

mistake estimations. Lag 1 is marked by the number of leads obtained for LR, FPR, AIC, SC, and HQ

The analysis has demonstrated the vector mistake estimations in the second step of VECM; here, the result specifies the positive connection between the FDI and the Pharmaceutical sector. Thus, the coefficient significance is 0.107719, i.e., positive. The research has also resulted in an r-square value of more than 0.6 means that the model is influential. Hence, there is a good connection between foreign direct investment and the pharmaceutical sector.

H0: There is no long-run association between FDI and with Pharmaceutical sector.
H1: There is a long-run association between FDI and with Pharmaceutical sector.

The analysis has explained the affinity between FDI investments and with Pharmaceutical sector. The review has been observed to be having a positive short-run association since the chi-square value tends to be less than the critical value. The examination indicates a meaningful connection between FDI and the pharmaceutical sector. The p-value tends to be less than 0.05, i.e., 0.0129.

FDI VS GDP

The above study indicates step 1 of the vector error correction model. Here, the results suggest that Lag order selection is at lag 0, stating there is a next step headed with the implication of lag 0 in vector error estimates. Lag 0 is determined by the number of stars denoted for LR, FPR, AIC, SC, and HQ.

Table 3. Vector Error Estimates of FDI with Pharmaceutical sector

Vector Error Correction Estimates		
Date: 07/20/21 Time: 15:09		
Sample (adjusted): 3 17		
Included observations: 15 after adjustments		
Standard errors in () & t-statistics in [ ]		
CointegratingEq	**CointEq1**	
FDI(-1)	1.000000	
PHARMA(-1)	0.074284	
	(0.09221)	
	[0.80558]	
C	-20559.09	
Error Correction	**D(FDI)**	**D(PHARMA)**
CointEq1	-0.872855	-4.073711
	(0.33415)	(3.17058)
	[-2.61220]	[-1.28485]
D(FDI(-1))	-0.020552	1.726444
	(0.28459)	(2.70033)
	[-0.07222]	[0.63935]
D(PHARMA(-1))	0.107719	-0.914050
	(0.04268)	(0.40498)
	[2.52385]	[-2.25702]
C	-2040.056	30731.65
	(3791.24)	(35973.7)
	[-0.53810]	[0.85428]
R-squared	0.604498	0.89974
Adj. R-squared	0.693621	0.78148
Sum sq. resides	2.01E+09	1.81E+11
S.E. equation	13522.11	128306.4
F-statistic	3.733242	5.275850
Log-likelihood	-161.6391	-195.3906
Akaike AIC	22.08522	26.58541
Schwarz SC	22.27403	26.77422
Mean dependent	1646.267	264.9511
S.D. dependent	17027.63	177613.0
Determinant resid covariance (of adj.)		2.92E+18
Determinant resid covariance		1.57E+18
Log-likelihood		-356.8104
Akaike information criterion		48.90805
Schwarz criterion		49.38008
Number of coefficients		10

Table 4. Wald test of FDI with Pharmaceutical sector

Wald Test			
System: %system			
Test Statistic	**Value**	**df**	**Probability**
Chi-square	8.702370	2	0.0129
Null Hypothesis: C(1)=C(3)=0			
Null Hypothesis Summary:			
Normalized Restriction (= 0)		**Value**	**Std. Err.**
C(1)		-0.872855	0.334145
C(3)		0.107719	0.042681
Restrictions are linear in coefficients.			

The analysis has demarcated the vector error estimations in the second step of VECM; here, the outcomes indicate the positive association between the FDI and Gross domestic product. Here the coefficient significance is observed to be 33416.04, i.e., optimistic. The examination has also resulted in an r-square value of more than 0.6 means that the model is influential. Therefore, there is a positive affinity between foreign direct investment and gross domestic product (GDP).

The analysis has examined the affinity between FDI acquisitions and the Indian Economy, i.e., GDP. The examination has been marked to be having a positive short-run association since the chi-square value tends to be less than the critical value,

Table 5. VAR lag order selection criteria of FDI with the Gross domestic product (GDP)

VAR Lag Order Selection Criteria						
Endogenous variables: FDI GDP Exogenous variables: C Date: 06/16/21 Time: 12:43 Sample: 1 10 Included observations: 10						
Lag	**LogL**	**LR**	**FPE**	**AIC**	**SC**	**HQ**
0	-520.7682	NA*	8.22e+25*	65.34602*	65.44259*	65.35097*
1	-518.3986	3.850525	1.02e+26	65.54983	65.83955	65.56466

* indicates lag order selected by the criterion
LR: sequential modified LR test statistic (each test at 5% level)
FPE: Finalpredictionerror
AIC: Akaikeinformationcriterion
SC: Schwarzinformationcriterion
HQ: HannanQuinn information criterion

Table 6. Vector Error Estimates of FDI with the Gross domestic product (GDP)

Vector Error Correction Estimates		
Date: 06/16/21 Time: 12:43		
Sample (adjusted): 3 10		
Included observations: 10 after adjustments		
Standard errors in () & t-statistics in [ ]		
CointegratingEq	**CointEq1**	
FDI(-1)	1.000000	
	2.55E-05	
GDP(-1)	(1.2E-05)	
	[2.15681]	
C	-19958.86	
Error Correction	**D(FDI)**	**D(GDP)**
	-0.516608	-16674.29
CointEq1	(0.28765)	(14397.4)
	[-1.79594]	[-1.15814]
	-0.266162	33416.04
D(FDI(-1))	(0.25230)	(12628.0)
	[-1.05494]	[2.64619]
	2.08E-06	-0.144131
D(GDP(-1))	(6.0E-06)	(0.29866)
	[0.34871]	[-0.48259]
	1785.724	-717875.7
C	(3875.71)	(1.9E+08)
	[0.46075]	[-0.00370]
R-squared	0.390122	0.542218
Adj. R-squared	0.223792	0.417368
Sum sq. resides	2.48E+09	6.20E+18
S.E. equation	15001.80	7.51E+08
F-statistic	2.345468	4.342964
Log-likelihood	-163.1968	-325.5088
Akaike AIC	22.29291	43.93451
Schwarz SC	22.48172	44.12333
Mean dependent	1646.267	16793331
S.D. dependent	17027.63	9.84E+08
Determinant resid covariance (of adj.)		1.04E+26
Determinant resid covariance		5.61E+25
Log-likelihood		-487.2344
Akaike information criterion		66.29792
Schwarz criterion		66.76996
Number of coefficients		10

Table 7. Wald test of FDI with the Gross domestic product (GDP)

Wald Test:			
System: %system			
Test Statistic	**Value**	**df**	**Probability**
Chi-square	5.007400	2	0.0218
Null Hypothesis: C(1)=C(3)=0			
Null Hypothesis Summary:			
Normalized Restriction (= 0)		**Value**	**Std. Err.**
C(1)		-0.516608	0.287654
C(3)		2.08E-06	5.97E-06
Restrictions are linear in coefficients.			

i.e., 5.007<5.991. The investigation implies a significant association between FDI and the Indian economy, i.e., GDP.

Objective: To know the effect of FDI flows on the Indian Economy and Pharmaceutical sector.

H0: There is no directional outcome between FDI and the Pharmaceutical sector
H1: There is a directional outcome between FDI and the Pharmaceutical sector

The table examined the unidirectional effect of the FDI on the pharmaceutical sector. The study estimated the p-value lesser than 0.05, meaning a positive influence between them and one side effect of FDI on the pharmaceutical industry. The results imply the number of observations as ten and the f-statistic value as 0.78410. Thus, it indicates a directional effect between the FDI (Foreign Direct Investment) and the Indian Economy, i.e., the pharmaceutical sector.

Table 8. Granger Causality Tests concerning FDI and Pharmaceutical sector

Pairwise Granger Causality Tests			
Date: 07/20/21 Time: 15:20			
Sample: 1 17			
Lags: 2			
Null Hypothesis	**Obs**	**F-Statistic**	**Prob.**
PHARMA does not Granger Cause FDI	10	0.78410	0.0427
FDI does not Granger Cause PHARMA		1.15339	0.3542

Table 9. Impact of FDI on the Pharmaceutical sector.

Dependent Variable: FDI Method: Least Squares Date: 07/20/21 Time: 15:25 Sample: 1 17 Included observations: 17				
Variable	**Coefficient**	**Std. Error**	**t-Statistic**	**Prob.**
C	15625.03	3633.065	4.300785	0.0006
PHARMA	0.001134	0.026187	0.043291	0.0460
Required	0.000125	Meandependentvar		15695.59
Adjusted R-squared	-0.066533	S.D.dependentvar		12963.28
S.E. of regression	13387.58	Akaikeinfocriterion		21.95217
Sum squared resid	2.69E+09	Schwarz criterion		22.05020
Loglikelihood	-184.5935	Hannan-Quinn criteria.		21.96192
F-statistic	0.001874	Durbin-Watson stat		1.540854
Prob(F-statistic)	0.966040			

H0: There is no effect of FDI flows on the pharmaceutical sector.
H1: There is an effect of FDI flows pharmaceutical sector.

The study above determines the effect of the FDI on the pharmaceutical sector. The study results have derived a positive influence, i.e., the coefficient value of 0.001134. The p-value is lesser than 0.05, meaning that the variables are significant. The independent variable is the pharmaceutical sector, and the dependent variable is FDI. The study has evaluated that FDI is being increased through the rise of the pharmaceutical industry. The study has implied a positive impact of the pharmaceutical sector on the dependent variable, i.e., FDI.

H0: There is no directional effect between FDI and the Indian Economy (GDP).
H1: There is a directional effect between FDI and the Indian Economy (GDP).

The table explains the unidirectional effect of the FDI on GDP. Here, it is estimated the p-value is lesser than 0.05, meaning that there is a positive influence between them and one side effect from FDI on the Indian economy, i.e., GDP. The results indicate the number of observations as ten and the f-statistic value as 0.0283. Hence, it implies a directional effect on the FDI (Foreign Direct Investment) and the Indian Economy, i.e., Gross domestic product.

The analysis above specifies the consequence of the FDI upon the Gross domestic product, that is, the Indian Economy factor. The examination results have

Table 10. Granger Causality Tests concerning FDI and Indian Economy (GDP)

Pairwise Granger Causality Tests			
Date: 06/16/21 Time: 12:59			
Sample: 1 17			
Lags: 2			
Null Hypothesis	**Obs**	**F-Statistic**	**Prob.**
GDP does not Granger Cause FDI	10	0.43600	0.0283
FDI does not Granger Cause GDP		1.32487	0.3087

derived a positive outcome, i.e., with the coefficient value of 2.9406. The p-value is more deficient than 0.05, meaning the independent variables are significant. The independent variable is GDP, and the dependent variable is FDI. The investigation has evaluated that FDI is rising through the rise of the GDP investments, and leverage plots are marked to increase their values. The research has implied an optimistic influence of the GDP flows on the Indian Economy, i.e., FDI.

Table 11. Gross domestic product impact on the Indian economy

Dependent Variable: FDI Method: Least Squares Date: 06/16/21 Time: 13:00 Sample: 1 10 Included observations: 10				
Variable	**Coefficient**	**Std. Error**	**t-Statistic**	**Prob.**
C	16201.82	3337.878	4.853927	0.0002
GDP	2.94E-06	5.25E-06	-0.561071	0.0030
R-squared	0.020555	Meandependentvar		15695.59
Adjusted R-squared	-0.044741	S.D. dependent var		12963.28
S.E. of regression	13250.10	Akaikeinfocriterion		21.93153
Sumsquaredresid	2.63E+09	Schwarz criterion		22.02955
Loglikelihood	-184.4180	HannanQuinncriter.		21.94127
F- statistic	0.314801	Durbin Watson stat		1.518660
Prob(F-statistic)	0.003034			

RESULTS AND FINDINGS OF THE STUDY

The analysis has found a long-run affinity between the FDI investments in the pharmaceutical sector with the p-value of 0.0129 and the coefficient value is 8.702370. When observed in the FDI to GDP, it tends to be a meaningful and long-term relationship.

1. The analysis demonstrates that GDP and the Pharmaceutical sector positively influence foreign direct investment, and the coefficient value of GDP is observed to be more than the pharmaceutical sector. Here, it implies that as GDP rises, FDI also increases and vice-versa.
2. The study has observed a positive increase in the further years for the GDP with the influence of Foreign direct investment through the survey.

Inference

1. Indian Pharmaceutical continues to leverage recent developments in biotechnology and IT for future markets, product commercialization, risk diversification across multiple regions, future and backward integration capabilities and R& D activities, merger integrations, and acquisitions'-marketing and licensing agreements.
2. R&D activities have been taken back by most domestic pharmaceutical companies. Indian companies must change their direction and invest heavily in R & D – AI and Machine learning to remain competitive in the future (Bhogaraju & Korupalli, 2020).
3. FDI inflows into the Indian pharmaceutical sector should improve the performance of profits and increase the efficiency of FDI-focused companies.

CONCLUSION

In the global pharmaceutical industry, India is prominent and rapidly expanding. It provides 20% of the world's global supply and supplies 62% of the worldwide demand for vaccines. It is the world's largest supplier of generic medicines. It is time to invest in this future for all stakeholders, government, academia, and industry so that the Indian government can achieve its target of becoming a $5 trillion economy in 2025. The current analysis analyzed the consequence of FDI on the Indian Economy in the Pharmaceutical sector. The examination has identified a good association between the FDI in the Pharmaceutical industry and FDI with gross domestic product. The results imply the positive effect of FDI has increased the pharmaceutical sector and the positive impact of FDI on GDP. It also concluded that there would be a future positive movement in the GDP with the effect of FDI. It is also supposed that the new drug industry will grow healthier as R&D expenditure increases significantly and new drug launches are proposed. Thus, for multinational companies and investors, the Indian pharmaceutical sector continues to be an attractive destination.

REFERENCES

Akhtar, G. (2014). Problem and Prospect of FDI Inflows in Indian Pharmaceutical Industry. *IOSR Journal Of Humanities And Social Science*, *19*(3), 69–73. doi:10.9790/0837-19316973

Bergman, A. (2006). *FDI and spillover effects in the Indian pharmaceutical industry.* Academic Press.

Bhogaraju, S. D., & Korupalli, V. R. K. (2020). Design of Smart Roads-A Vision on Indian Smart Infrastructure Development. *2020 International Conference on COMmunication Systems & NETworkS (COMSNETS)*, 773–778. 10.1109/COMSNETS48256.2020.9027404

Bhogaraju, S. D., Kumar, K. V. R., Anjaiah, P., Shaik, J. H., & ... (2021). Advanced Predictive Analytics for Control of Industrial Automation Process. In *Innovations in the Industrial Internet of Things (IIoT) and Smart Factory* (pp. 33–49). IGI Global.

Dhande, N. C., & Magar, A. V. (2015). A Study of Foreign Direct Investment in Indian Pharmaceutical Industry. *International Journal (Toronto, Ont.)*, *3*(7).

Dhar, B., & Joseph, R. K. (2019). India's information technology industry: A tale of two halves. In *Innovation, Economic Development, and Intellectual Property in India and China* (pp. 93–117). Springer.

Granger, C. W. (1969). Some recent developments in a concept of causality. *Journal of Econometrics, 39*.

Jain, H., & Rautela, M. (2018). *FDI in Indian pharmaceutical sector.* Available at SSRN 3153434.

Joseph, R. K., & Ranganathan, K. V. K. (2016). *Trends in Foreign Investment in Healthcare Sector of India.* ISID Working Paper No. 187. Institute for Studies in Industrial Development (ISID).

Kathuria, V., & Das, S. (2005). Impact of FDI on R\&D strategies of firms in the post-1991 era. *IIMB Management Review*, *17*(2), 17–28.

Maathai, K. D. (2005). *Mathiyazhagan, Impact of foreign direct investment on Indian economy: A sectoral level analysis*. Academic Press.

Mehta, R. (2012). *The role of FDI in Indian growth and infrastructure development*. Academic Press.

Mudassir, M. M., & Safiuddin, S. K. (2015). Does digital marketing replace the personal selling: An empirical study of the marketers. *International Journal of Management Research and Reviews*, *5*(12), 1142.

Pawar, M. M., & Argade, N. (n.d.). *Impact of foreign direct investment on drugs & pharmaceuticals industry: An Indian outlook*. Academic Press.

Safiuddin, S. K., & Samad, M. A. (2015). Impact of FDI on the Growth of Selected Pharmaceutical Firms-An Aggregate Analysis. *Sumedha Journal of Management*, *4*(3), 47.

Seeja, G., Reddy, O., Kumar, K. V. R., Mounika, S., & ... (2021). Internet of Things and Robotic Applications in the Industrial Automation Process. In *Innovations in the Industrial Internet of Things (IIoT) and Smart Factory* (pp. 50–64). IGI Global.

Yadav, D. V. (2017). An Analytical Study of Foreign Direct Investment in Pharma Sector of India. *International Journal of Law*, *3*(5), 40–42.

Chapter 12

Local Brand Impact During COVID-19

Sai Sreeja Nainala
Woxsen University, India

Snehamayee Gowribidanur Matam
Woxsen University, India

ABSTRACT

This chapter explores the role of local brands during the COVID-19 pandemic, the expansion of SMEs all throughout the pandemic, and the needs for all start-ups during the pandemic. The authors have also done research and written about how startups and small businesses have adapted to and used digitalization. This chapter will discuss the effects of regional brands during a pandemic.

INTRODUCTION

Pandemic! We've all been through too many challenging times and the quarantine. Industries are being severely impacted by this pandemic. During an outbreak, many people favor locally produced goods over imported ones. Everyone has encountered supply shortages, and during that period, many local businesses entered the market, overtaking the established brands and earning profit. In terms of market growth, economic conditions, and market competitiveness, consumers are the primary market drivers. Everyone saw how consumer purchasing behaviors and decision-making changed as a result of the pandemic (Mehta et al., 2020).

The primary cause of the rise in local brands is the lack of a sufficient supply of brand products globally. Production was halted due to pandemics and lockdowns; as

DOI: 10.4018/978-1-6684-4246-3.ch012

a result, there was a shortage of goods; as a result, customers turned to local brands, which led to an increase in local brand sales (Christa et al., 2021).

Covid-19 had a significant impact on business sales, the worldwide market experienced various issues, and several nations' economies experienced significant declines. Due to their losses, the business owners began to close their doorways. Online sales eventually increased, but because of lockdown in several countries, the supply chain was impacted, and both buyers and sellers experienced issues with the delivery of the products (Fairlie et al., 2022). For the local firms, being able to ship their goods within the price range they were producing has been a great benefit.

When compared to the pharmaceutical and medical industries, sectors like tourism, manufacturing,

vehicles, construction, restaurants, retail, IT, and airlines had been more negatively impacted. Except for healthcare, practically all types of enterprises had closed due to COVID-19.

Changes in Consumer Decision Making and Expectations and Purchase Behaviour During Covid-19

Consumer perceptions, behavior intentions, and purchasing decisions are not constant; they change in response to the circumstances of the moment. Consumers are also impacted by the trends and events that are taking place in the actual world. Consumer motivation has shifted as a result of the pandemic, increasing the sensation of deliberate consumption. The fear of the economy failing must have been one of the elements influencing decision-making because it inspired customers to purchase the goods they needed and to use them responsibly (Vázquez-Mart\'\inez et al., 2021), (Kim et al., 2022).

The pandemic had many people in fragile mental states, thus consumers sought human touch from any medium. Online buyers likely assumed that the chatbot-generated messages would have a human touch because they were missing out on actual emotions while away from their families. Consumers have always viewed online buying as self-service, and they were drawn in by the personalized texts that were automatically generated (Westerman, 2022). Since income level significantly influences consumers' motivation to buy, Covid 19 has had an influence on customers' purchasing decisions. During the crisis, many individuals lost their jobs, and the economy was shaken by lower per capita income, which affected consumer choices. Markets had difficulty collecting sales value, which eventually resulted in the major breakdown. The fundamental driving force behind consumers' motivation and purchasing choices has always been their way of life and economic level (Usunier et al., 2007).

Market Trends During Covid-19

During the pandemic, markets were penetrated, numerous trends emerged, and preexisting trends lost their significance. After the epidemic, MSMEs and other small businesses started to go digital. Many small and medium-sized firms began modernizing their operations technologically as soon as the government unveiled the "no human interaction" programmed in the midst of the economic crisis. Prior to the pandemic, the majority of businesses adopted digital payment methods utilizing UPI IDs. However, even small businesses switched to digital payment methods after the Covid-19 outbreak, using services like Google Pay, Phonepe, Paytm, BHIM, Paypal, etc.

Online purchasing has grown throughout the pandemic, and people have started setting up online profiles. Numerous small businesses set up their own websites and began marketing their goods on social media sites like Instagram, Facebook, YouTube, and others. Numerous young people have launched their own clothing lines, retail businesses, and accessory suppliers, and they have begun shipping their goods all over India.

Since there was a manpower constraint during the epidemic, supply chain logistics were altered. Businesses started employing software that periodically updates information on the track of supplies and became totally digital for keeping track of their inventory. The primary shift that occurred during the pandemic was the decrease in theatrical releases, while OTT platforms like Netflix, Amazon Prime Video, Hotstar, Sony Liv, etc. saw a rise in subscribers and significant financial gains.

How Prominent Brands Affected During Covid -19

Several people, businesses, families, and industries suffered by COVID-19. However, several well-known companies also encountered numerous issues throughout the epidemic. The performance of the corporations was poor, and the net growth of many industries had decreased. It led to the business's closure, winding up, and bankruptcy. People have seen the effects of the pandemic firsthand all around the world. Less amenities were offered to the populace. The stock market had experienced a significant decline; many businesses had lost their shares because of a lack of funding and declining sales. The government's decision to declare a state of emergency and impose a curfew on numerous countries had a significant impact on the large corporations.

Despite the problems faced by various businesses, including the automotive, construction, tourist, manufacturing, aviation, retail, and restaurant sectors. However, subscriptions to internet streaming services like Netflix, Amazon Prime, Hotstar, Sony liv, and others had increased significantly. As everything moved online, whether it be for business or educational purposes, video meeting platforms like Zoom, Microsoft Teams, Google Meet, etc., also profited from the epidemic.

Case Study: The pandemic had a significant impact on stores, including Tailored Brands, the parent company of Men's Warehouse and jobs. Initially, this business had close to 500 outlets and ran smoothly and profitably. The company's financial situation was altered by Covid-19, and as a result, the company incurred bank debt. To get back on track, customized brands took on approximately $365 million in exit term loans in August 2020 and closed about 500 outlets in order to pay off $686 million in debt (Morris, 2021).

Pharmaceuticals vs. Other Industries

Coronavirus outbreak in 2019 had a significant impact on a number of businesses. The healthcare and pharmaceutical industries were primarily affected by COVID. During the pandemic, pharmaceutical items were in crisis. People became cautious and began purchasing medications for the disease, which caused a supply and demand issue. However, the sales that occurred during the epidemic helped the health care sector make a lot of money (Ayati et al., 2020).

Curfews and lockdowns caused a lot of problems for non-pharmaceutical industries. Production was halted, and many companies had issues making sales. This had a detrimental influence on the global economy and decreased the non-pharmaceutical industries' share of the global market. (Hu et al., 2021) Airlines primarily encountered issues because many nations restricted foreign travelers and discouraged cross-border travel. This resulted in significant losses for the airlines and the loss of many employments.

Because more individuals started working from home and as a result held meetings online, OTT platforms and online video meeting applications made much more money than they did before COVID, excluding from non-pharmaceuticals. Education institutions have also begun offering online courses.

How Local Brands Impacted Consumer Purchase Choice Over Big Brand Products

People were afraid to visit malls, massive super stores, and other public locations since there were so many people there during the pandemic. This resulted in a decline in sales at large retailers and supermarkets. People were looking for the neighboring Kirana stores and purchased the goods, which astonished them with extremely high quality, cleanliness, and purity. People started to favor localized brands over national ones (Landa, 2021).

The largest issue for the leading brands during the epidemic was logistics, which made it more difficult for them to supply and distribute their goods. As a result of the stock shortages in the hypermarkets, consumers were compelled to shop locally. Purchase preferences have shifted from big brands to regional ones.

Independent retailers embraced digitalization; they started to accept UPI payments, take and deliver online orders, and embrace new technologies. All of these factors encouraged companies to continue with local brands.

Case study- The case study by Velicia Ferren Widjaja, Rionaldi Budianto, and Doni Purnama Alamsyah from 2021 demonstrates that local businesses in Indonesia are severely impacted by the pandemic. Since starting a business is regarded to provide a solid income, numerous start-ups entered the Indonesian market by 2019. As a result, several people in Indonesia wish to left their jobs and pursue entrepreneurial. The pandemic's first effects on business were not nearly as severe as in other regions because of their excessive number of small firms. The Indonesian government forbade citizens from leaving the country unless strictly necessary. This led to losses in the transportation and hospitality businesses. Industries saw financial success when the government permitted people to leave whenever they needed to. The researchers concluded that while a small number of businesses generated profits, a minor number of industries and brands made a loss and filed for bankruptcy. It is a wise decision and has many advantages that many local firms had embraced digitization and gone online. During the crisis, many businesses had obstacles with their business models and began to change their business models and marketing techniques in order to benefit from the situation in the present, increase the company's worth, and create wealth. The economy of Indonesia grew as a result.

How SME'S Number Increased During Covid -19

People started their enterprises as a result of the pandemic. As a result, between April and June 2021, almost 17200 start-ups are launched. In 2021, business owners will conduct a survey to learn why people start new companies amid pandemics. People responded that the pandemic is the right time for their company or organization as they have opportunity and time to focus on their start-up and they additionally see there is a possibilities to their business in the pandemic as people have time and many established businesses are failing in stocking the products, this is a gap where there is start-ups can fit in.

The percent of start-ups pick B2C since during the pandemic, buyers had greater needs and requirements for items like clothing, home goods, software apps, and advertising. Customers got time, and they spend more of it online. As a result, practically all start-ups adopted a simple and efficient digital strategy (Keh et al., 2001).

In India, a significant number of small businesses choose to sell their products and services online, particularly on Instagram. Their Instagram influencer marketing, videos, and advertising captured consumers. Incredibly, 44 Indian start-ups became unicorns in 2021. Even if there were more SME's

during the epidemic in India, it was extremely hard for them to tackle some issues. The SMEs have numerous issues, and it was somewhat challenging for them to tackle them all. To make their company steady and prosperous, they must work on these. For SMEs, handling capital is both a tough challenge and an essential one. The protection of their business and finances is something that SMEs must work on because cybercrime instances are on the rise these days. As a result, it is important for small and medium-sized businesses to concentrate more on their economic freedom as payments and transactions move online. Companies must be explicit about the amounts their need in order for banks to lend to them. Since every business will have unique financial needs, businesses should think about borrowing the money before accepting a bank loan. Notwithstanding being a long-term loan, the interest rate is still rather expensive. As a result, businesses need to be mindful of the perceptions of financial institutions and banks.

Does Local Kirana Stores Will Continue to Be Dominated by Large Supermarkets and E- Commerce

E-commerce brought huge problems for Kirana businesses. The local Kirana has traditionally been dominated by e-commerce owing to its modern technology and digitization. However, during the pandemic, nearly all neighboring Kirana stores developed technologies and went digital. Due to e-commerce and supermarket delivery delays during the pandemic, this helped companies draw in customers. Consumers were made to feel protected, sanitary, and secure by the local Kirana's home delivery service during the pandemic. And when it comes to any other businesses besides Kirana stores, clients were more drawn to their goods and services during the pandemic at nice house bakers and clothing shops.

I hate to confess that the pandemic also performed some positive things. Nonetheless, we are witnessing a variety of positive improvements that have occurred and continue to occur as a result of Kirana stores as well as other small- and medium-sized businesses implementing digitalization, which was not the case prior to the pandemic.

As local businesses and Kirana's innovate and adopt new technology, we must support them. For them, digitization is the initial step. We must force learners to recognize a wide range of topics, including planograms, goods assortments, and numerous others (Widjaja et al., 2021). It's a beneficial move that Kirana's and other general stores sell goods in reaction to clients who are present on their site. Luxury goods cannot be sold in urban or slum areas. They have a consumer product list. Therefore, if they adopt other tactics and learn a few new things such planograms and assortations, they will certainly be dominated by this group of major e-commerce shops.

If they don't receive any commodities, consumers normally switch to another e-channel, but for local Kirana's, switching to another shop is not common or routine. Consequently, there is a good probability that neighboring shops will continue to make money, flourish, and draw in new consumers (Hu et al., 2021). Local Kirana stores can easily adapt their products to consumers' multiple changes in their purchasing behavior since it is much easier for them to do so than for huge e-retailers. Customers' wants and demands in products typically vary rapidly.

I can't be sure that Kirana stores will keep taking over the large supermarkets, but I can guarantee that they won't be adversely harmed. Future earnings and sales for Kirana stores will tend to be positive.

Vocal for Local Campaigns by Brands

It is crucial to support homegrown goods and services because doing so has many rewards and stimulates the economy of our nation. Almost all brands have adopted this and conducted numerous marketing initiatives focused on local voices. This was a great success and affected a lot of people. In many nations, fostering local products and inspiring others to follow suit has been done and is being done. Here are a few instances of outspoken local marketing initiatives from various countries.

NIKE

Nike excels in marketing. It ran a regional advertising campaign in London dubbed "Nothing Beats a Londoner." They created a campaign in which all the Londoners from the area have been seen participating in sports and other activities that Londoners often engage in, such as football, basketball, skating, swimming, ice hockey, scatting, tennis, etc. This promotional campaign was a resounding success.

H&M

In Amsterdam, H&M ran a small-scale marketing campaign titled "The new recipe." H&M canvassed Amsterdam residents for this campaign to get their opinions on the stores. Then they came up with the idea of recycling the used clothes that their customers brought in and starting renting out their clothing; this campaign was a big success and well-liked by the locals. They appreciated the move toward ecology that renting clothes and recycling them represented. Renting is an option for those who cannot afford the clothes. With posters and commercials on social media channels, several Indian firms took part in the #voice for local advertising campaign.

A few Indian marketing campaigns are listed below

- **Parle**: "Swadeshi" delicious snacks made by Indians for Indians. And mentioned we were Indians and will always.
- **Balaji wafers**: "snack local be vocal". And mentioned "We sure are local and our crunchy snacks will make you go vocal!".
- **Chai Kappi**: They have made a post where they describe images of transparent glasses of Indian chai and opaque glasses of coffee with the words "swadeshi and vidheshi" on them.
- **Dabur honey**: "Naturally Health, Naturally Indian".

Start-Ups During Covid-19

During the pandemic, numerous small- and medium-sized businesses emerged. It's necessary and difficult to tell people about company brand. It may seem difficult to target your customer, but the digital age has made it much easier for brands to connect with consumers. Due to their youth, start-ups are more adaptable and can adjust and respond to changes more easily. Most all small-scale businesses pick social media, particularly Instagram, as their marketing tool. They have marketed their goods through reels, hashtags, ads, and Instagram influencer marketing. Because everyone had more time to use social media during the pandemic than at previous times, brands took advantage of this and had a significant impact on customers. Customers have difficulty trusting the brands since there were too many start-ups during the pandemic. Nowadays, having an online presence is crucial for any brand to succeed. Because buyers now trust companies with websites, many small brands have websites as well. Beginning businesses found everything to be simple thanks to digitalization.

During the pandemic, there were little changes in consumer preference, shopping patterns, and habits.

Start-ups saw these possibilities and seized them to establish their businesses. Due to their youth, start-ups find this simple, but non-startups find it challenging. People are supporting the start-ups because, so few local start-ups were thriving internationally.

Here are few Sri Lankan stary-ups who gained global recognition and appreciation.

- **Telehealth Sector**: Odoc, Mydoc
- **Delivery platforms**: Simplex, Grasshopper
- **E-learning**: Siplo, Online accounting

- **Online shopping**: Takas.lk, Catchme.lk
- **FinTech**: DirectPlay, OgoPay, Iloan, HeliosP2P
- **Food and Agtech:** Sozo, Spectrify.AI, Honest Greens, Ananta Sustainable

Start-ups provide employment to people and this also helped in the economy of the country.

CONCLUSION

Local brands were significantly affected by Pandemic and were forced to move digital, which helped them become highly successful. We can't be certain if local brands or supermarkets will predominate because we understand the market is dynamic and difficult to predict. In the end, it doesn't seem whether a company is a tiny or large brand—all rather than how well they use the online to meet the requirements and wishes of their customers. People saw the pandemic as a chance to begin their own business, and many SMEs have emerged in the previous two years. The growth of start-ups is beneficial for the economy of the country and for the promotion of regional goods. Although certain industries, including as tourism, hospitality, and travel, had numerous difficulties and loses as a result of the epidemic, others, including such pharmaceuticals, online learning, telemedicine, etc., saw huge opportunity. Though local brands have their pros and negatives, local brands are generally more successful.

REFERENCES

Ayati, N., Saiyarsarai, P., & Nikfar, S. (2020). Short and long term impacts of COVID-19 on the pharmaceutical sector. *Daru: Journal of Faculty of Pharmacy, Tehran University of Medical Sciences*, 28(2), 799–805. doi:10.100740199-020-00358-5 PMID:32617864

Christa, U., & Kristinae, V. (2021). The effect of product innovation on business performance during COVID 19 pandemic. *Uncertain Supply Chain Management*, 9(1), 151–158. doi:10.5267/j.uscm.2020.10.006

Fairlie, R., & Fossen, F. M. (2022). The early impacts of the COVID-19 pandemic on business sales. *Small Business Economics*, 58(4), 1853–1864. doi:10.100711187-021-00479-4

Hu, S., Xiong, C., Yang, M., Younes, H., Luo, W., & Zhang, L. (2021). A big-data driven approach to analyzing and modeling human mobility trend under non-pharmaceutical interventions during COVID-19 pandemic. *Transportation Research Part C, Emerging Technologies, 124*, 102955. doi:10.1016/j.trc.2020.102955 PMID:33456212

Keh, H. T., & Shieh, E. (2001). Online grocery retailing: Success factors and potential pitfalls. *Business Horizons, 44*(4), 73–83. doi:10.1016/S0007-6813(01)80050-1

Kim, J., Yang, K., Min, J., & White, B. (2022). Hope, fear, and consumer behavioral change amid COVID-19: Application of protection motivation theory. *International Journal of Consumer Studies, 46*(2), 558–574. doi:10.1111/ijcs.12700 PMID:34220343

Landa, R. (2021). *Advertising by design: Generating and designing creative ideas across media*. John Wiley & Sons.

Mehta, S., Saxena, T., & Purohit, N. (2020). The new consumer behaviour paradigm amid COVID-19: Permanent or transient? *Journal of Health Management, 22*(2), 291–301. doi:10.1177/0972063420940834

Morris, A. N. (2021). Small Business Debt in the Age of COVID-19. *Am. Bankr. Inst. L. Rev., 29*, 131.

Usunier, J.-C., & Cestre, G. (2007). Product ethnicity: Revisiting the match between products and countries. *Journal of International Marketing, 15*(3), 32–72. doi:10.1509/jimk.15.3.32

Vázquez-Martinez, U. J., Morales-Mediano, J., & Leal-Rodriguez, A. L. (2021). The impact of the COVID-19 crisis on consumer purchasing motivation and behavior. *European Research on Management and Business Economics, 27*(3), 100166.

Westerman, G. (2022). Developing Strategy for New Customer Expectations. *MIT Sloan Management Review, 63*(2), 1–4.

Widjaja, V. F., Budianto, R., & Alamsyah, D. P. (2021). Local Business in Mid of Covid-19 Pandemic: A Prominent Case Study in Bandung Indonesia. *Proceedings of the 11th Annual International Conference on Industrial Engineering and Operations Management*, 4589–4595.

Chapter 13
Machine Learning–Based Stock Price Prediction for Business Intelligence

Bhavya K. R.
Reva University, India

L. N. C. Prakash K.
CVR College of Engineering, India

Malla Sudhakara
Reva University, India

Rupa Devi B.
AITS, India

G. Ramasubba Reddy
Sai Rajeswari Institute of Technology, India

Sangeetha M.
Reva University, India

ABSTRACT

The act of digital marketing uses a variety of traditional methods such as analyst consensus, earnings per share estimation, or fundamental intrinsic valuation. Also, social media management, automation, content marketing, and community development are some of the most popular uses for digital marketing. Stock price prediction is a challenging task since there are so many factors to take into account, such as economic conditions, political events, and other environmental elements that might influence the stock price. Due to these considerations, determining the dependency of a single factor on future pricing and patterns is challenging. The authors examine Apple's stock data from Yahoo API and use sentiment categorization to predict its future stock movement and to find the impact of "public sentiment" on "market trends." The main purpose of this chapter is to predict the rise and fall with high accuracy degrees. The authors use an artificial intelligence-based machine learning model to train, evaluate, and improve the performance of digital marketing strategies.

DOI: 10.4018/978-1-6684-4246-3.ch013

INTRODUCTION

Forecasting of stock prices is vital for financial backers and is quite possibly the most fascinating issues for scientist. As per the proficient market speculation (EMH) and irregular walk hypothesis, stock costs are considered to not have anything to do with chronicled patterns Notwithstanding, according to the viewpoint of conduct finance, financial backers' way of behaving and independent direction is frequently impacted by silly factors and commotion. The market by and large shows consistency. The forecast of monetary time series is a vital assignment. Analysts have directed a great deal of chips away at stock cost prediction. From one perspective, the customary technique is to utilize verifiable cost information inside the business sectors to foresee stock costs (Yang and Parwada, 2012). Then again, More and more peculiarities show that data outside the exchanging market ay essentially affect resource costs; Twitter's opinion condition of financial backers frequently influences stock returns (Nofer and Hinz, 2015). Prices are not set in stone by the essential worth and deviations brought about by financial backers' silly way of behaving (Szyszka, 2007). In these examinations, an ordinary strategy is to utilize monetary information, declarations, budget summaries, and other data to foresee stock costs (Shang and Wang, 2020). Nonetheless, news, reports, and declarations, as a rule, happen haphazardly, so the coherence of such sort of data is effectively impacted by time stretches, bringing about incomplete loss of significant data. Another technique is to utilize online information sources via web-based media stages to foresee the stock costs.

These examinations utilize online information from interpersonal organizations, for example, Twitter to assess financial backer feeling and dissect the connection among opinion and securities exchanges (Renault, 2020). Yet, the characterization of feeling is typically outrageous, like good and pessimistic. Additionally, it isn't permitted to quantify financial backer' social connection data in manners aside from the particular opinion aspect. Interpersonal organizations contain a great deal of significant data; however, the financial backer' social association information actually needs proper devices and innovations to change it into important data.

As of the end of October 2021, Microsoft posted revenue of $45.3bn for the first quarter to September - 22% higher than the same period last year. Operating income rose 27% to $20.2bn, while profits totalled $20.5bn in GAAP and $17.2bn in non-GAAP and $17.2lbn non-GAAP increased by 48% and 24%. Microsoft 365 commercial revenue increased by 23%, driving an 18% increase in Office commercial products and cloud services. Microsoft 365 consumer subscribers increased to 54.1 million, driving a 10% increase in Office consumer products and cloud services. As a result, LinkedIn revenue rose by 42%, fuelled in part by Marketing Solutions growth of 61%. Up to date apple stock performance is shown in Figure 1.

Figure 1. Up to date stock performance

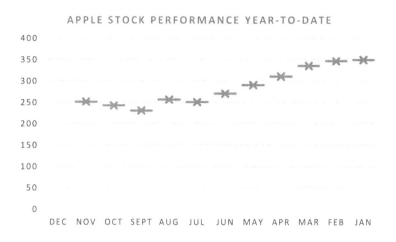

More normal service at software and cloud giant Microsoft (MSFT) has been resumed after a rocky start to 2022. Its stock had dropped around 20% over January but today, is showing a 10% improvement from that low at $304.56.In fairness the tech sector in general had taken a pounding in the new year but Microsoft was able to dispel some of the gloom by posting strong results for the second quarter. Microsoft projected third-quarter 2022 revenue growth of 17%, the mid-point of the company's range, while the projected mid-point for operating income was for $19.9bn both of which are ahead of analyst forecasts. At the time of writing (9 February), Microsoft had a market cap of $2.28trn, just behind Apple, which had a market cap of $2.85trn, according to Companies Market Cap.

Microsoft's stock is currently trading at $305. Major challenge is that it regains its upward momentum? According to the algorithmic forecasts of Wallet Investor, MSFT stock could rise to $377 within the next year investment. It doesn't provide a 10-year forecast for MSFT stock, but it predicts that MSFT could reach $669 within five years and the graphical representation of the corresponding statistics is shown in Figure 2.

According to Market Beat, 33 analysts rated MSFT stock as a 'buy', with just one saying it is a 'hold.' Analysts expect MSFT stock to rise 17% to $358 over the next year. The highest analyst forecast is $411, while the lowest is $290.

To analyse the strength of the correlation between Twitter sentiment and stock performance, we are collecting Apple's stock data from yahoo API in different sectors. Due to practical reasons, like the limited time interval and relevant data, we are focusing to only analyse data from social media Twitter during a six-week period

Figure 2. Year wise apple stock performance

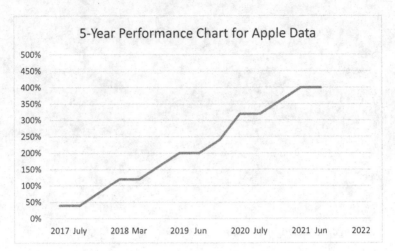

The objective of this study is to utilize advanced AI method to work on the precision of offer cost prediction in industry. The Implementation of the interpersonal organization variable to expand the impact of stock value forecast is our key commitment. We study in the event that the interpersonal organization variable coming about because of financial backers' unconstrained consideration could give new explanations behind stock cost expectation. We concentrate on social networks, which use the "word of mouth" impact to propagate ideas, views, and trends. Other internet data sources, on the other hand, are unable to assess investor social interaction information in any way other than the unique dimension.

RELATED WORK

A stock's price depends on supply and demand, which in turn depends on fundamental factors and market sentiment and examples of fundamental aspects include the stock's perceived risk, discount rate and expected growth, inflation the strength of the economy, trends and stocks liquidity are among the technical factors while market sentiment refers to the psychology of the stock market participate.

Major examination is the method involved with checking out at a business at the most essential or key monetary level. This will inspect the critical proportions of a business to decide its monetary wellbeing. Key examination can give a thought of the worth of what an organization's stock ought to be. Henceforth, crucial investigation concerns the actual stock, like the resources, liabilities, and salaries of the objective organizations by examining their fiscal reports, as well as the proportions of past execution, like Price-to-Earnings Ratio (P/E proportion) (Harrington, 2009), which is the proportion for esteeming an organization that actions its present offer value, connected with its profit per-share (EPS). Principal examination depends on the faith in the business needs for the cash-flow to continue to work. On the off chance that the organization runs well, it ought to get extra capital honours which will prompt stock cost took off. Essential examination is directed from the worldwide economy initially and afterward public economy prior to breaking down a particular industry and a particular organization. It is a hierarchical interaction. As the essential examination is a moderately sensible and technique, it is utilized broadly (Harrington, 2010).

Crossover models generally perform better compared to single AI models, and the brain organizations and SVMs are regularly a significant part in numerous mixture models, for instance, the mix of brain organization and choice tree for the expectation of advanced game substance stocks value (Chang, 2011), the reconciliation of dim calculation and RBF brain organization, prepared by 4 different learning methodologies (Lei, 2018), fluffy time series investigation with brain networks for the estimate of the Taiwan Stock Exchange Capitalization. Developmental improvement with covering strategies is frequently used to advance AI models or select elements for stock cost (pattern) forecast. For instance, Harmony Search and Genetic Algorithm was utilized to track down the best design of brain organization (G¨oçken et al., 2016), brain network with avaricious calculation in light of the component decrease with covering procedures at the expectation of stock cost pattern (Lertyingyod and Benjamas, 2017), recreated tempering calculation was utilized to streamline include space and model boundaries (Torun, 2011), and a Markov choice interaction was joined on hereditary calculations to foster stock exchanging methodologies (Chang and Lee, 2017).

Following quite a while of stock exploration, in excess of 100 pointers and proportions have been produced for crucial and specialized investigation, individually. In this exploration, information is gathered from the data sets, it is the most famous stock data set. 30 elements are chosen, as they are the most prominently utilized in existing exploration. For the essential investigation, 15 highlights in 6 classes are chosen, though for the specialized examination, 15 elements in 10 gatherings are chosen. The gathered crude information will go through two phases of information handling. For the essential elements, information is gathered each quarter after the organizations distributing their monetary reports. For the specialized highlights, information is gathered each exchanging day, synchronized with the nearby cost. An example is the information on each exchanging day. To analyse the effect of two arrangements of elements on specialized investigation, the quarterly essential information is changed to day-to-day information by utilizing the univariate straight handling, which is chosen by the start and the closure upsides of the element in the quarter, as displayed in Fig. 1, where accept all the difference in a central component in a quarter is straight. While handling the specialized information, to keep the uprightness of the example information, the examples that miss some component values are erased. Simultaneously, the relating exchanging day tests moved from the principal information are likewise erased to keep up with the consistency of the key information and specialized information.

Recent studies show that investors can get early indicators of news by scraping different data sources such as blogs, social media and search engines. For example, Google used their software called Google Trends and showed that Google search queries could be used in order to predict consumer spending (Torsten Schmidt et al.2009). A previous paper by Bollen, Mao and Zeng show that mood and emotions are difficult in financial decision making,therefore it is safe to assume that mood and emotions also may impact asset pricing (Pagolu et al. 2018). Mao, Wang found that it is a important correlation between the daily number of tweets that mentions stocks in the stock index Standard & Poor 500 and stock pointers that are related to the price and volume. They also identified correlation between the daily number of tweets and the daily traded volume for 8 out of 10 industry sectors. (Shuyuan Deng et.al 2018).

Machine Learning techniques have becoming widely used in stock research due to their intrinsic potential to extract information from vast amounts of data (Kumar, Dogra, Utreja, & Yadav, 2018). Supervised Learning, Unsupervised Learning, and Reinforcement Learning are the three types of machine learning, according to Khadka (2019). Analysing and extracting meaningful patterns from massive raw input data is at the core of machine learning. Higher degrees of understanding for decision-making and trend prediction are the consequence. As a result, many companies place a high value on obtaining these insights and information from data since it allows them to achieve competitive advantages (Mohammadi, Al-Fuqaha, Sorour, & Guizani, 2018). Machine learning approaches, according to Sodhi, Awasthi, and Sharma (2019), can address difficulties.

Efficient-Market Hypothesis

Stock market prediction has been on the table for decades and has brought attention both from business and in science. One of the first theories on the subject was the Efficient-Market Hypothesis (EMH) which states that asset pricing reflects all available information. According to the EMH assets always trade on a fair value and markets only reacts on new information such as news, therefore is it impossible to beat the market over time on a risk-adjusted basis. News are unpredictable and this suggest that asset pricing follows a random walk with a 50% chance of going either up or down (Kenton 2018). EMH and The Random Walk Theory has received a lot of criticism and evidence show that asset pricing does not follow a random walk and in other words asset pricing can be predicted to some degree. For example, Warren Buffett wrote a article arguing that if several funds managed to beat the index year after year it cannot be an random event (Buffett, Warren 1984). The NYU Stern School of Business professor Aswath Damodaran referred this as a proof that the market is not always efficient (Damodaran 2014).

Correlation and Causality

Correlation is commonly defined as how close two variables are to having a linear relationship with each other. The co-variance of two events A and B is defined below and E[A] is the expected value:

C (A, B) = E [(A - E[A])(B - E[B])

If C (A, B) = 0 then they are said to be uncorrelated [7].
The correlation is defined as:

$$\rho \ (A, B) = {}_{D(A)D(B)}^{C(A;B)} C\left(A; B\right) \text{€}\left[-1, 1\right]$$

where D(A) and D(B) represent the standard deviation of A and B.
If ρ (A, B) = 1 there is a true positive relationship between both A and B and if A increases B also increases.
If ρ (A, B) = -1 there is a true negative relation between both A and B and if A increases Y decreases.
Even-though the correlation coefficient is -1 or +1 it does not have to imply that one causes the other. Causality refers to when one thing, often referred to the cause, gives rise to another cause which is often called the effect. It is important to differentiate association with causation, association refers to event which happen together more regularly than others, but that does not mean that the relationship is meaningful. In this chapter we will identify the correlation between public sentiment and stock price in general and if any of the two causes the other in particular.

Figure 3. Year wise apple stock performance

1	Date	Open	High	Low	Close	Adj Close	Volume
2	2012-01-03	58.485714	58.928570	58.428570	58.747143	50.857235	75555200
3	2012-01-04	58.571430	59.240002	58.468571	59.062859	51.130558	65005500
4	2012-01-05	59.278572	59.792858	58.952858	59.718571	51.698215	67817400
5	2012-01-06	59.967144	60.392857	59.888573	60.342857	52.238651	79573200
6	2012-01-09	60.785713	61.107143	60.192856	60.247143	52.155792	98506100
7	2012-01-10	60.844284	60.857143	60.214287	60.462856	52.342537	64549100
8	2012-01-11	60.382858	60.407143	59.901428	60.364285	52.257195	53771200
9	2012-01-12	60.325714	60.414288	59.821430	60.198570	52.113747	53146800
10	2012-01-13	59.957142	60.064285	59.808571	59.972858	51.918343	56505400
11	2012-01-17	60.599998	60.855713	60.422855	60.671429	52.523098	60724300
12	2012-01-18	60.994286	61.352856	60.900002	61.301430	53.068489	69197800
13	2012-01-19	61.450001	61.624287	60.930000	61.107143	52.900303	65434600
14	2012-01-20	61.070000	61.071430	59.964287	60.042858	51.978935	103493600
15	2012-01-23	60.361428	61.207142	60.328571	61.058571	52.858246	76515600
16	2012-01-24	60.728573	60.728573	59.935715	60.058571	51.992550	136909500

METHODS

Data Collection

To be able to perform the sentiment analysis and calculate the correlation, Twitter and stock data sets is necessary. The collection of these data sets is described and shown in figure 3 below

Stock Data Collection

The stock information has been gathered pandas_datareader library permits us to interface with the site and concentrate information straightforwardly from web sources, for this situation we are removing information from Yahoo Finance API AAPL US Equity.

In order to ensure a varied set of companies in different industries, the companies presented below were selected. American International Group AIG is a worldwide insurance agency with tasks in excess of 80 countries and locales. They provide a range of insurance products in business and in life, including: life insurance, general property and financial services. AIG's industry is Insurance (AIG 2019). Apple Inc. Apple designs and manufactures electronics such as phones, computers and smart watches and sells a range of related software. Apple's segments include the Americas, Europe, Japan, Greater China and Rest of Asia Pacific. Apples industry is Consumer Electronics [About Apple 2019].

World's biggest aviation organization is the Boeing Company. They are a creator of business jetliners, guard, space and safety frameworks, and high-quality group of subordinate vending support. Boeing upholds aircrafts and U.S. what's more, partnered government clients in excess of 150 nations. The Boeing's industry is Aerospace and Défense (About Boeing 2019). Facebook Inc. Facebook is a web-based web-based entertainment and informal communication administration organization. They are building items that empower individuals to interface through PCs, cell phones and different surfaces. Facebook's industry is Internet Content and Information (About Facebook 2019). Netflix Inc. Netflix is a web diversion administration and are usable in excess of 190 nations. Clients can sit in front of the TV series, narratives and element films across a wide assortment of types and dialects on any web associated screen. Netflix's industry is Media (About Netflix 2019). Home Depot Inc. Home Depot is a home improvement retailer. They sell Home Depot's industry is Home Improvement Stores (About Home Depot 2019).

Data Pre-Processing

The pre-processing stage is critical in order to obtain a high accuracy in the sentiment analysis [10]. Before the data is cleaned there are a lot of spam, special characters and other unnecessary data which not are required or can be classified in the analysis. Tweets were classified as spam if a user tweeted the same content several times. These tweets were deleted during this stage. Then blank spaces at the beginning and the end, usernames, punctuations, links, tabs and tweets made in other languages than English were deleted.

Sentiment Analysis

After the pre-processing stage, the data is stored as a Jupiter data frame since the following work also was done in python. Sentiment was selected to perform the sentiment analysis. The package is well used to calculate text polarity on a row-level. Sentiment also provides the opportunity to take valence shifters in consideration, e.g., negators, adversative conjunctions, amplifiers and de-amplifiers. The words of each sentence are compared to a polarity dictionary and then tagged with a number between -1 and +1. Sentiment have weights on valence shifters and the standard weights provided by the creator was chosen. The final result is the divided by the number of words in order to get a value which is not dependent on the length of the sentence.

Data Aggregation

When the sentiment analysis was completed, the daily sentiment was calculated for each stock during the period. This was done by calculating the mean value of all sentiments from all tweets during each day. One day is defined as one minute after the closing of the stock exchange until the next day's closing. The sentiment values were inserted into a matrix with two columns where column one contained the stock's daily sentiment, and where column two contained the close price of the stock on the corresponding day.

Correlation Calculation

Correlation is a proportion of affiliation or relation between two highlights for example the amount B will shift with a variety in A. The connection technique will make use of Pearson Correlation and it is shown in figure 4.

Using PC coefficient:

corr=df. corr(method='pearson')

PC Coefficient is the most well-known method for estimating connection, the scope of values shifts from - 1 to 1. In arithmetic/physical science terms it tends to be perceived as though two elements are emphatically associated then they are straightforwardly relative and in the event that they share negative connection, they are contrarily corresponding.

EDA (Explanatory Data Analysis)

EDA indicates to the basic sequence of performing beginning inspections on data in order to find designs, to detect peculiarities, to test theory and to actually take a look at suspicions with the support of synopsis insights and graphical portrayals. The fair practice to fathom the data first and endeavour to collect as various encounters from it. Hence EDA is tied in with figuring out information close by, prior to getting them messy with it and it is certifiably not a conventional interaction with a severe arrangement of rules. More than anything, EDA is a perspective. During the underlying periods of EDA, we should go ahead and explore each thought that happens. A portion of these thoughts will work out, and some will be impasses. As your investigation proceeds, you will home in on a couple of especially useful regions that you'll ultimately review and convey to other people.

EDA is also a significant piece of any information examination, regardless of whether the inquiries are given to we on a platter, since we generally need to explore the nature of our information. Information cleaning is only one use of EDA. To do information cleaning, we want to convey every one of the devices of EDA: perception, change, and displaying.

Figure 4. Pearson correlation calculation

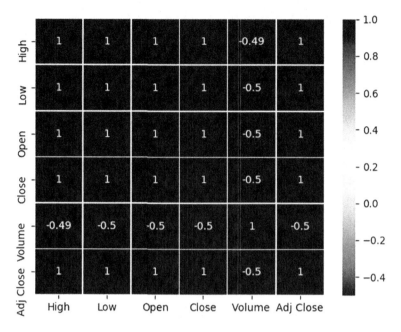

The detailed pictorial approaches used in EDA are regularly very forthright, comprising of different procedures of:

1. Charting the simple data, (for ex, data follows, histograms, bi-histograms, likelihood plots, slack plots, block plots, and Youden plots.
2. Charting upfront insights, for ex, mean plots, standard deviation plots, box plots, and primary impacts plots of the crude information.
3. Aligning charts in order to enlarge capacities, for example, utilizing various plots per page.

Below EDA shows the year wise Apple price prediction with dependent and independent variable.

Visualize the Dependent Variable With Independent Variable

See Figure 5.

Bar Plot of Open Price vs. Close Price (Year 2012)

Let us take a look at the bar plot of top 50 data which is from 2012 year

Figure 5.

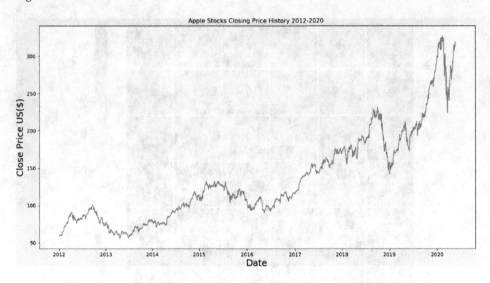

Figure 6.

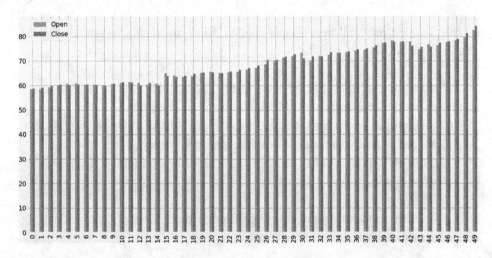

Bar Plot of Open Price vs. Close Price (Year 2020)

Let us take a look at the bar plot of top 50 data which is from 2020 year

All of the above bar plot represents year-wise open price and close price for the apple stock from 2012 to 2020. Now by applying a machine-learning algorithm to identify the rise and fall with high accuracy degrees.

Figure 7.

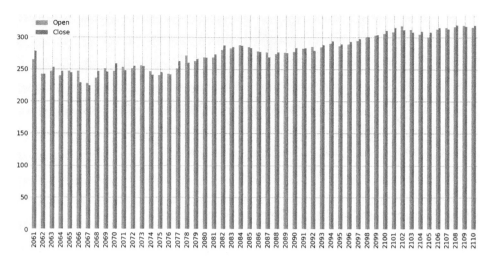

LINEAR REGRESSION MODEL

Separation of two variables to examine the one relationship and also it is used to measure the technical and quantitative analysis in market fields. Initially, we use Explanatory variables to predict the apple stock price along with average and correlation for making the prediction. Next is to define a dependent variable and it is the outcome for which the ML model will predict the stock price based on the explanatory variables.

The next step is to split the data into train and test. Train data is to create the linear regression by grouping the input and expected output. Test data is to show how well the model has been trained. Finally, cross-validation has been done for the model. Basically, Cross Validation is a procedure utilizing which a Model is assessed on the dataset on which it isn't prepared for example it tends to be test information or can be one more set according to accessibility or possibility.

number of splits: 20 and Accuracy: 99.99743780203187

Plot Actual vs. Predicted Value of Linear Regression Model

See Figure 8.

Figure 8.

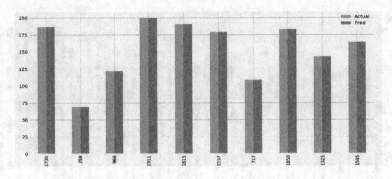

KNN: K-nearest Neighbor Regression Model

KNN is used for both regression and classification, it finds the association between the independent variable and continuous result by averaging the observations.

It chooses the feature similarity to predict the values from new data points.

k neighbours = 4

Accuracy: 99.91435220285842

Plot Actual vs. Predicted Value of kNN Model

See Figure 9.

Figure 9.

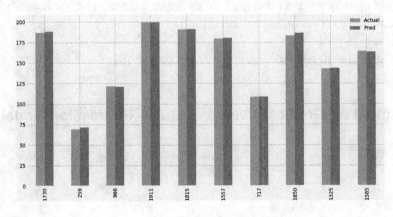

SVM Support Vector Machine Regression Model

Accuracy: 99.99301338392715

Plot Actual vs. Predicted Value of SVM

See Figure 10.

Figure 10.

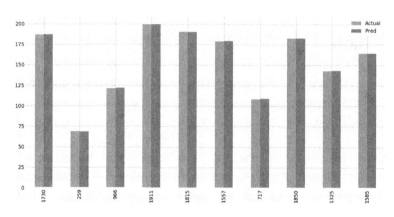

RMSE (Root Mean Square Error)

RMS is the Standard Deviation of residuals, which are a proportion of how far information focuses are from the relapse. Or then again in straightforward terms how thought the information focuses are around the best fit line.

Linear Model RMSE: 3.0534992716871643e-14

KNN Model RMSE: 1.191675778610913

SVM Model RMSE: 0.5182098703394772

R-Squared Error

R-Squared score differs between 0 to 100%.

Mathematical Formula for R-squared score:(y_test[i] — y_pred[i]) **2

Linear R-Squared: 1.0

KNN R-Squared: 0.999629726665711

SVM R-Squared: 0.9999299807307482

CONCLUSION

One cannot say that there is a clear correlation between the Apple data and the stock price. In order to get more reliable results much more data would be needed and also a better method to clean up the data. There are some evidences suggesting that if the quality of the data is good then there is a correlation between the Twitter sentiment and the stock price. But in most cases, there are other factors driving the stock price. Also, the results suggests that the importance of sentiment is fluctuating and could increase if a significant event has occurred which might affect the stability of the correlation. There are no or little evidence showing that the correlation of Twitter sentiment and stock price has any relation to a specific industry or product type. Regarding the certainty of our results, the correlation seems to be significant, but the found results does not prove causality between the two. An investor should not solely base their analysis on these results but it could be used as an extra layer in their analysis improving accuracy or to monitor company sentiments in long term, considering the high correlation on the clean data sets.

REFERENCES

About Apple Inc. (2019). https://www.reuters.com/finance/stocks/company-profile/AAPL.O

Boeing, A. (2019). https://www.boeing.com/company/general-info/

Chang, Y.-H., & Lee, M.-S. (2017). Incorporating Markov decision process on genetic algorithms to formulate trading strategies for stock markets. *Applied Soft Computing, 52*, 1143–1153. doi:10.1016/j.asoc.2016.09.016

Damodaran, A. (2014). *Session 7: Market Efficiency - Laying the Groundwork.* Academic Press.

Depot, A. H. (2019). https://www.reuters.com/finance/stocks/company-profile/HD.N

Facebook, A. (2019). https://www.reuters.com/finance/stocks/company-profile/FB.OQ

Focus, F. (2011). *Profit Margin Analysis. Third Quarter 2011.* http://search. credoreference.com.ezproxy.westminster.ac.uk/content/entry/ultimatebusiness/pr ofit_margin/0/

Harrington, C. (2003). *Fundamental vs. Technical Analysis. CFA Institute Magazine.* doi:10.2469/cfm.v14.n1.2789

Huang, Sinha, & Zhao. (2018). The Interaction between croblog. *Sentiment and Stock Return: An Empirical Examination.*

Netflix, A. (2019). https: / / www. reuters. com / finance / stocks / company -profile/ NFLX.OQ

Nisar, T. M., & Yeung, M. (2018). Twitter as a tool for forecasting stock market movements: A short-window event study. *J. Finance Data Sci., 4*(2), 101–119. doi:10.1016/j.jfds.2017.11.002

Nofer, M., & Hinz, O. (2015). Using twitter to predict the stock market. *Business & Information Systems Engineering, 57*(4), 229–242. doi:10.100712599-015-0390-4

Nofsinger, J. R. (2005). Social Mood and Financial Economics. *Journal of Behavioral Finance, 6*(3), 144–160.

Pagolu, V. S. (2016). *Sentiment Analysis of Twitter Data for Predicting Stock Market Movements.* https://arxiv.org/pdf/1610.09225.pdf

Renault, T. (2020). Sentiment analysis and machine learning in finance: A comparison of methods and models on one million messages. *Digit. Finance, 2*(1), 1–13. doi:10.100742521-019-00014-x

Rowe, M., Stankovic, M., Dadzie, A.-S., & Hardey, M. (Eds.). F. °A. Nielsen. A new ANEW: evaluation of a word list for sentiment analysis in microblogs. In M. Rowe, M. Stankovic, A.-S. Dadzie, & M. Hardey (Eds.), *Proceedings of the ESWC2011 Workshop on Making.* Academic Press.

Schmidt, T., & Vosen, S. (2009). *Forecasting Private Consumption: Survey-based Indicators vs. Google Trends.* https://pdfs. semanticscholar.org/66f2/b2cfe56fc2414d3036cb6e 28098bfa55216f.pdf

Sense of Microposts. (2011). Big things come in small packages. *CEUR Workshop Proceedings, 718*, 93–98.

Shang, Y., & Wang, Y. (2020). Study of CNN-based news-driven stock price movement prediction in the A-share market. In *International Conference of Pioneering Computer Scientists, Engineers and Educators.* Springer. 10.1007/978-981-15-7984-4_35

Smith, A., & Andersson, M. (2018). Social Media Use in 2018. Academic Press.

Szyszka, A. (2007). *Wycena papierów wartościowych na rynku kapitałowym w świetle finansów behawioralnych. Prace Habilitacyjne/Akademia Ekonomiczna w Poznaniu 35* [Valuation of Securities on the Capital market in the light of Behavioral Finance. Habilitation Theses]. University of Economics in Poznah.

Thelwall, M. (2009). MySpace Comments. *Online Information Review*, *33*(1), 58–76. doi:10.1108/14684520910944391

Tumasjan, A. (2010). *Predicting Elections with Twitter: What 140 Characters Reveal about Political Sentiment.* Academic Press.

Yang, J. W., & Parwada, J. (2012). *Predicting stock price movements: An ordered probit analysis.* Academic Press.

Chapter 14

Transformation and Future Directions of the Integrated Chip (IC) Manufacturing Industry Using Artificial Intelligence Models

G. S. Siva Kumar
Pragati Engineering College, India

Srinivas Akula
Pragati Engineering College, India

Suneetha P.
Pragati Engineering College, India

Vasantha Lakshmi B.
Pragati Engineering College, India

Sailaja V.
Pragati Engineering College, India

Ravi Kumar M.
Pragati Engineering College, India

ABSTRACT

The era of the semi-conductor manufacturing industry is from 1970 to recent times. During these decades, the manufacturing process has achieved its greatest heights. At present, it reached its saturation level in terms of VLSI, ULSI, SOC manufacturing techniques. Recently artificial intelligence models are expanding their domains and applications in all the sectors. In this regard, changes in the hardware modeling also play a crucial role. In this chapter, the authors present artificial intelligence on hardware models, how the IC manufacturing industry is turning its conventional methods to add new features, and future directions at the business level.

DOI: 10.4018/978-1-6684-4246-3.ch014

Critic high tech minerals (CHTMs) are unrefined substances that are fundamental for a future clean-energy change and the assembling of very good quality items. Electronic devices, one of the quickest developing electronic items, contain different CHTMs. Starting around 2019, India has outperformed the United States to turn into the second biggest electronic gadget market on the planet. An expanding and disturbing number of unreasonable waste electronic contraptions will be created in India soon. In this review, the powerful material stream investigation approach and the Weibull dissemination are taken on to examine the volumes of collected squander electronic devices and the contained CHTMs in light of the separation among electronic gadgets and component telephones in India. Also, a market supply model is embraced to anticipate the future patterns of CHTMs in squander electronic devices. The outcomes show an overall vertical propensity of waste electronic devices volume in India, which demonstrates that different CHTMs contained in electronic devices waste can be appropriately reused or reused. Future ramifications in light of the investigation results are accommodated proficient electronic devices the executives in India.

INTRODUCTION

Basic cutting-edge minerals (chtms) are ''minor'' metals on which present day innovation is in total dependent to fill roles. The loads of chtms on earth are restricted, and gaining them from normal virgin metal is troublesome because of specialized and monetary impediments. The accessibility of these chtms is, in this manner, dependent on not just the particular mining creation of their host mineral(s) yet in addition whether the friend minerals are appropriately recuperated instead of disposed of without having been handled Furthermore, requests for materials and metals will increment with innovative turn of events, in light of the fact that the World Bank revealed that ''the perfect energy progress will be fundamentally mineral concentrated'' Urban mining is a likely option for addressing the difficulties connected with the proceeded with solid interest for chtms and delicate stock of chtms. Metropolitan mining has been effectively used for asset extraction of electrical and electronic items and modern Waste The quick headway of mechanical development has prompted a significant expansion in the interest for chtms The Indian economy has been developing quickly at a yearly pace of 7.1% in the previous ten years, which positions India as an arising world economy In the Indian economy, the electronic business, including creation, inside utilization and product, is one of the quickest developing areas .

India as of late outperformed the United States as the second-biggest electronic gadget market behind China, when it arrived at 158 million shipments in 2019.

Electronic devices, one of the fastest growing electronic items, contain different chtms. Two sorts of electronic devices exist, in particular, include telephones and electronic gadgets. In particular, the major chtms, like cobalt and palladium, are contained n squander include telephones, while antimony, beryllium, praseodymium, neodymium, and platinum are likewise contained in squander electronic gadgets. Regardless of being a moderately rich country as far as mineral assets, India's reliance on imported minerals is high, next just to oil. Subsequently, squander electronic contraptions address an expected essential supply of chtms for metropolitan mining in ongoing many years. In the worldwide setting, past examination on squander electronic devices has essentially centred around squander age and different minerals contained in squander. They assessed that roughly 3.7 million electronic contraptions are stored by college understudies in the UK, while around 28.1 million electronic devices and 29.3 million electronic devices are accumulated, for the USA and Europe, separately. They assessed that the Czech Republic created 45 thousand waste electronic gadgets from 1990 to 2000; this number expanded to 6.5 million from 2000 to 2010 and is They assessed to increment to around 26.3 million telephones from 2010 to 2020. Shown that roughly 39 million waste electronic gadgets collected in 2014 in Iran, yet the part that might actually be reused segment was just 4.2 million. Through the finish of 2035, it is projected that around 90 million waste electronic gadgets will be disposed of in Iran used the deals and new technique and they assessed that roughly 47.92 million waste electronic contraptions were produced in 2002 and around 739.98 million waste electronic devices were created in 2012 in China anticipated future amounts of waste metals/minerals from squander electronic gadgets in 2025 in China with 100 percent reusing, roughly 9.01 huge loads of Au and 14.91 huge loads of Ag might possibly be removed from printed circuit sheets (pcbs) demonstrated that roughly 54,050 tons of electronic gadgets have been shipped to Nigeria during 2001 and 2013; these telephones contained 8920 tons of copper, 270 tons of nickel, 120 tons of lead, 40 tons of chromium and 1310 tons of bromine from brominated fire retardants. Examined the metal/mineral substance of waste electronic gadgets and waste component telephones in Sweden and found that the lead content in electronic gadgets is lower than that in include telephones, while the substance of other harmful metals/minerals are comparable. Led a concentrate on htms in squander electronic gadgets and estimated an impressive amount of htms put away in squander electronic devices that could be reused in the Chinese market. Inferred that non-PCB parts of waste electronic gadgets represent over half of the all-out monetary worth regarding the recuperation potential. They assessed that the financial worth of almost 1.72 million USD and 37.6 million USD could be produced from reusing essential metals and valuable metals in pcbs used the base distance most extreme getting (MDMR) calculation and announced that in excess of 400 million units of waste electronic gadgets could be reused in China (Hsu et al., 2008; Lau et al., 2009).

Conceptualization

Material stream examination (MFA) is a powerful device to dissect the streams and loads of any material-based framework. In this review, the item life cycle incorporates the whole market life from beginning business sector passage to conclusive market leave, that is to say, the full ''support to-grave'' process. Squander electronic devices allude to electronic contraptions that have completed their whole help to clients, and will not reappear the dynamic use stage. The normal help long periods of electronic contraptions are viewed as the electronic devices life expectancy. Various nations characterize CHTMs in an unexpected way. For instance, in China, CHTMs are made out of an assortment of metals characterized by the Ministry of Natural Resources and Key Laboratory of Strategic Studies, including 17 uncommon earth metals. In India, the minerals of uncommon metals, tantalum, tungsten, barium, cobalt, lithium, niobium, rubidium, cesium, tin, cadmium, mercury, molybdenum, and vanadium, notwithstanding nickel and zircon are viewed as essential super advanced minerals. Mineral asset accessibility has different definitions; in this review, it is characterized as the optional asset stores of a specific mineral that could possibly be given to society. The mineral worth can be determined through a particular financial and specialized appraisal framework. This framework considers a few topographical, financial and innovative elements related with mines or mineral stores In this review, the asset accessibility of different CHTMs alludes to the social supplies of CHTMS.

System Boundary

In this paper, the geological limit is restricted to India. The framework limit of the waste electronic devices' material stream process. The Indian telecom market incorporates two primary classes of electronic devices: electronic gadgets and component telephones. The substance of CHTMs in the two classes contrast significantly. As displayed in the framework limit, CHTMs initial come into the creation method of electronic contraptions as unrefined components in the wake of being extricated and handled and stay in the electronic devices during the dynamic use stage. Toward the finish of the electronic devices life expectancy, CHTMs contained in these electronic contraptions can be reused or reused as optional mineral assets to return the assembling step. Subsequently, this interaction is a ''support to-grave'' process.

Distribution of Electronic Gadgets Lifespan

Estimation of Waste Electronic Gadgets Generation

The Weibull circulation is generally applied for item life expectancy displaying, and many examinations have utilized this dispersion to assess the life expectancy of electronic and electrical items. In this review, the twofold boundary Weibull conveyance was taken on to investigate the electronic contraptions' life expectancy circulation all through the assigned years utilizing Minitab 17.0 The likelihood thickness work f(t) and appropriation work F(t) of the twofold boundary.

Estimation of the Social Stock of Critical High-Tech Minerals

The amount of CHTMs contained in squander electronic contraptions is resolved utilizing.

Future Trends Analysis

In this part, the expectation of future waste electronic devices age was directed through the market supply strategy. (Huang et al., 2021; Kossukhina, 2021; Pan et al., 2022)

Data Source and Collection

The information in this exploration were acquired from the sites of reusing organizations, public written works, and modern reports. The quantity of electronic contraptions transported was utilized as an intermediary for electronic devices deals in light of the presumption that ''all electronic devices in the market are probably going to be sold consistently''. Albeit electronic contraptions were first presented in Quite a while from 1995 to 1996, they required 10 years to turn into the prevailing method for correspondence. The shipment data of two kinds of electronic devices in India was acquired from International Data Corporation (IDC) announcements (IDC, 2009-2019), and the normal life expectancy of electronic devices in India depended on information from Stevens. Explicit substance data in regard to the CHTMs contained in various electronic contraptions was gotten from recently distributed writing and the information extent of this study was confined to India. In extending the deals of electronic devices from 2020 to 2035, unique classifications of electronic contraptions share a few similitudes, yet additionally particular patterns. Be that as it may, the absolute electronic contraptions shipments in 2020 are expected to decline by 10% because of the Coronavirus Disease 2019 (COVID-19) pandemic. As indicated by a worldwide electronic devices shipment forecast delivered by Canalys, the yearly electronic devices shipment development rate will be 35.5%, 17.75%, and 8.88%, separately, in 2020, 2021 and 2022. The shipment development pace of component telephones and electronic gadgets in India is thought to be reliable with the worldwide situation. Besides, we expected that the effect of the pandemic will keep going for something like three successive years; at the end of the day, the yearly electronic contraptions shipment development rate will get back to business as usual after 2022. For the element telephones, we used the 10-year normal development rate (3.86%) and determined the information in light of verifiable. We accept that this approach is a level-headed methodology, uncovered that a huge populace in India is as yet utilizing highlight telephones due to monetary and expertise limitations and will keep on utilizing highlight telephones in ongoing many years. With respect to electronic gadgets, we applied a 2-year normal development rate (10.82%) because of emotional vacillation throughout recent years. We accepted that these development rates are steady and will stay consistent until 2035.The amounts of the two kinds of electronic contraptions that were sent. Minitab 17.0 was chosen to show the shape (b) and scale (d) boundaries of the Weibull appropriation. The lifetime data of the electronic contraptions was gotten from past investigations and reports and point by point data about the lifetime dispersion of electronic devices. The different CHTMs contained in highlight telephones and electronic gadgets in India are introduced (Abalansa et al., 2021; He et al., 2021, 2021; Qahtan et al., 2022).

Sensitivity Analysis

In this review, an awareness investigation was directed to distinguish factors that impact the assessment results. Five situations were considered to evaluate the awareness. "B" was utilized to address the essential situation. Situations 1 and 2 were utilized to look at the impact of more limited and longer electronic contraptions life expectancies on the quantity of produced squander electronic devices. Situations 3 and 4 were applied to approve the effects of material synthesis by diminishing and expanding the gauge esteem by 10%. An itemized portrayal of the responsiveness investigation is given in the outcomes area.

RESULTS

Generation of Waste Electronic Gadgets

The volumes of waste electronic devices in India from 2009 to 2035, which were assessed utilizing Eqs. (1) to (5) examined in the past segment. By and large, the outcomes show that squander electronic contraptions improvement in India from

2009 to 2035 can be sorted into two periods, specifically, the recorded period and the future time frame. In the chronicled period, from 2009 to 2019, the amount of waste electronic contraptions showed a fast ascent from almost 1.65 million units in 2010 to around 157 million units in 2019, and the whole number of waste electronic devices surpassed 632 million. In this period, roughly 134 million units of electronic gadgets and 499 million units of element telephones aggregated. The outcomes show comparable patterns for squander include telephones and waste electronic gadgets, yet with somewhat changing degrees. Squander highlight telephones showed a rising course of ''consistent development advancement''. The quantity of waste element telephones, which was around 1.6 million units in 2009, constantly expanded to roughly 109 million units in 2019, which uncovers a course of ''continuous development improvement''. The outcomes show that in 2010, somewhat more than 46,600 squander electronic gadgets were created; this number expanded to 48 million by 2019. Later on period, from 2020 to 2035, the age of waste electronic devices is projected to arrive at roughly 181 million units in 2020 and 224 million units in 2035, while the combined amount of waste electronic contraptions is anticipated to surpass 3.34 billion units. During this period, the aggregate number of waste electronic contraptions is supposed to be roughly 1.7 billion element telephones and around 1.64 billion electronic gadgets, which represents 51.02% of the aggregate and 48.98% of the aggregate, individually. The future formative ways of electronic gadgets and waste element telephones vary impressively relying upon their administration life expectancies and changed or accepted yearly development rates. By and large, squander highlight telephones show a course of ''moderate growth decline''. The quantity of waste component telephones is anticipated to expand consistently to a top in 2023 of 132 million units. This amount is supposed to diminish bit by bit and at last arrive at 77.5 million units in 2035.

The yearly figure for highlight telephones is projected to change between 77.52 million units and 131.95 million units. Nonetheless, include telephones are not supposed to be eliminated during this period. On the other hand, squander electronic gadgets show a course of ''moderate development'' as it were. The figure for electronic gadgets is supposed to increment from 61.73 million units in 2020 to 146.87 million units in 2035, which demonstrates that electronic gadgets are anticipated to develop consistently and persistently. In addition, these figures demonstrate that the utilization of component telephones is diminishing yet that of electronic gadgets is expanding. Just in years almost 2030 are the numbers comparable, however the hole then, at that point, keeps on expanding. The CHTMs contained in squander electronic devices were assessed; the outcomes showed that more than 19.8 thousand tons of CHTMs were put away in squander electronic contraptions in India from 2009 to 2035. In particular, the social supplies of palladium and cobalt put away in squander electronic devices from 2009 to 2035. These outcomes are likewise ordered into two periods, specifically, recorded period and future period. In the recorded period, from 2009 to 2019, the total social supplies of palladium and cobalt contained in squander electronic contraptions were roughly 6.5 tons and 2738.7 tons, separately. As a general rule, the social supplies of palladium and cobalt contained in both component telephones and electronic gadgets and the deals of electronic contraptions in this period expanded consistently.

The absolute amount of palladium and cobalt safeguarded in squander electronic devices likewise expanded significantly because of the consistent expansion in the deals of electronic devices. The total social supplies of palladium put away in squander electronic devices in India outperformed 1.7 tons in 2019, which is equivalent to roughly 21.13% of the worldwide palladium yield - with the exception of Canada, Russia, South Africa, the United States, and Zimbabwe - which was around 8 tons as indicated by information delivered by the United States Geological Survey (USGS, 2012). In India, the amount of cobalt contained in squander electronic contraptions appropriately reuse or reuse the CHTMs in squander electronic devices, almost certainly, the reliance on essential mineral will be altogether decreased, and the asset supply imperatives will be feeling better in India. Later on period, with the expansion in the creation and utilization of different electronic items, the auxiliary asset impacts of palladium and cobalt put away in squander electronic contraptions will turn out to be progressively evident. From 2009 to 2035, the outcomes show that the all-out amount of palladium and the complete amount of cobalt put away in squander electronic devices will be around 46.4 tons and 19,525.6 tons, individually. With mechanical advances and electronic devices practical redesigns, an assortment of CHTMs, for example, antimony, beryllium, neodymium, praseodymium and platinum, which are not put away in highlight telephones are right now being utilized to create electronic gadgets.

The individual social loads of these five CHTMs contained in squander electronic gadgets from 2009 to 2035. The outcomes can be classified into two periods the verifiable surpassed 713.9 tons in 2019, which represents 22.84% of the cobalt put away in squander electronic contraptions in China in 2016. If the Indian government can go to successful lengths to period and the future time frame. In the verifiable period, from 2009 to 2019, an aggregate of 20.2 huge loads of these CHTMs collected in squander electronic gadgets, including 11.2 huge loads of antimony, 0.4 huge loads of beryllium, 6.7 huge loads of neodymium, 1.3tons of praseodymium, and 0.5 huge loads of platinum. In 2019, the social loads of beryllium, neodymium, praseodymium, platinum and antimony were 0.1 tons, 2.4 tons, 0.5 tons, 0.2tons and 4 tons, individually. Proficient reusing and the board of these CHTM stocks contained in electronic gadgets would produce positive asset impacts. A rising measure of different auxiliary CHTM assets can be procured if other CHTM-rich side-effects are reused properly and successfully. Later on period, from 2020 to

2035, a greater number of than 247.1 huge loads of CHTMs are supposed to be protected in squander electronic gadgets. In particular, more than 137.5 huge loads of antimony, 4.9 huge loads of beryllium, 16.4 huge loads of praseodymium, 81.8 huge loads of neodymium, and 6.6 huge loads of platinum will be contained in squander electronic gadgets. With the fast headway of man-made brainpower and future 5G-related foundation development, it is predictable that undeniably different CHTMs will be gathered or put away in future normal waste electronic items, for example, squander electronic gadgets and workstations.

Sensitivity Analysis

Assessment results generally have some degree of vulnerability. Suppositions were made with respect to the proposed assessment toward the start of the review. Responsiveness investigation is essential for assessment and future projection utilizing numerical models. It is enthusiastically prescribed to research the vulnerability of the projection brings about the accepted scope of conceivable boundary values. One significant boundary that requires thought is the electronic devices life expectancy conveyance, which is a dynamic, undulating, and developing worth with the headway of new advances The life expectancy dissemination is a main consideration that impacts the projection consequences of the quantity of waste electronic contraptions that are produced, for both electronic gadgets and element telephones. In this paper, the responsiveness of the numerical model to boundaries was broke down in the Weibull circulation work with a scope of ± 1.0 years.

The assessed outcomes for various electronic contraptions lifetime suppositions in situation 1 (7 years) and situation 2 (9 years) are recorded in the Supplementary Material. The normal life expectancy variety of ± 1.0 years causes a change in yearly waste component telephone of roughly 3.21% to 1.52%. Expecting that the normal life expectancy of component telephones diminishes to 7.0 years in situation 1 and increments to 9.0 years in situation 2, the normal life expectancy variety of ± 1.0 years will probably cause vacillations of between roughly 3.21% and 1.52% in the yearly number of waste element telephones that are created. For electronic gadgets, the normal life expectancy is accepted to diminish to 5.0 years in situation 1 and increment to 7.0 years in situation 2, which produces changes of 6.93% and 6.85% later on yearly number of waste electronic gadgets that are created. The definite assessment consequences of electronic contraptions in various situations are displayed in the Supplementary Material. Material piece is another basic affecting component. Parts and metals will show various vacillations as indicated by the patterns in innovation restoration or electronic devices refreshes. For example,the content of CHTMs in the various classes of electronic devices shows up altogether unique. This investigation expected that the normal material substance extents are reliable while assessing the CHTMs in squander electronic contraptions. This supposition that is probably going to lead to a deviation in the substance of CHTM amounts in various kinds of waste electronic contraptions. Along these lines, situations 3 and 4 considered various loads of CHTMs substance to lead an awareness examination. The nitty gritty aftereffects of the awareness investigation in squander electronic devices In various situations are introduced in the Supplementary Material.

DISCUSSION

Estimated Quantities of Waste Electronic Gadgets

The awareness examination shows that the electronic contraptions life expectancy is a key element that impacts the quantity of waste electronic devices. Numerous past examinations have shown that the electronic devices life expectancy changes considerably among nations and districts. For instance, found that the normal life expectancy of electronic contraptions in the Czech Republic is around 7.99 years, which is longer than that in many nations. They observed that the normal life expectancy of electronic contraptions in Brazil is roughly 4.5 years, which surpasses the normal most authorities on the matter would agree. They assessed that the normal life expectancy of electronic contraptions in Iran is roughly 3 years. They uncovered that the normal electronic devices life expectancy is under three years in China. They revealed that the normal life expectancy of electronic devices is under two years in China.

One of the significant explanations behind these outcomes is the particular shopper conduct in various locales and nations. Nonetheless, the circumstance in the Indian setting is captivating. In the first place, the prevalence of electronic gadgets is developing at a high speed, and most of the Indian populace has all the earmarks of being keen on supplanting old electronic devices with the most cutting-edge electronic gadgets. Be that as it may, the e-garbage removal ways of behaving of Indian purchasers fluctuates significantly in various pieces of the country. Most of the Indian populace will in general utilize electronic items until they are harmed or new innovation is accessible at a reasonable cost. Furthermore, the casual economy is sizeable and contributes fundamentally to the long life expectancy of electronic gadgets in India. In this manner, the normal life expectancy of electronic contraptions in India is significantly longer than that in most different nations and districts of the world. Concentrates on show that electronic gadgets in India have the longest life expectancy and can last six to eight years. Apparently, scarcely any investigations have assessed the age and future patterns of waste electronic devices in India while considering the distinctions between include telephones and electronic gadgets. Restricted research concentrates on zeroed in on broad waste electrical and electronic hardware (WEEE) items have been led for the Indian market. As per our assessment, during the time of 2009 to 2019, the all out total age of waste element telephones and electronic gadgets was roughly 498.9 million units and 133.8million units, separately.

Further extended that from 2020 to 2035, the all-out aggregate waste age of element telephones and electronic gadgets will be around 1.7 billion units and 1.6 billion units, individually. We accept that these outcomes give a strong premise and apply beneficial outcomes on squander electronic contraptions the board in India. Nonetheless, the assessment precision would be significantly improved by information of better quality. We trust that sooner rather than later, better information can be gotten for an intensive comprehension of Indian electronic devices shopper conduct to give a more solid assessment of the waste sum and a more clear understanding of dynamic electronic devices lifetime data (Debnath, 2022; He et al., 2021, 2021).

Strategic Value of High-Tech Minerals

With the pattern of computerization, media transmission and electronic gadget innovation advancement around the world, the Indian hardware industry has become one of the quickest developing businesses in the country specifically, electronic contraptions have turned into a close vital thing in roughly 10 years they have become one of the quickest developing items in the gadgets business. CHTMs contained in electronic devices have encountered emotional changes during this period. In this review, while inspecting the accessibility of CHTMs in electronic devices squander, the tremendous changes in the electronic contraptions industry and the intricacy of the CHTMs remembered for telephones were completely evaluated and thought of. CHTMs are significant natural substances for some worldwide arising enterprises.

The interest for different CHTMs is supposed to keep filling in the long haul because of the quick headway of media transmission and battery development. Notwithstanding, the steady and persistent inventory of different CHTMs is probably going to be impacted by a few variables. One variable is that the inventory of CHTMs is enormously dependent on the specific transporter mineral. For instance, the double-dealing of gallium to a great extent depends on the limit of its transporter mineral aluminium. Another significant variable is surprising world occasions or worldwide crises. For example, the new episode of the COVID-19 pandemic has considerably impacted worldwide stockpile chains. In outrageous conditions, squander electronic contraptions have turned into a bountiful auxiliary CHTM repository with extensive vital worth. In India, the amassed social supply of cobalt put away in squander electronic devices outperformed 2738.7 tons in 2019 and is projected to surpass 16786.8 tons in 2035. Moreover, the grade of cobalt in squander electronic contraptions is altogether higher than that in normal mineral. A past report uncovered that main roughly 1.2 kg of cobalt material can be procured from mining one ton of normal cobalt mineral; yet around 63 kg of cobalt can be recognized in one ton of waste electronic gadgets. Along these lines, the legitimate taking care of and reusing of CHTMs in squander electronic devices has huge vital worth.

Comparing India With China

China and India are right now the two biggest dynamic Internet markets; they create a gigantic amount of waste gadgets yearly. Reports show that China and India are supposed to twofold the age of e-squander amounts in the following not many years. Electronic devices are one of the quickest developing classes of WEEE items in both the Chinese and Indian settings. In China, around 2.3 billion units of waste component telephones and 1.0 billion units of waste electronic gadgets were created from 1987 to 2016, and beyond what 15 thousand tons of CHTMs could be reused from these waste electronic contraptions. Later on, the age of more than 1 billion units of waste electronic devices is normal in 2035, which will make north of 90 thousand tons of CHTM safeguarding. As per our assessment, the gathered number of waste electronic contraptions in India has outperformed 632.7 million units, including around 499 million units of waste component telephones and 133.8 million units of waste electronic gadgets from 2009 to 2019. Additionally, beyond what 2765.4 huge loads of CHTMs could be reused from these waste electronic contraptions. Guaging demonstrates the age of waste electronic contraptions is projected to be 181.2 million units in 2020 and to arrive at 224.4 million units in 2035, with more than 17,073.8 huge loads of CHTMs. As recently talked about, concerning the present and future accessibility, an unprecedented number of waste electronic devices are accessible in China and India, and a huge amount of CHTMs is put away in electronic devices squander, which addresses a bountiful auxiliary CHTM supply.

Remarkably, in later many years, the age of waste component telephones is supposed to diminish quickly in China; be that as it may, the circumstance in India is altogether unique. In 2035, it is anticipated that over almost 100% of waste electronic devices in the Chinese market will be electronic gadgets, and the level of waste element telephones will be under 1%. Highlight telephones will in any case play a significant part in the Indian electronic contraptions market. One potential justification behind the present circumstance is that most of the Indian populace is as yet confronting imperatives in updating their element telephones to electronic gadgets. A definite realistic examination of India and China is remembered for the Supplementary Material. Future pertinent examinations can be directed in light of other nations' datasets utilizing the philosophy used in this review. For instance, our outcomes can be reached out to other emerging nations, like Brazil, Mexico, Vietnam, and so on A more extensive examination of these arising nations could uncover valuable examples of electronic devices reusing and assist with distinguishing the legitimate electronic devices administrative methodologies. Above all, this more extensive correlation would contribute enormously to other nations' electronic contraptions vital preparation.

CONCLUSION AND IMPLICATIONS

Concluding Remarks

The point of this study was to gauge the previous volumes and foresee the future volumes of waste electronic devices and different CHTMs contained in them in India from 2009 to 2035. No past review has determined the quantity of electronic contraptions and future patterns of electronic devices in India. In this review, material stream examination and the Weibull appropriation were utilized to assess the amount of waste electronic contraptions age and related CHTM stocks by independently considering electronic gadgets and component telephones. Since India turned into the second-biggest electronic gadget market following China, it is critical to concentrate on the current status and future pattern of the electronic contraptions market in India. This article gives gauge information to fill the information hole in this field and to assist partners with upgrading how they might interpret this field. In view of this investigation, the accompanying ends can be reached: (1) Waste electronic contraptions contain different CHTMs, and the substance of CHTMs changes among electronic gadgets and component telephones; (2) From 2009 to 2019, the collected number of waste electronic contraptions in India outperformed 632.7 million units, including around 130 million units and 500 million units of waste electronic gadgets and element telephones, separately. In excess of 27 thousand tons of CHTMs are accessible for reusing. Later on, it is anticipated that in excess of 180 million units of waste electronic devices will be produced in 2020. This number will surpass 220 million out of 2035, which makes in excess of 170 thousand tons of CHTM conservation in squander electronic devices. (3) Electronic contraptions squander volumes in India show an overall vertical propensity, which demonstrates that different potential CHTMs contained in electronic devices waste ought to be fittingly reused or reused (Bhogaraju et al., 2020; Reddy et al., 2022; Satheesh et al., n.d.).

Implications

In light of the outcomes, a few proposals can be made to assist with further developing waste electronic contraptions the board in India: (1) From an administration viewpoint, the Indian government ought to propose an exhaustive bundle intend to work on significant WEEE reusing regulations and guidelines, zeroing in particularly on squander electronic devices reusing. In the first place, the electronic contraptions reusing industry ought to be planned and controlled since the essential e-squander reusing technique in India is casual which is destructive to the climate and human wellbeing. Second, the Indian government ought to perceive the essential significance of different CHTMs contained in squander electronic contraptions, which involve a plentiful potential HTM repository that is basic for public safety. Third, the Indian government ought to carry out strategies with respect to a roundabout and feasible WEEE reusing framework and contribute bureaucratic assets to help online WEEE reusing exercises. (2) From an organization point of view, different electronic devices organizations ought to put forth attempts to address what is happening. In the first place, the item biological plan ought to be improved by assembling organizations to guarantee that future waste electronic devices can be destroyed or reused with a standard structure. Research-based organizations ought to put adequate assets into innovative work (R&D) to further develop destroying or refining advances. Second, homegrown organizations ought to draw in unfamiliar speculations. With some inside and out activities among partners, empowering organizations to effectively gather squander electronic devices and around handle squander electronic contraptions fittingly will have long haul benefits. (3) From a shopper viewpoint, neighbourhood customers have gigantic potential for development. Shoppers' cognizance, mindfulness, acknowledgment and disposition will straightforwardly and in a roundabout way influence their conduct propensities. In the first place, Indian buyers ought to work on their consciousness of waste electronic gadget reusing and effectively progress from that point customary way to deal with natural insurance and proficiency. Second, real electronic devices utilization ways of behaving can be changed by changes in awareness. In addition, assuming most of shoppers in the public arena were wilful good examples, the finish of-life reusing rate would almost certainly get to the next level.

Limitations and Future Directions

This study means to dissect the volume of gathered squander electronic devices and the volume of the CHTMs contained in these electronic devices by independently considering highlight telephones and electronic gadgets in the Indian setting. Additionally, a market supply model was taken on to foresee the future patterns of

CHTMs in squander electronic devices in India. Be that as it may, there are still a constraints and vulnerabilities in this article because of restricted assets, like time and information accessibility. To start with, the electronic devices life expectancy data was acquired from past distributions and may not be substantial for India. Second, our assessment and forecast outcomes are hypothetical. In spite of the fact that is the outcomes depend on a generally recognized numerical model, they could in any case display a few deviations. Besides, the material synthesis may move after some time; in any case, we utilized fixed values announced in the writing on the grounds that precisely it is almost difficult to project future changes. Last, more information ought to be given to investigate the effect of the source and supply of vital metals on electronic contraptions according to the point of view of the upstream and downstream businesses of key minerals in electronic devices. Considering these restrictions, future examinations ought to lead a public poll overview to straightforwardly acquire direct electronic devices life expectancy data from Indian electronic devices customers. Moreover, future examinations ought to likewise consider the plans of cutting edge electronic contraptions, which will probably have different CHTM pieces (Bhogaraju et al., 2021; Seeja et al., 2021).

REFERENCES

Abalansa, S., El Mahrad, B., Icely, J., & Newton, A. (2021). Electronic waste, an environmental problem exported to developing countries: The GOOD, the BAD and the UGLY. *Sustainability*, *13*(9), 5302. doi:10.3390u13095302

Bhogaraju, S. D., & Korupalli, V. R. K. (2020). Design of Smart Roads-A Vision on Indian Smart Infrastructure Development. *2020 International Conference on COMmunication Systems & NETworkS (COMSNETS)*, 773–778. 10.1109/COMSNETS48256.2020.9027404

Bhogaraju, S. D., Kumar, K. V. R., Anjaiah, P., & Shaik, J. H. (2021). Advanced Predictive Analytics for Control of Industrial Automation Process. In Innovations in the Industrial Internet of Things (IIoT) and Smart Factory (pp. 33–49). IGI Global. doi:10.4018/978-1-7998-3375-8.ch003

Debnath, B. (2022). Sustainability of WEEE recycling in India. In *Re-Use and Recycling of Materials* (pp. 15–32). River Publishers. doi:10.1201/9781003339304-3

He, P., Hu, G., Wang, C., Hewage, K., Sadiq, R., & Feng, H. (2021). Analyzing present and future availability of critical high-tech minerals in waste cellphones: A case study of India. *Waste Management (New York, N.Y.)*, *119*, 275–284. doi:10.1016/j.wasman.2020.10.001 PMID:33099072

Hsu, C.-W., & Hu, A. H. (2008). Green supply chain management in the electronic industry. *International Journal of Environmental Science & Technology, 5*(2), 205–216.

Huang, Y.-C., Borazon, E. Q., & Liu, J.-M. (2021). Antecedents and consequences of green supply chain management in Taiwan's electric and electronic industry. *Journal of Manufacturing Technology Management, 32*(5), 1066–1093. doi:10.1108/JMTM-05-2020-0201

Kossukhina, M. A. (2021). Digital transformation technologies of the enterprises in the electronic industry of Russia. *2021 IEEE Conference of Russian Young Researchers in Electrical and Electronic Engineering (ElConRus)*, 1898–1900. 10.1109/ElConRus51938.2021.9396528

Lau, K. H., & Wang, Y. (2009). Reverse logistics in the electronic industry of China: A case study. *Supply Chain Management*.

Pan, X., Wong, C. W. Y., & Li, C. (2022). Circular economy practices in the waste electrical and electronic equipment (WEEE) industry: A systematic review and future research agendas. *Journal of Cleaner Production, 365*, 132671. doi:10.1016/j.jclepro.2022.132671

Qahtan, S., Alsattar, H. A., Zaidan, A. A., Pamucar, D., & Deveci, M. (2022). Integrated sustainable transportation modelling approaches for electronic passenger vehicle in the context of industry 5.0. *Journal of Innovation & Knowledge, 7*(4), 100277.

Reddy, E. M. K., Gurrala, A., Hasitha, V. B., & Kumar, K. V. R. (2022). Introduction to Naive Bayes and a Review on Its Subtypes with Applications. *Bayesian Reasoning and Gaussian Processes for Machine Learning Applications*, 1–14.

Satheesh, M. K., & Kumar, K. V. R. (n.d.). Addressing the Utilization of Popular Regression Models in Business Applications. In Machine Learning for Business Analytics (pp. 29–43). Productivity Press. doi:10.4324/9781003206316-3

Seeja, G., Reddy, O., Kumar, K. V. R., Mounika, S., & ... (2021). Internet of Things and Robotic Applications in the Industrial Automation Process. In *Innovations in the Industrial Internet of Things (IIoT) and Smart Factory* (pp. 50–64). IGI Global.

Compilation of References

Abalansa, S., El Mahrad, B., Icely, J., & Newton, A. (2021). Electronic waste, an environmental problem exported to developing countries: The GOOD, the BAD and the UGLY. *Sustainability*, *13*(9), 5302. doi:10.3390u13095302

Abdullah, M., Al-Ayyoub, M., AlRawashdeh, S., & Shatnawi, F. (2021). E-learningDJUST: E-learning dataset from Jordan university of science and technology toward investigating the impact of COVID-19 pandemic on education. *Neural Computing & Applications*, 1–15. doi:10.100700521-021-06712-1 PMID:34803236

About Apple Inc. (2019). https://www.reuters.com/finance/stocks/company-profile/AAPL.O

Adornato, A. C. (2016). Forces at the gate: Social media's influence on editorial and production decisions in local television newsrooms. *Electronic News*, *10*(2), 87–104. doi:10.1177/1931243116647768

Agrawal, A., Gans, J., & Goldfarb, A. (2018). *Prediction machines: the simple economics of artificial intelligence*. Harvard Business Press.

Agrawal, M. L. (2004). Customer Relationship Management (CRM) & Corporate Renaissance. *Journal of Service Research*, *3*(2), 149–167.

Akhtar, G. (2014). Problem and Prospect of FDI Inflows in Indian Pharmaceutical Industry. *IOSR Journal Of Humanities And Social Science*, *19*(3), 69–73. doi:10.9790/0837-19316973

Alhumaid, K., Habes, M., & Salloum, S. A. (2021). Examining the factors influencing the mobile learning usage during COVID-19 Pandemic: An Integrated SEM-ANN Method. *IEEE Access: Practical Innovations, Open Solutions*, *9*, 102567–102578. doi:10.1109/ACCESS.2021.3097753

An, J., & Rau, R. (2021). Finance, technology and disruption. *European Journal of Finance*, *27*(4–5), 334–345. doi:10.1080/1351847X.2019.1703024

Asghar, N. (2016). Yelp dataset challenge: Review rating prediction doi:10.48550/arXiv.1605.05362

Ayati, N., Saiyarsarai, P., & Nikfar, S. (2020). Short and long term impacts of COVID-19 on the pharmaceutical sector. *Daru: Journal of Faculty of Pharmacy, Tehran University of Medical Sciences*, *28*(2), 799–805. doi:10.100740199-020-00358-5 PMID:32617864

Baber, H. (2021). Modelling the acceptance of e-learning during the pandemic of COVID-19-A study of South Korea. *The International Journal of Management Education*. doi:. doi:10.1016/j.ijme.2021.100503

Baderiya, M. S. H., & Chawan, P. M. (2018). Customer buying Prediction Using Machine-Learning Techniques. *Survey (London, England)*.

Balaji, G. N., & Rajesh, D. (2017). Smart Vehicle Number Plate Detection System for Different Countries Using an Improved Segmentation Method. *Imperial Journal of Interdisciplinary Research (IJIR)*.

Ballestar, M. T., Grau-Carles, P., & Sainz, J. (2019). Predicting customer quality in e-commerce social networks: A machine learning approach. *Review of Managerial Science*, *13*(3), 589–603. doi:10.100711846-018-0316-x

Bandy, J., & Diakopoulos, N. (2019). Auditing News Curation Systems: A Case Study Examining Algorithmic and Editorial Logic in Apple News.

Baral, P. K., Das, D., & Kumar, K. (2016). Mutual Funds Industry in India: A Growth Trend Analysis. *International Journal of Multidisciplinary Research and Development*, *3*(1), 1–13.

Batra, R., & Keller, K. L. (2016). Integrating marketing communications: New findings, new lessons, and new ideas. *Journal of Marketing*, *80*(6), 122–145. doi:10.1509/jm.15.0419

Batt, S., Grealis, T., Harmon, O., & Tomolonis, P. (2020). Learning Tableau: A data visualization tool. *The Journal of Economic Education*, *51*(3–4), 317–328. doi:10.1080/00220485.2020.1804503

Baumann, A., Haupt, J., Gebert, F., & Lessmann, S. (2018). Changing perspectives: Using graph metrics to predict purchase probabilities. *Expert Systems with Applications*, *94*, 137–148. doi:10.1016/j.eswa.2017.10.046

Bergman, A. (2006). *FDI and spillover effects in the Indian pharmaceutical industry*. Academic Press.

Bhogaraju, S. D., & Korupalli, V. R. K. (2020, January). Design of smart roads-a vision on indian smart infrastructure development. In *2020 International Conference on COMmunication Systems & NETworkS (COMSNETS)* (pp. 773-778). IEEE. 10.1109/COMSNETS48256.2020.9027404

Bhogaraju, S. D., Kumar, K. V. R., Anjaiah, P., & Shaik, J. H. (2021). Advanced Predictive Analytics for Control of Industrial Automation Process. In Innovations in the Industrial Internet of Things (IIoT) and Smart Factory (pp. 33-49). IGI Global. doi:10.4018/978-1-7998-3375-8.ch003

Bhogaraju, S. D., Kumar, K. V. R., Anjaiah, P., Shaik, J. H., & ... (2021). Advanced Predictive Analytics for Control of Industrial Automation Process. In *Innovations in the Industrial Internet of Things (IIoT) and Smart Factory* (pp. 33–49). IGI Global.

Biong, H., Parvatiyar, A., & Wathne, K. (1996). Are Customer Satisfaction Measures Appropriate to Measure Relationship Satisfaction? In A. Parvatiyar & J. N. Sheth (Eds.), *Contemporary Knowledge of Relationship Marketing* (pp. 258–275). Emory University Centre for Relationship Marketing.

Bock, M. A. (2016). Showing versus telling: Comparing online video from newspaper and television websites. *Journalism*, *17*(4), 493–510. doi:10.1177/1464884914568076

Boeing, A. (2019). https://www.boeing.com/company/general-info/

Bruns, A., & Nuernbergk, C. (2019). Political journalists and their social media audiences: New power relations. *Media and Communication*, *7*(1), 198–212. doi:10.17645/mac.v7i1.1759

Campbell, D., Wells, J., & Valacich, J. S. (2009). Diagnosing and Managing Online Business-to-Consumer (B2C) Relationships: Toward an eCommerce B2C Relationship Stage Theory. *AIS Transactions on Human-Computer Interaction*, *1*(4), 108–132. doi:10.17705/1thci.00008

Cha, S. H., Steemers, K., & Kim, T. W. (2018). Modeling space preferences for accurate occupancy prediction during the design phase. Automation in Construction, 93, 135–147. doi:10.1016/j.autcon.2018.05.001

Chakraborty, I., Kim, M., & Sudhir, K. (2019). Attribute sentiment scoring with online text reviews: Accounting for language structure and attribute self-selection.

Chang, Y.-H., & Lee, M.-S. (2017). Incorporating Markov decision process on genetic algorithms to formulate trading strategies for stock markets. *Applied Soft Computing*, *52*, 1143–1153. doi:10.1016/j.asoc.2016.09.016

Chen, Y., Hong, T. & Luo, X. (2018). An agent-based stochastic Occupancy Simulator. *Building Simulation*, *11*(1), 37–49.

Cheng, C., Mei1, L., & Zhang, J. (2018). License Plate Recognition via Deep Convolutional Neural Network. *IOP Conference Series: Earth and Environmental Science, Volume 189, Traffic Engineering and Transportation System*.

Chen, I. J., & Popvich, K. (2003). Understanding customer relationship management (CRM): People, process and technology. *Business Process Management Journal*, *9*(5), 672–688. doi:10.1108/14637150310496758

Chou, P., Chuang, H. H. C., Chou, Y. C., & Liang, T. P. (2022). Predictive analytics for customer repurchase: Interdisciplinary integration of buy till you die modeling and machine learning. *European Journal of Operational Research*, *296*(2), 635–651. doi:10.1016/j.ejor.2021.04.021

Christa, U., & Kristinae, V. (2021). The effect of product innovation on business performance during COVID 19 pandemic. *Uncertain Supply Chain Management*, *9*(1), 151–158. doi:10.5267/j.uscm.2020.10.006

Crosby, L. A. (2002). Exploding some myths about customer relationship management. *Journal of Service Theory and Practice*, *12*(5), 271–277. doi:10.1108/09604520210442056

Cui, D., & Curry, D. (2005). Prediction in marketing using the support vector machine. *Marketing Science*, *24*(4), 595–615. doi:10.1287/mksc.1050.0123

Dalal, N., & Triggs, B. (2005). Histograms of oriented gradients for human detection. *IEEE Computer Society Conference on Computer Vision and Pattern Recognition (CVPR'05)*, pp. 886-893 vol. 1, 10.1109/CVPR.2005.177

Damodaran, A. (2014). *Session 7: Market Efficiency - Laying the Groundwork*. Academic Press.

Davis, D. F., Golicic, S. L., & Marquardt, A. (2012). *Business-to-business Marketing Management: Strategies, Cases, and Solutions*. Emerald Group Publishing. doi:10.1108/S1069-0964(2012)18

Day, G. S. (2000). Managing Market Relationships. *Journal of the Academy of Marketing Science*, *28*(1), 24–30. doi:10.1177/0092070300281003

de Pauli, Z. T., Suellen, M. K., & Bonat, W. H. (2020). Comparing artificial neural network architectures for Brazilian stock market prediction. *Annals of Data Science*, *7*(4), 613–628. doi:10.100740745-020-00305-w

Dean, T., Ruzon, M., Segal, M., Shlens, J., Vijaya-Narasimhan, S., Yagnik, J. (2013). Fast accurate detection of 100000 object classes on a single machine. *Computer Vision and Pattern Recognition (CVPR)*, pp. 1814-1821, 2013.

Debnath, B. (2022). Sustainability of WEEE recycling in India. In *Re-Use and Recycling of Materials* (pp. 15–32). River Publishers. doi:10.1201/9781003339304-3

Depot, A. H. (2019). https://www.reuters.com/finance/stocks/company-profile/HD.N

Dhande, N. C., & Magar, A. V. (2015). A Study of Foreign Direct Investment in Indian Pharmaceutical Industry. *International Journal (Toronto, Ont.)*, *3*(7).

Dhar, B., & Joseph, R. K. (2019). India's information technology industry: A tale of two halves. In *Innovation, Economic Development, and Intellectual Property in India and China* (pp. 93–117). Springer.

Dimovski, W., Brooks, R., & van Eekelen, A. (2007). The costs of raising equity capital for closed-end fund IPOs. *Applied Financial Economics Letters*, *3*(5), 295–299. doi:10.1080/17446540701222391

Dowling, G. (2002). *Customer Relationship Management: In B2C Markets Often Less Is More*. doi:10.2307/41166134

Ellikkal, A., Rajamohan, S., & Prakash, M. O. (2022). IPOs in Indian Stock Market: Analyzing Pricing and Performance of IPO Listed in 2021. *Journal of Management*, *10*(2), 1–8.

Elzamly, A. (2017). Predicting critical cloud computing security issues using Artificial Neural Network (ANNs) algorithms in banking organizations. http://dstore.alazhar.edu.ps/xmlui/handle/123456789/445

Engel, J., Agrawal, K. K., Chen, S., Gulrajani, I., Donahue, C., & Roberts, A. (2019). Gansynth: Adversarial neural audio synthesis.

Erhan, D., Szegedy, C., Toshev, A., & Anguelov, D. (2014). Scalable object detection using deep neural networks. *Computer Vision and Pattern Recognition,* pp. 2155-2162. 10.1109/CVPR.2014.276

Evolution of CRM. (n.d.). *AgileCRM.* Retrieved from https://www.agilecrm.com/crm/evolution-of-crm#:~:text=In%20t he%20last%20decade%20or,to%20interactive%20client%20relation ship%20management

Facebook, A. (2019). https://www.reuters.com/finance/stocks/company-profile/FB.OQ

Fairlie, R., & Fossen, F. M. (2022). The early impacts of the COVID-19 pandemic on business sales. *Small Business Economics*, *58*(4), 1853–1864. doi:10.100711187-021-00479-4

Felzenszwalb, P. F., Girshick, R. B., McAllester, D., & Ramanan, D. (2010, September). Object Detection with Discriminatively Trained Part-Based Models. *IEEE Transactions on Pattern Analysis and Machine Intelligence*, *32*(9), 1627–1645. doi:10.1109/TPAMI.2009.167 PMID:20634557

Fink, K. & Schudson, M. (2020). The Algorithm Method. *Columbia Journalism Review.* https://archives.cjr.org/the_research_report/the_algorithm_m ethod.php

Focus, F. (2011). *Profit Margin Analysis. Third Quarter 2011.* http://search. credoreference.com.ezproxy.westminster.ac.uk/ content/entry/ultimatebusiness/pr ofit_margin/0/

Frankowska-Takhari, S. (2020). Selecting and tailoring of images for visual impact in online journalism. *IR Information Research.* http://informationr.net/ir/22-1/colis/colis1619.html

GAMMA. (2020). Crowd and Multi-agent Simulation. GAMMA. http://gamma.cs.unc.edu/research/crowds/

Ghosh, B., Basu, B. & O'Mahony, M. (2009). Multivariate short-term traffic flow forecasting using time-series analysis. *IEEE Transactions on Intelligent Transportation Systems*, *10*(2), 246–254.

Gillick, J., & Bamman, D. (2018, June). Telling stories with soundtracks: an empirical analysis of music in film. In *Proceedings of the First Workshop on Storytelling,* (pp. 33-42). 10.18653/v1/W18-1504

Girshick, R., Donahue, J., Darrell, T., & Malik, J. (2014). Rich Feature Hierarchies for Accurate Object Detection and Semantic Segmentation. *IEEE Conference on Computer Vision and Pattern Recognition*, pp. 580-587, 10.1109/CVPR.2014.81

Granger, C. W. (1969). Some recent developments in a concept of causality. *Journal of Econometrics, 39.*

Gummesson, E. (2008). Quality, service-dominant logic and many-to-many marketing. *The TQM Journal*, *20*(2), 143–153. doi:10.1108/17542730810857372

Hammond, P. (2017). From computer-assisted to data-driven: Journalism and Big Data. *Journalism*, *18*(4), 408–424. doi:10.1177/1464884915620205

Harman, R. (2020). How technology is changing the Craft of Screenwriting. *Raindance*. https://www.raindance.org/how-technology-is-changing-the-craft-of-screenwriting/

Harrington, C. (2003). *Fundamental vs. Technical Analysis. CFA Institute Magazine*. doi:10.2469/cfm.v14.n1.2789

Hartmann, J., Huppertz, J., Schamp, C., & Heitmann, M. (2019). Comparing automated text classification methods. *International Journal of Research in Marketing*, *36*(1), 20–38. doi:10.1016/j.ijresmar.2018.09.009

Heidari, M., Zad, S., & Rafatirad, S. (2021). Ensemble of supervised and unsupervised learning models to predict a profitable business decision. *IEEE International IOT, Electronics and Mechatronics Conference (IEMTRONICS)*, IEEE. 10.1109/IEMTRONICS52119.2021.9422649

Hellerstein, J.L., Zhang, F. & Shahabuddin, P. (2001). Statistical approach to predictive detection. *Computer Networks*, *35*(1), 77–95.

He, P., Hu, G., Wang, C., Hewage, K., Sadiq, R., & Feng, H. (2021). Analyzing present and future availability of critical high-tech minerals in waste cellphones: A case study of India. *Waste Management (New York, N.Y.)*, *119*, 275–284. doi:10.1016/j.wasman.2020.10.001 PMID:33099072

Hilpisch, Y. (2014). *Python for Finance: Analyze big financial data*. O'Reilly Media, Inc.

Hilpisch, Y. (2018). *Python for finance: mastering data-driven finance*. O'Reilly Media.

Hossain, N. (2020). Sentiment analysis of restaurant reviews using combined CNN-LSTM. *11th International Conference on Computing, Communication and Networking Technologies (ICCCNT)*, IEEE. 10.1109/ICCCNT49239.2020.9225328

Hsu, C.-W., & Hu, A. H. (2008). Green supply chain management in the electronic industry. *International Journal of Environmental Science & Technology, 5*(2), 205–216.

Huang, L. (2015). Auto regressive moving average (ARMA) modeling method for gyro random noise using a robust kalman filter. *Sensors, 15*(10), 25277–25286.

Huang, Sinha, & Zhao. (2018). The Interaction between croblog. *Sentiment and Stock Return: An Empirical Examination*.

Huang, D., & Luo, L. (2016). Consumer preference elicitation of complex products using fuzzy support vector machine active learning. *Marketing Science*, *35*(3), 445–464. doi:10.1287/mksc.2015.0946

Huang, Y.-C., Borazon, E. Q., & Liu, J.-M. (2021). Antecedents and consequences of green supply chain management in Taiwan's electric and electronic industry. *Journal of Manufacturing Technology Management*, *32*(5), 1066–1093. doi:10.1108/JMTM-05-2020-0201

Hu, S., Xiong, C., Yang, M., Younes, H., Luo, W., & Zhang, L. (2021). A big-data driven approach to analyzing and modeling human mobility trend under non-pharmaceutical interventions during COVID-19 pandemic. *Transportation Research Part C, Emerging Technologies*, *124*, 102955. doi:10.1016/j.trc.2020.102955 PMID:33456212

Jacobs, B. J., Donkers, B., & Fok, D. (2016). Model-based purchase predictions for large assortments. *Marketing Science*, *35*(3), 389–404. doi:10.1287/mksc.2016.0985

Jain, H., & Rautela, M. (2018). *FDI in Indian pharmaceutical sector*. Available at SSRN 3153434.

Jena, P. R., Majhi, R., Kalli, R., Managi, S., & Majhi, B. (2021). Impact of COVID-19 on GDP of major economies: Application of the artificial neural network forecaster. *Economic Analysis and Policy*, *69*, 324–339. doi:10.1016/j.eap.2020.12.013

Johnson, Clark, & Barczak. (2012). Customer relationship management processes: How faithful are business-to-business firms to customer profitability? *Industrial Marketing Management*. Advance online publication. doi:10.1016/j.indmarman.2012.04.001

Jones, S.S., Evans, R.S., Allen, T.L., Thomas, A., Haug, P.J., Welch, S.J. & Snow, G.L. (2009). A multivariate time series approach to modeling and forecasting demand in the emergency department. *Journal of Biomedical Informatics*, *42*(1), 123–139.

Joo, M. H., Nishikawa, Y., & Dandapani, K. (2019). Cryptocurrency, a successful application of blockchain technology. *Managerial Finance*.

Joseph, R. K., & Ranganathan, K. V. K. (2016). *Trends in Foreign Investment in Healthcare Sector of India*. ISID Working Paper No. 187. Institute for Studies in Industrial Development (ISID).

Kalekar, P. (2004). Time series forecasting using Holt-Winters exponential smoothing. *Kanwal Rekhi School of Information Technology*, 1–13. Available from: https://www.it.iitb.ac.in/~praj/acads/seminar/04329008_ExponentialSmoothing.pdf

Kam, H. J., & Sung, J. O. (2010). *Prediction of Daily ED Patient Numbers*. Available from: www.e-hir.org

Kaplan, R. S., & Norton, D. (1992, January-February). The Balanced Scorecard – Measures that Drive Performance. *Harvard Business Review*, *70*, 71–79. https://hbr.org/1992/01/the-balanced-scorecard-measures-that-drive-performance-2 PMID:10119714

Karwal, H., & Girdhar, A. (2015). Vehicle Number Plate Detection System for Indian Vehicles. *IEEE International Conference on Computational Intelligence & Communication Technology*, pp. 8-12, 10.1109/CICT.2015.13

Kashyap, A., Suresh, B., Patil, A., Sharma, S., & Jaiswal, A. (2018). Automatic Number Plate Recognition. *International Conference on Advances in Computing, Communication Control and Networking (ICACCCN)*, pp. 838-843, doi:10.1109/ICACCCN.2018.8748287

Kathuria, V., & Das, S. (2005). Impact of FDI on R\&D strategies of firms in the post-1991 era. *IIMB Management Review*, *17*(2), 17–28.

Keh, H. T., & Shieh, E. (2001). Online grocery retailing: Success factors and potential pitfalls. *Business Horizons*, *44*(4), 73–83. doi:10.1016/S0007-6813(01)80050-1

Kim, K.J. (2003). Financial time series forecasting using support vector machines. *Neurocomputing*, *55*(1–2), 307–319.

Kim, K.-J., & Han, I. (2010). *Genetic algorithms approach to feature discretization in artificial neural networks for the prediction of stock price index*. Available from: www.elsevier.com/locate/eswa

Kim, D. H., Lee, S., Jeon, J., & Song, B. C. (2020). Real-time purchase behavior recognition system based on deep learningbased object detection and tracking for an unmanned product cabinet. *Expert Systems with Applications*, *143*, 11306. doi:10.1016/j.eswa.2019.113063

Kim, J., Yang, K., Min, J., & White, B. (2022). Hope, fear, and consumer behavioral change amid COVID-19: Application of protection motivation theory. *International Journal of Consumer Studies*, *46*(2), 558–574. doi:10.1111/ijcs.12700 PMID:34220343

Kim, S., & Lee, H. (2022). Customer Churn Prediction in Influencer Commerce: An Application of Decision Trees. *Procedia Computer Science*, *199*, 1332–1339. doi:10.1016/j.procs.2022.01.169

Koehrsen, W. (n.d.). *Histograms and Density Plots in Python. Towards Data Science*. Available from: https://towardsdatascience.com/histograms-and-density-plots-in-python-f6bda88f5ac0

Kossukhina, M. A. (2021). Digital transformation technologies of the enterprises in the electronic industry of Russia. *2021 IEEE Conference of Russian Young Researchers in Electrical and Electronic Engineering (ElConRus)*, 1898–1900. 10.1109/ElConRus51938.2021.9396528

Kulkarni, Y., Bodkhe, S., Kamthe, A., & Patil, A. (2018). Automatic number plate recognition for motorcyclists riding without helmet. *International Conference on Current Trends towards Converging Technologies (ICCTCT)*, pp. 1-6, 10.1109/ICCTCT.2018.8551001

Kumar, K.V.R., & Elias, S. (n.d.). Use Case To Simulation: Muscular Fatigue Modeling And Analysis Using Openism. *Turkish Journal of Physiotherapy and Rehabilitation, 32, 2.*

Kumar, K.V.R., Zachariah, A.A., & Elias, S. (n.d.). *Quantitative Analysis of Athlete Performance in Artistic Skating using IMU, and Machine Learning Algorithms*. Academic Press.

Kumar, I., Rawat, J., Mohd, N., & Husain, S. (2021). Opportunities of artificial intelligence and machine learning in the food industry. *Journal of Food Quality*, *2021*, 1–10. doi:10.1155/2021/4535567

Kumar, V., & Reinartz, W. (2012). *Customer Relationship Management: Concept, Strategy, and Tools*. Springer. doi:10.1007/978-3-642-20110-3

Landa, R. (2021). *Advertising by design: Generating and designing creative ideas across media.* John Wiley & Sons.

Lau, K. H., & Wang, Y. (2009). Reverse logistics in the electronic industry of China: A case study. *Supply Chain Management.*

Lawson, R., C. M. A., C. S. C. A., Smith, D., C. A. E., C. M. A., & C. P. A. (2018). Developing data fluency. *Strategic Finance*, *100*(3), 68–69.

Lee, J., Jung, O., Lee, Y., Kim, O., & Park, C. (2021). A Comparison and Interpretation of Machine Learning Algorithm for the Prediction of Online Purchase Conversion. *Journal of Theoretical and Applied Electronic Commerce Research*, *16*(5), 1472–1491. doi:10.3390/jtaer16050083

Li, Q., Gu, M., Zhou, K., & Sun, X. (2016). Multi-classes feature engineering with sliding window for purchase prediction in mobile commerce. In *Proceedings - 15th IEEE international conference on data mining workshop, ICDMW*, (pp. 1048–1054)

Li, S., Joe, J., Hu, J., & Karava, P. (2015). System identification and model-predictive control of office buildings with integrated photovoltaic-thermal collectors, radiant floor heating and active thermal storage. Solar Energy, 113, 139–157. doi:10.1016/j.solener.2014.11.024

Lik Lau, B.P., Wijerathne, N., Kiat Ng, B.K., & Yuen, C. (2017). *Sensor fusion for public space utilization monitoring in a smart city.* Academic Press.

Li, K., Yang, D., Ji, S., & Liu, L. (2018, December). The Impacts of Subtitles on 360-Degree Video Journalism Watching. In *International Joint Conference on Information, Media and Engineering (ICIME)*, (pp. 130-134). IEEE. 10.1109/ICIME.2018.00035

Lindén, C. G. (2017). Algorithms for journalism: The future of news work. *The journal of media innovations, 4*(1), 60-76.

Lin, T. C. W. (2016). Compliance, technology, and modern finance. *Brook. J. Corp. Fin. \&. Com. L.*, *11*, 159.

Liu, X., Lee, D., & Srinivasan, K. (2019). Large-scale cross-category analysis of consumer review content on sales conversion leveraging deep learning. *JMR, Journal of Marketing Research*, *56*(6), 918–943. doi:10.1177/0022243719866690

Lo, C., Frankowski, D., & Leskovec, J. (2016). Understanding behaviors that lead to purchasing: a case study of pinterest. In *Proceedings of the ACM SIGKDD international conference on knowledge discovery and data mining*, (pp. 531–540) 10.1145/2939672.2939729

Luo, Y., & Xu, X. (2021). Comparative study of deep learning models for analyzing online restaurant reviews in the era of the COVID-19 pandemic. *International Journal of Hospitality Management*, *94*, 102849. doi:10.1016/j.ijhm.2020.102849 PMID:34785843

Ma, R., Boubrahimi, S. F., Hamdi, S. M., & Angryk, R. A. (2017). Solar flare prediction using multivariate time series decision trees. In: *Proceedings - 2017 IEEE International Conference on Big Data, Big Data 2017*. Institute of Electrical and Electronics Engineers Inc. 10.1109/BigData.2017.8258216

Maathai, K. D. (2005). *Mathiyazhagan, Impact of foreign direct investment on Indian economy: A sectoral level analysis*. Academic Press.

Madhumitha, M., & Dhivya, P. (2020). Vehicle Recognition and Compilation in Database Software. *International Conference on System, Computation, Automation and Networking (ICSCAN)*, pp. 1-5, 10.1109/ICSCAN49426.2020.9262286

Mahajan, S. (2022). Paytm IPO: Case of Failure and the Behemoth. *JBIMS*.

Ma, L., & Sun, B. (2020). Machine learning and AI in marketing–Connecting computing power to human insights. *International Journal of Research in Marketing*, *37*(3), 481–504. doi:10.1016/j.ijresmar.2020.04.005

Manoff, R. S., Houck, T., & Squire, J. D., & SoMo Audience Corp, (2019). *Content manipulation using swipe gesture recognition technology*. U.S. Patent Application 16/116,459.

Markets, R. (2020). Global Gesture Recognition Market to Reach $23.55 Billion by 2023: Analysis by Technology, Industry and Region. *PR Newswire*. https://www.prnewswire.com/news-releases/global-gesture-reco gnition-market-to-reach-23-55-billion-by-2023-analysis-by-te chnology-industry-and-region-300699427.html

Mart'ınez, A., Schmuck, C., Pereverzyev, S. Jr, Pirker, C., & Haltmeier, M. (2020). A machine learning framework for customer purchase prediction in the non-contractual setting. *European Journal of Operational Research*, *281*(3), 588–596. doi:10.1016/j.ejor.2018.04.034

Material, M. (2016). *The Evolution of Office Space Utilization in the U.S.* Academic Press.

Media and Entertainment|Vault.com. (2020). Overview. *Firsthand*. https://www.vault.com/industries-professions/industries/medi a-and-entertainment

Mehta, R. (2012). *The role of FDI in Indian growth and infrastructure development*. Academic Press.

Mehta, S., Saxena, T., & Purohit, N. (2020). The new consumer behaviour paradigm amid COVID-19: Permanent or transient? *Journal of Health Management*, *22*(2), 291–301. doi:10.1177/0972063420940834

Mhamdi, C. (2016). Transgressing media boundaries: News creation and dissemination in a globalized world. *Mediterranean Journal of Social Sciences*, *7*(5), 272–272. doi:10.5901/mjss.2016.v7n5p272

Miguéis, V. L., Camanho, A. S., & Borges, J. (2017). Predicting direct marketing response in banking: Comparison of class imbalance methods. *Service Business*, *11*(4), 831–849. doi:10.100711628-016-0332-3

Miles, N. (2020). How to Analyze a Film Script. *Pen and the Pad.* https://penandthepad.com/analyze-film-script-12069589.html

Mithas, S., Krishnan, M. S., & Fornell, C. (2005). Why do customer relationship management applications affect customer satisfaction? *Journal of Marketing*, *69*(4), 201–209. doi:10.1509/jmkg.2005.69.4.201

Mokryn, O., Bogina, V., Kuflik, T. (2019). Will this session end with a purchase? Inferring current purchase intent of anonymous visitors. *Electronic Commerce Research and Applications*, *34*, 100 836

Morris, A. N. (2021). Small Business Debt in the Age of COVID-19. *Am. Bankr. Inst. L. Rev.*, *29*, 131.

Mottaghi, N., & Farhangdoost, S. (2021). Stock Price Forecasting in Presence of Covid-19 Pandemic and Evaluating Performances of Machine Learning Models for Time-Series Forecasting. https://arxiv.org/abs/2105.02785

Mudassir, M. M., & Safiuddin, S. K. (2015). Does digital marketing replace the personal selling: An empirical study of the marketers. *International Journal of Management Research and Reviews*, *5*(12), 1142.

Mukherji, P., & Sengupta, S. (2020). Media & Entertainment Industry: An Overview. https://avasant.com/insights/publications/technology-optimiz ation/media-entertainment-industry-an-overveiw/

Murphy, S. A. (2013). Data visualization and rapid analytics: Applying tableau desktop to support library decision-making. *Journal of Web Librarianship*, *7*(4), 465–476. doi:10.1080/1 9322909.2013.825148

Netflix, A. (2019). https: / / www. reuters. com / finance / stocks / company -profile/NFLX.OQ

Nisar, T. M., & Yeung, M. (2018). Twitter as a tool for forecasting stock market movements: A short-window event study. *J. Finance Data Sci.*, *4*(2), 101–119. doi:10.1016/j.jfds.2017.11.002

Niu, J., & Niu, P. (2019). An intelligent automatic valuation system for real estate based on machine learning. *Proceedings of the International Conference on Artificial Intelligence, Information Processing and Cloud Computing.* 10.1145/3371425.3371454

Nofer, M., & Hinz, O. (2015). Using twitter to predict the stock market. *Business & Information Systems Engineering*, *57*(4), 229–242. doi:10.100712599-015-0390-4

Nofsinger, J. R. (2005). Social Mood and Financial Economics. *Journal of Behavioral Finance*, *6*(3), 144–160.

Pagolu, V. S. (2016). *Sentiment Analysis of Twitter Data for Predicting Stock Market Movements.* https://arxiv.org/pdf/1610.09225.pdf

Palekar, R. R., Parab, S. U., Parikh, D. P., & Kamble, V. N. (2017). Real time license plate detection using openCV and tesseract. *International Conference on Communication and Signal Processing (ICCSP),* pp. 2111-2115. 10.1109/ICCSP.2017.8286778

Pandey, D. (2021). Coronavirus Impact on Indian IPO Market. *IUP Journal of Accounting Research \& Audit Practices, 20*(4), 603–609.

Pan, X., Wong, C. W. Y., & Li, C. (2022). Circular economy practices in the waste electrical and electronic equipment (WEEE) industry: A systematic review and future research agendas. *Journal of Cleaner Production, 365,* 132671. doi:10.1016/j.jclepro.2022.132671

Park, C. H., & Park, Y. H. (2016). Investigating purchase conversion by uncovering online visit patterns. *Marketing Science, 35*(6), 894–914. doi:10.1287/mksc.2016.0990

Paule-Vianez, J., Gutiérrez-Fernández, M., & Coca-Pérez, J. L. (2019). *Prediction of financial distress in the Spanish banking system: An application using artificial neural networks.* Applied Economic Analysis. doi:10.1108/AEA-10-2019-0039

Pawar, M. M., & Argade, N. (n.d.). *Impact of foreign direct investment on drugs & pharmaceuticals industry: An Indian outlook.* Academic Press.

Payne, A., & Frow, P. (2005). A strategic framework for customer relationship management. *Journal of Marketing, 69*(4), 167–176. doi:10.1509/jmkg.2005.69.4.167

Peppers, D., & Rogers, M. (2011). *Managing Customer Relationships: A Strategic Framework.* John Miley & Sons. doi:10.1002/9781119239833.fmatter

Plum, K. (n.d.). *What is a Workplace Utilisation Study?* Available from: https://www.advanced-workplace.com/what-is-a-workplace-utilisation-study/

Pukala, R., Hlibko, S., Vnukova, N., & Korvat, O. (2020). Power BI in ICT for Monitoring of Insurance Activity Based on Indicators of Insurance Portfolios. *IEEE International Conference on Problems of Infocommunications. Science and Technology (PIC S\&T),* 393–401. 10.1109/PICST51311.2020.9467993

Puranic, A., K, D., & V, U. (2016). Vehicle Number Plate Recognition System: A Literature Review and Implementation using Template Matching. *International Journal of Computers and Applications, 134*(1), 12–16. doi:10.5120/ijca2016907652

Qahtan, S., Alsattar, H. A., Zaidan, A. A., Pamucar, D., & Deveci, M. (2022). Integrated sustainable transportation modelling approaches for electronic passenger vehicle in the context of industry 5.0. *Journal of Innovation & Knowledge, 7*(4), 100277.

Rader, E., & Gray, R. (2015, April). Understanding user beliefs about algorithmic curation in the Facebook news feed. In *Proceedings of the 33rd annual ACM conference on human factors in computing systems,* (pp. 173-182). 10.1145/2702123.2702174

Rafay, A., Suleman, M., & Alim, A. (2020). Robust review rating prediction model based on machine and deep learning: Yelp dataset. *International Conference on Emerging Trends in Smart Technologies (ICETST)*, IEEE. 10.1109/ICETST49965.2020.9080713

Rafique, M. I. S. & Habib, H. A. (2009). Space Invariant Vehicle Recognition for Toll Plaza Monitoring and Auditing System. *Multitopic Conference INMIC 13th International,* pp. 1-6.

Rai, A. (2020). Explainable AI: From black box to glass box. *Journal of the Academy of Marketing Science*, *48*(1), 137–141. doi:10.100711747-019-00710-5

Rajan, A. (1990). *Information technology in the finance sector: an international perspective.*

Rajkumar, K., & Sudheer, D. (2016). A review of visual information retrieval on massive image data using hadoop. *Int. J. Control Theor. Appl*, *9*, 425–430.

Reagan Nickl (SpacelQ). (2019). *Sapce Utilization Metrics*. Available from: https://spaceiq.com/blog/space-utilization-metrics/

Reddy, E. M. K., Gurrala, A., Hasitha, V. B., & Kumar, K. V. R. (2022). Introduction to Naive Bayes and a Review on Its Subtypes with Applications. *Bayesian Reasoning and Gaussian Processes for Machine Learning Applications*, 1–14.

Reddy, C. S., Sangam, R. S., & Srinivasa Rao, B. (2019). A survey on business intelligence tools for marketing, financial, and transportation services. In *Smart intelligent computing and applications,* (pp. 495–504). Springer. doi:10.1007/978-981-13-1927-3_53

Reddy, E. M. K., Gurrala, A., Hasitha, V. B., & Kumar, K. V. R. (2022). Introduction to Naive Bayes and a Review on Its Subtypes with Applications. In *Bayesian Reasoning and Gaussian Processes for Machine Learning Applications* (pp. 1–14). Chapman and Hall/CRC. doi:10.1201/9781003164265-1

Redmon, J., Divvala, S., Girshick, R., & Farhadi, A. (2016). You Only Look Once: Unified, Real-Time Object Detection. *IEEE Conference on Computer Vision and Pattern Recognition (CVPR)*, pp. 779-788, 10.1109/CVPR.2016.91

Renault, T. (2020). Sentiment analysis and machine learning in finance: A comparison of methods and models on one million messages. *Digit. Finance*, *2*(1), 1–13. doi:10.100742521-019-00014-x

Ren, S., He, K., Girshick, R., & Sun, J. (2017, June 1). Faster R-CNN: Towards Real-Time Object Detection with Region Proposal Networks. *IEEE Transactions on Pattern Analysis and Machine Intelligence*, *39*(6), 1137–1149. doi:10.1109/TPAMI.2016.2577031 PMID:27295650

Rockenbach, G., Boeira, C., Schaffer, D., Antonitsch, A., & Musse, S. R. (2018, November). Simulating crowd evacuation: From comfort to panic situations. In *Proceedings of the 18th International Conference on Intelligent Virtual Agents,* (pp. 295-300). 10.1145/3267851.3267872

Rowe, M., Stankovic, M., Dadzie, A.-S., & Hardey, M. (Eds.). F. °A. Nielsen. A new ANEW: evaluation of a word list for sentiment analysis in microblogs. In M. Rowe, M. Stankovic, A.-S. Dadzie, & M. Hardey (Eds.), *Proceedings of the ESWC2011 Workshop on Making*. Academic Press.

Ryu, S. H., & Moon, H. J. (2016). Development of an occupancy prediction model using indoor environmental data based on machine learning techniques. Building and Environment, 107, 1–9. doi:10.1016/j.buildenv.2016.06.039

Safiuddin, S. K., & Samad, M. A. (2015). Impact of FDI on the Growth of Selected Pharmaceutical Firms-An Aggregate Analysis. *Sumedha Journal of Management, 4*(3), 47.

Saini, A., Grewal, R., & Johnson, J. L. (2010). Putting market-facing technology to work: Organizational drivers of CRM performance. *Marketing Letters, 21*(4), 365–383. doi:10.100711002-009-9096-z

Salesforce. (2021a). *The B2B Sales Funnel and the Role of CRM Systems*. Retrieved from https://www.salesforce.com/uk/learning-centre/crm/b2b-crm

Salesforce. (2021b). *The complete history of CRM*. Retrieved from https://www.salesforce.com/in/hub/crm/the-complete-crm-history

Salkind, N. (2012). Time-Series Study. In *Encyclopedia of Research Design*. SAGE Publications, Inc.

Salo, T. (2020). *Incorporating CSR Activities into the Company's Financial Strategy: A Case Study* [Thesis]. Metropolia University of Applied Sciences.

Sankar, S., Ramasubbareddy, S., Luhach, A. K., & Chatterjee, P. (2022). NCCLA: New caledonian crow learning algorithm based cluster head selection for Internet of Things in smart cities. *Journal of Ambient Intelligence and Humanized Computing, 13*(10), 1–11. doi:10.100712652-021-03503-3

Sankar, S., Somula, R., Parvathala, B., Kolli, S., & Pulipati, S. (2022). SOA-EACR: Seagull optimization algorithm based energy aware cluster routing protocol for wireless sensor networks in the livestock industry. *Sustainable Computing: Informatics and Systems, 33*, 100645.

Satheesh, M. K., & Kumar, K. V. R. (n.d.). Addressing the Utilization of Popular Regression Models in Business Applications. In Machine Learning for Business Analytics (pp. 29–43). Productivity Press. doi:10.4324/9781003206316-3

Schmidt, T., & Vosen, S. (2009). *Forecasting Private Consumption: Survey-based Indicators vs. Google Trends*. https://pdfs.semanticscholar.org/66f2/b2cfe56fc2414d3036cb6e28098bfa55216f.pdf

Scott, B. (2016). *How can cryptocurrency and blockchain technology play a role in building social and solidarity finance?* Shahrokhi, M. (2008). E-finance: Status, innovations, resources and future challenges. *Managerial Finance*.

Seeja, G., Reddy, O., Kumar, K. V. R., Mounika, S., & ... (2021). Internet of Things and Robotic Applications in the Industrial Automation Process. In *Innovations in the Industrial Internet of Things (IIoT) and Smart Factory* (pp. 50–64). IGI Global.

Seippel, H. S. (2018). *Customer purchase prediction through machine learning* [Master's thesis]. University of Twente.

Selvam, M. (2022). Lic IPO. *SMART Journal of Business Management Studies*, *18*(2), 6–7.

Sense of Microposts. (2011). Big things come in small packages. *CEUR Workshop Proceedings*, *718*, 93–98.

Shang, Y., & Wang, Y. (2020). Study of CNN-based news-driven stock price movement prediction in the A-share market. In *International Conference of Pioneering Computer Scientists, Engineers and Educators*. Springer. 10.1007/978-981-15-7984-4_35

Shariff, M. A. S., Bhatia, R., Kuma, R., & Jha, S. (2021). Vehicle Number Plate Detection Using Python and Open CV. *International Conference on Advance Computing and Innovative Technologies in Engineering (ICACITE)*, pp. 525-529, 10.1109/ICACITE51222.2021.9404556

Singh, D., Denesh, R., Balakrishnan, J., Vijayan, N., & Ghosh, D. (2017). Department of Management Studies. *International Journal of Mental Health and Addiction*, *16*, 15.

Singh, J., & Bhushan, B. (2019). Real Time Indian License Plate Detection using Deep Neural Networks and Optical Character Recognition using LSTM Tesseract. *International Conference on Computing, Communication, and Intelligent Systems (ICCCIS)*, pp. 347-352, 10.1109/ICCCIS48478.2019.8974469

Singhmar, M. K. (n.d.). *Why Customer Relationship Management is Important for Your Business*. Retrieved from https://seeresponse.com/blog/why-customer-relationship-management-is-important-for-your-business/

Sin, L. Y. M., Tse, A. C. B., & Yim, F. H. K. (2005). CRM: Conceptualization and scale development. *European Journal of Marketing*, *39*(11/12), 1264–1290. doi:10.1108/03090560510623253

Smith, A., & Andersson, M. (2018). Social Media Use in 2018. Academic Press.

Stamos Katsigiannis, W. A., & Ramzan, N. (2019). 5G: Disruption in Media and Entertainment. *Enabling 5G Communication Systems to Support Vertical Industries*.

Stock, J. H. (2001). Time Series: Economic Forecasting. In *International Encyclopedia of the Social & Behavioral Sciences* (pp. 15721–15724). Elsevier. doi:10.1016/B0-08-043076-7/00526-X

Sudheer, D., & Lakshmi, A. R. (2015). Performance evaluation of Hadoop distributed file system. *Pseudo Distrib Mode Fully Distrib Mode*, (9), 81-86.

Sudheer, D., & Krishnan, R. (2019). Multiscale texture analysis and color coherence vector based feature descriptor for multispectral image retrieval. *Advances in Science, Technology and Engineering Systems Journal*, *4*(6), 270–279. doi:10.25046/aj040634

Suh, E., Lim, S., Hwang, H., & Kim, S. (2004). A prediction model for the purchase probability of anonymous customers to support real time web marketing: A case study. *Expert Systems with Applications*, *27*(2), 245–255. doi:10.1016/j.eswa.2004.01.008

Sulaiman & Said Musnadi. (2018). Customer Relationship Management, Customer Satisfaction and Its Impact on Customer Loyalty. *ICMR 2018*, 692-698. Doi:10.5220/0008892606920698

Sun, H., Fu, M., Abdussalam, A., Huang, Z., Sun, S., & Wang, W. (2018). License Plate Detection and Recognition Based on the YOLO Detector and CRNN-12. *International Conference On Signal And Information Processing, Networking And Computers ICSINC*, pp 66-74

Szyszka, A. (2007). *Wycena papierów wartościowych na rynku kapitałowym wświetle finansów behawioralnych. Prace Habilitacyjne/Akademia Ekonomiczna w Poznaniu 35* [Valuation of Securities on the Capital market in the light of Behavioral Finance. Habilitation Theses]. University of Economics in Poznah.

Tabak, V. & de Vries, B. (2010). Methods for the prediction of intermediate activities by office occupants. *Building and Environment*, *45*(6), 1366–1372.

Tabak, V. (2009). *User Simulation of Space Utilisation: System for Office Building Usage Simulation*. Academic Press.

Talwar, M., Talwar, S., Kaur, P., Tripathy, N., & Dhir, A. (2021). Has financial attitude impacted the trading activity of retail investors during the COVID-19 pandemic? *Journal of Retailing and Consumer Services*, *58*, 102341. doi:10.1016/j.jretconser.2020.102341

Techopedia. (2020). What is Gesture Recognition? *Techopedia*. https://www.techopedia.com/definition/618/gesture-recognitio n

Teng, K. L., Ong, S. G., & Ching, P. W. (2007). The Use of Customer Relationship Management (CRM) by Manufacturing Firms in Different Industries: A Malaysian Survey. *International Journal of Management*, *24*, 386.

Thelwall, M. (2009). MySpace Comments. *Online Information Review*, *33*(1), 58–76. doi:10.1108/14684520910944391

Treleaven, P., Barnett, J., Knight, A., & Serrano, W. (2021). Real estate data marketplace. *AI and Ethics*, *1*(4), 445–462. doi:10.100743681-021-00053-4

Tsagkias, M., King, T. H., Kallumadi, S., Murdock, V., & de Rijke, M. (2021, February). Challenges and research opportunities in ecommerce search and recommendations. In *ACM SIGIR Forum*, *54*(1), pp. 1-23. ACM.

Tumasjan, A. (2010). *Predicting Elections with Twitter: What 140 Characters Reveal about Political Sentiment*. Academic Press.

Usunier, J.-C., & Cestre, G. (2007). Product ethnicity: Revisiting the match between products and countries. *Journal of International Marketing*, *15*(3), 32–72. doi:10.1509/jimk.15.3.32

Compilation of References

Vărzaru, A. A., & Bocean, C. G. (2021). A two-stage SEM–artificial neural network analysis of mobile commerce and its drivers. *Journal of Theoretical and Applied Electronic Commerce Research, 16*(6), 2304–2318. doi:10.3390/jtaer16060127

Vázquez-Martinez, U. J., Morales-Mediano, J., & Leal-Rodriguez, A. L. (2021). The impact of the COVID-19 crisis on consumer purchasing motivation and behavior. *European Research on Management and Business Economics, 27*(3), 100166.

Vidya, C. T., & Prabheesh, K. P. (2020). Implications of COVID-19 pandemic on the global trade networks. *Emerging Markets Finance & Trade, 56*(10), 2408–2421. doi:10.1080/154049 6X.2020.1785426

Walstra, R., Drougas, A., & Harrington, S. (2015). Integrating Excel, SQL, and SPSS within an Introductory Finance Intrinsic Value Assignment. *Journal of Finance and Accountancy, 20*, 1.

Wang, Z., Zhang, M., Wang, D., Song, C., Liu, M., Li, J., Lou, L., & Liu, Z. (2017). Failure prediction using machine learning and time series in optical network. *Optics Express, 25*(16), 18553. doi:10.1364/OE.25.018553 PMID:29041054

Westerman, G. (2022). Developing Strategy for New Customer Expectations. *MIT Sloan Management Review, 63*(2), 1–4.

Widjaja, V. F., Budianto, R., & Alamsyah, D. P. (2021). Local Business in Mid of Covid-19 Pandemic: A Prominent Case Study in Bandung Indonesia. *Proceedings of the 11th Annual International Conference on Industrial Engineering and Operations Management*, 4589–4595.

Woodburn, D. (2002). Customer relationship management: Hard lessons learned in B2B pose tough questions for B2C. *Journal of Direct, Data and Digital Marketing Practice, 4*(1), 19–32. doi:10.1057/palgrave.im.4340160

Wu, H., & Li, B. (2022, January). Customer Purchase Prediction Based on Improved Gradient Boosting Decision Tree Algorithm. In *2nd International Conference on Consumer Electronics and Computer Engineering (ICCECE)*, (pp. 795-798). IEEE. 10.1109/ICCECE54139.2022.9712779

Wu, C. Y., Singhal, N., & Krahenbuhl, P. (2018). Video compression through image interpolation. In *Proceedings of the European Conference on Computer Vision (ECCV)*, (pp. 416-431).

Wu, Z., Tan, B. H., Duan, R., Liu, Y., & Mong Goh, R. S. (2015). Neural modeling of buying behaviour for E-commerce from clicking patterns. In *Proceedings of the international ACM recommender systems challenge 2015*, (p. 12). 10.1145/2813448.2813521

Yadav, D. V. (2017). An Analytical Study of Foreign Direct Investment in Pharma Sector of India. *International Journal of Law, 3*(5), 40–42.

Yadav, N., & Goyal, S. (2022). *Regaining partner trust in the food delivery business: case of Zomato*. Emerald Emerging Markets Case Studies.

Yang, J. W., & Parwada, J. (2012). *Predicting stock price movements: An ordered probit analysis*. Academic Press.

Yao, J., & Jiang, K. (2019). A fast intra prediction algorithm with simplified prediction modes based on utilization rates. In *Proceedings - 18th IEEE/ACIS International Conference on Computer and Information Science, ICIS 2019*. Institute of Electrical and Electronics Engineers Inc. 10.1109/ICIS46139.2019.8940153

Zahoor, K., Bawany, N. Z., & Hamid, S. (2020). Sentiment analysis and classification of restaurant reviews using machine learning. *21st International Arab Conference on Information Technology (ACIT)*, IEEE. 10.1109/ACIT50332.2020.9300098

Zeng, M., Cao, H., Chen, M., & Li, Y. (2019). User behaviour modeling, recommendations, and purchase prediction during shopping festivals. *Electronic Markets*, *29*(2), 263–274. doi:10.100712525-018-0311-8

Zetzsche, D. A., Arner, D. W., & Buckley, R. P. (2020). Decentralized finance. *Journal of Financial Regulation*, *6*(2), 172–203. doi:10.1093/jfr/fjaa010

Zhai, X., & Bensaali, F. (2013). Standard Definition ANPR System on FPGA and an Approach to Extend it to HD. *IEEE GCC Conference and exhibition*, pp. 214. 10.1109/IEEEGCC.2013.6705778

Zhang, M., & Luo, L. (2018). Can user-posted photos serve as a leading indicator of restaurant survival? Evidence from Yelp. *Evidence from Yelp*.

Zhao, M., Cai, W., & Turner, S. J. (2018, February). Clust: Simulating realistic crowd behaviour by mining pattern from crowd videos. *Computer Graphics Forum*, *37*(1), 184–201. doi:10.1111/cgf.13259

Zheng, X., Zhu, M., Li, Q., Chen, C., & Tan, Y. (2019). FinBrain: when finance meets AI 2.0. *Frontiers of Information Technology \& Electronic Engineering, 20*(7), 914–924.

Zhou, Y., Tagliaro, C. & Hua, Y. (n.d.). *From Hour to Minute: Non-technical Challenges for Measuring Office Space Utilization with Smart Technologies*. Academic Press.

Zia Ullah, Q., Hassan, S., & Khan, G. M. (2017). Adaptive Resource Utilization Prediction System for Infrastructure as a Service Cloud. *Computational Intelligence and Neuroscience*. doi:10.1155/2017/4873459 PMID:28811819

About the Contributors

Samala Nagaraj is a Ph.D. in Marketing from University of Hyderabad. He is currently working as Assistant Professor in Woxsen School of Business. He has over 10 years of teaching experience and 5 years of research experience. He is awarded UGC-NET & JRF in the year 2012. He currently teaches subjects related to Marketing and Business Analytics (using SPSS, Python, and Tableau). He has research publication is reputed national and international journals. He has published papers in journals indexed in Scopus, ABDC-B & C, SSCI. He is an editorial reviewer for many Scopus and ABDC-B & C journals.

Korupalli V. Rajesh Kumar is currently working as Assistant Professor in School of Business, Woxsen University, Hyderabad, Telangana. He earned his M. Tech in Embedded Systems from JNTU, Kakinada, and AMIE in ECE from the Institution of Engineers, Kolkata. He is pursuing his Ph.D. from VIT University, Chennai. He was earlier associated with VIT as Junior Research Fellow and upGrad Educational Private Limited where he was guiding students in selecting research problems and in writing a thesis, to deal with AI/ML models, for those who are pursuing M.Sc. in Data Science / AI ML courses from Liverpool John Moores University through upGrad. His research specialization is signals and sensor-based Data Analytics for Bio-Medical Applications.

* * *

Preethi Christina A. is an MTech Computer Science Big Data Analytics Student at VIT University.

N. Badrinath has 19 years of opulent experience with 9 years in teaching, 5 years in research, and 5 years of industrial exposure with research activities. Holding 3 patents. Published several papers in international & national journals and conferences and delivered guest lectures in many national & international seminars.

Satyam Chaurasia is an MTech Computer Science Big Data Analytics Student at VIT University.

Sudheer Devulapalli completed Master's in JNTUK University and submitted thesis for PhD program in VIT Deemed to be University, Vellore, India. He has published three Indian patents and many papers in national and international journals, Scopus and high impact factor publications. He presented many papers at international and national conferences. He obtained a good knowledge of image retrieval and bigdata processing.

Md. Shamim Hossain is an Associate Professor in the Department of Marketing at Hajee Mohammad Danesh Science and Technology University (HSTU), Bangladesh. In 2019, he received his Ph.D. in Business Management from the University of International Business and Economics (UIBE), Beijing, China. His research interests include operations management, online business, e-marketing, self-service technologies (SSTs), e-commerce, m-banking, online customer behavior, and machine learning in marketing. Dr. Hossain is concentrating his efforts on how to apply machine learning to business areas, notably marketing. Many of his studies have been published in prestigious journals such as the Journal of Retailing and Consumer Services, the Journal of Food Quality, the Mathematical Problems in Engineering, the Journal of Healthcare Engineering, the Journal of Sport Psychology, The Economic Research-Ekonomska Istraivanja, The Management & Marketing, Challenges for the Knowledge Society, and the International Journal of Engineering Business Management. Dr. Hossain has also contributed book chapters to high-quality textbooks published by IGI-Global, USA.

Bharathi K. is an MTech Computer Science Big Data Analytics Student at VIT University.

Bhavya K. R. is currently working as Assistant Professor at REVA University Bengaluru. She finished her master's degree in Computer Science and Engineering in 2018 from VTU. She finished graduation from the same university in the year 2012. Her research interests include image processing and deep learning in computer vision.

Madapuri Kumar received B. Tech. in Computer Science and Engineering from Sri Venkateswara University, Tirupati, Andhra Pradesh, India. He received M. Tech. degree from Jawaharlal Nehru Technological University, Anantapur, Andhra Pradesh, India. He received PhD from Jawaharlal Nehru Technological University, Anantapur, Andhra Pradesh, India. Rudra Kumar published many research papers in national and international journals, conferences and authored three books. His main research interest includes Software Engineering, Data Mining and IoT.

Ravi Kumar M. is an M. Tech in Embedded systems Practical experience in the area of internet of things with good knowledge in Arduino boards and Raspberry Pi with Arduino C (C++) and Python languages. Knowledgeable in artificial intelligence with machine learning tools.

Sangeetha M., Assistant Professor, REVA University, Bengaluru, did B.E. (CSE) in Anna University, Chennai. She did M.E(CSE) in Anna University, Chennai. She was awarded PhD (ISE) in VTU.

Suneetha P. completed B.Tech in Electronics and Communication Engineering in2006 from JNTU college of engineering, M.Tech, Ph.D from JNTUK in 2010&2020respectively.She published more than 25 papers in national and international. Her research interests include signal processing, image processing, speech processing, and communications.

B. Rupa Devi has teaching experience of 19 years. She has been ratified as Associate Professor by JNTUA, Anantapuramu. She has published many international journals. She is pursuing her research in SVU, Tirupati in the field of Machine Learning under the guidance of Dr Ch Subba Rao.

Ramasubbareddy Somula is now working as Assistant Professor in VIT University. Done BTech in Alfa College of Engineering & Technology, Andhra Pradesh. His MTech was in Srirama Engg College, Andhra Pradesh.

Malla Sudhakara is currently working as Assistant Professor in the school of computing and information technology. He finished his master's degree in Computer Science and Engineering in 2012 from JNTU University, Anantapur. He finished graduation from the same university in the year 2010. He has four years of teaching experience as an Assistant Professor in reputed engineering colleges in Andhra Pradesh, India. He started his research career in 2015 in Computing Science and Engineering at VIT Chennai Campus. He published articles in several UGC and Scopus Indexed journals. His research interests include Image Analytics, Image Processing, and Deep Learning in computer vision.

Murat Pasa Uysal is a faculty member at the Department of Management Information Systems, Baskent University, Turkey. He holds a B.S degree in electrical & electronic engineering, a M.S degree in computer engineering, and a Ph.D. degree in educational technology. He completed his post-doctoral studies at Rochester Institute of Technology in New York, USA. His research interest is in the areas of information systems, software engineering, machine learning and project management.

Sailaja V. received her B.Tech. in Electronics & communications engineering from VR Siddhartha Engineering College, ME degree in Electronic Instrumentation from AU college of Engineering , Ph.D from Andhra University, Presently working as professor at Pragati Engineering College, Surampalem, India Previously worked as HOD and professor at Godavari Institute Of Engineering and Technology. Her current research interests are in speech processing, Signal processing with big data.

Index

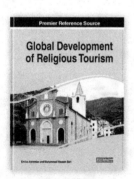

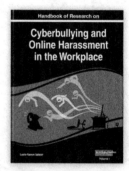

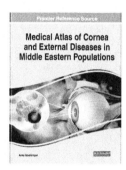
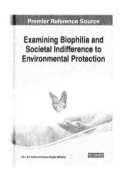
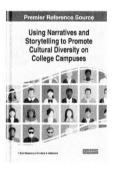

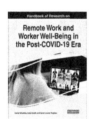

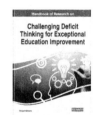